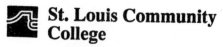

HEMINGWAY AND
THE NATURAL WORLD

HEMINGWAY AND THE
NATURAL WORLD

EDITED BY ROBERT E. FLEMING

UNIVERSITY OF IDAHO PRESS

MOSCOW, IDAHO / 1999

03 02 01 00 99   5 4 3 2 1

Library of Congress Cataloging-in-Publication Data

Hemingway and the natural world / edited and with an introduction by
    Robert E. Fleming.
        p.   cm.
    Includes bibliographical references and index.
    ISBN 0-89301-214-9 (hard cover)
    1. Hemingway, Ernest, 1899–1961—Knowledge—Natural history.
    2. Nature in literature.   I. Fleming, Robert E. (Robert Edward),
    1936–   .
    PS3515.E37   Z5–999
    813'.52—dc21   98-42679
                                                         CIP

TO PAUL SMITH

OTHER TITLES OF INTEREST

Reading the Earth
New Directions in the Study of Literature and the Environment
Edited by Michael P. Branch, Rochelle Johnson, Daniel Patterson,
and Scott Slovic

Green Cultural Studies
Nature in Film, Novel, and Theory
Jhan Hochman

Tricky Tribal Discourse
The Poetry, Short Stories, and Fus Fixico Letters of Creek Writer
Alex Posey
Alexia Kosmider

Wise Economies
Brevity and Storytelling in American Short Stories
Kirk Curnutt

The Great Poem of the Earth
A Study of the Poetry of Thomas Hornsby Ferril
Andrew Elkins

Loaded Fictions
Social Critique in the Twentieth-Century Western
Scott Emmert

Parallel Expeditions
Charles Darwin and the Art of John Steinbeck
Brian E. Railsback

The World of David Wagoner
Ron McFarland

CONTENTS

ILLUSTRATIONS

Introduction

ROBERT E. FLEMING

Few authors in history have been so closely identified with the natural world as Ernest Hemingway. As a small child he was taken every summer from his home in Oak Park, which in 1899 was more a rural village than the busy suburb it has since become, to his parents' northern Michigan vacation property, where he would later spend the happiest times of his boyhood. There and in the woods and prairies of northern Illinois, Hemingway would pursue the outdoor activities to which his father, Clarence Edmonds Hemingway, had introduced him—fishing, hunting, hiking, and camping. He loved animals, but he loved them as a young man of his generation loved them. That is, like many distinguished naturalists of the nineteenth century, he learned about wild birds, mammals, and fish by hunting or catching them. The taxidermy that he and his father studied allowed him to preserve his specimens; later he would preserve his prey eternally by enclosing it in the amber of his prose.

Because he was the son of educated parents, the young Hemingway did not confine himself to physical observation of the natural world but also approached nature through books. Mark Spilka has emphasized young Ernest's indoctrination into nineteenth-century moral standards by the Victorian novels favored by his conservative parents,[1] but other books were also important to the boy. Michael Reynolds first commented on the importance to young Hemingway of Theodore Roosevelt's articles and books: the former appeared in *National Geographic* and *Century* during Ernest's formative years; *African Game Trails* was first published in 1910.[2] Hemingway would go on to amass an excellent outdoorsman's and naturalist's library, ranging from copies of the *American Rifleman* and *Field and Stream* to Colonel Townsend Whelan's *Wilderness Hunting and Wildcraft*, from Harold Elmer Anthony's *Field Book of North American Mammals* and Roger Tory Peterson's *Field Guide to the Birds* to Louis Roule's *Fishes, Their Journeys and Migrations*.[3] If, as Gertrude Stein said, Hemingway looked like a modern and smelled of museums,[4] he was also a hunter, fisherman, and naturalist who smelled of libraries.

As Hemingway's world was enlarged by his travels in Europe, Africa, the Caribbean, and the American West, his concept of nature expanded to include sights, experiences, and activities that he could only imagine during his sheltered Oak Park and Petoskey boyhood. As his concept of the world changed, so did his concept of nature. The African animals that had been part of his imaginative experience now became reality. Dreams of adventure in far-off, exotic locations gave way to actual adventure. New experiences, such as the *corridas* of Spain, expanded his concept of how mankind related to nature.

Yet through it all, there were always books to help him. When it came time to write a book defining the *corrida de toros* for the Anglo-American world, he relied not only on his own considerable experience and on the word of the expert matadors he had come to know by the early 1930s but on "2077 books and pamphlets in Spanish dealing with or touching on tauromaquia," as a bibliographical note at the end of *Death in the Afternoon* acknowledges.[5] When writing about Africa, he found not only Roosevelt but Arthur Blayney Percival and Arthur H. Neumann to use as models or as foils for his own work.

Hemingway's imaginative use of the natural world began with high school apprentice pieces set in the north woods. Short stories such as "Sepi Jingan" and "Judgment of Manitou," both of which appeared in his high school literary magazine *Tabula*, show the dual influence of his personal exposure to the forests and Native Americans of northern Michigan and of the works of Stewart Edward White and Owen Wister.[6] So does an unpublished postwar story of Billy Gilbert's return from the Great War in "Cross Roads: An Anthology."

After his move to France in 1921, it might have been expected that Hemingway would become urbanized. He was, after all, living in Paris and making a conscious effort to obtain an informal cultural education to make up for the formal education he had skipped by not attending college. But while he read the books recommended by Gertrude Stein and Ezra Pound and viewed the pictures at the Louvre and the Luxembourg Gardens, Hemingway continued to pursue the outdoor life, as his published journalism from the period attests. Articles on tuna fishing in Spain, trout fishing in Switzerland, hiking in Germany, skiing in Switzerland, and game shooting across the continent appear along with articles on the Genoa Conference and the Greco-Turkish war. Currently, hunting and fishing are regarded by some as barbaric sports, and self-styled animal rights activists and friends of animals see these activities as diametrically opposed to the welfare of the fish and game on which they depend. But Hemingway had been taught by his father to respect the animals he killed and to utilize them fully. As a boy, Ernest was forced to eat a porcupine he shot, and his semiautobiographical character Nick Adams is careful to release an unwanted trout he has caught only after wetting his hand to avoid disturbing the protective coating of the fish. It is not surprising, therefore, to find that early in his journalistic career, Hemingway compared game management in Europe very favorably to North American practices.

In "Game-Shooting in Europe" (1923), Hemingway examines the shooting scene in France, Italy, and Germany. Game is plentiful because it is carefully protected by closed seasons, and the forests are owned by the government and maintained rather than harvested. Only in Italy does he find game laws as lax as in Canada, where, he laments to Canadian readers, "Ontario's supply of game seems inexhaustible. But wait until the steady hunting, the destruction of timber and the forest fires have kept up for fifty years."[7] He points to practices in his native Midwest, where the prairie chicken and the quail have nearly been "wiped out," and where the wild turkey and curlew have been exterminated. Hemingway would take a similar conservationist approach to the hunting of big game a decade later, when he wrote for *Esquire*'s readership about the difference between "Shootism vs. Sport." The latter is achieved by the man who hunts lions on foot; whether or not he shoots a lion, he will be successful: "You will be more of a sportsman to come back from Africa without a lion than to shoot one from the protection of a motor car, or from a blind at night when the lion is blinded by the light and cannot see his assailant."[8]

Upon moving to Key West, Florida, Hemingway became a noted big game fisherman. Once again, books supplemented his direct observation of nature. He read Zane Grey, first to learn from him and later to compete with him. When Hemingway moved his books to Cuba in 1940, his inventory included three fishing books by the western writer: *An American Angler in Australia*, *Tales of Tahitian Waters*, and *Tales of the Angler's Eldorado, New Zealand*. Michael Reynolds has also determined that Hemingway had read a fourth Grey book, *Tales of Swordfish and Tuna*.[9] But as he had done with literary mentors, Hemingway measured his own writing on fishing against Grey's and soon found the popular writer lacking in comparison to himself.[10]

In 1933 Hemingway realized a hunter's dream by taking an African safari. He was fortunate enough to have as his guide Philip Percival, whose brother Blayney had written two books based on his experiences as an African game warden, *A Game Ranger's Note Book* (1924) and *A Game Ranger on Safari* (1928). Both books were in Hemingway's library when he moved it to Cuba.[11] When he produced his own literary rendering of the experience, *Green Hills of Africa* (1935), Hemingway was guided not only by his own experiences in Africa but by the accounts of

[3]

Blayney Percival and other writers of safari literature. In 1953–1954, Ernest and Mary Hemingway attempted to recreate the earlier safari—with almost tragic results. First their small airplane crashed near Murchison Falls in Uganda and then, after their rescue from that accident, a second plane caught fire during takeoff. The literary result, however, was a manuscript for "The African Book," a sort of sequel to *Green Hills of Africa*. Although he seems to have considered the second African book virtually finished and stored it in a bank vault as a precaution, the African book has yet to be published in its entirety.[12]

As Hemingway aged, he turned toward home. In a 1933 short story, Nick Adams replies to his son's suggestion that "'We could all be buried in France'" by saying "'I don't want to be buried in France.'" Nick and his son agree that they should all be buried "'at the ranch.'"[13] As he approached the age of sixty, Hemingway too returned to live and die in his native land. In the late 1950s, after Castro's revolution had left Cuba an armed camp, Hemingway moved to central Idaho, the scene of many happy times in the past. There he would have his final union with nature, lying under the pine trees in the small country cemetery of Ketchum, across the river from his last American home.

At Ketchum and Sun Valley, Idaho, the Seventh International Hemingway Conference was convened July 20–25, 1996. Selected from conference papers, the following essays document and reflect on Hemingway's firsthand and literary relationship with the natural world. They trace his actual wanderings across the globe—from Oak Park to Petoskey, from France to Spain, from Key West to Africa, and from Cuba to Idaho—and document the richness of the heritage that Hemingway left behind in his observation and response to nature. The keynote address by Terry Tempest Williams suggests that Hemingway has spoken to her, and that his dual relationship to the natural world—through direct observation and through books—has passed that heritage on to a modern nature writer.

NOTES

1. Mark Spilka, *Hemingway's Quarrel with Androgyny* (Lincoln: University of Nebraska Press, 1990).

2. Michael Reynolds, *The Young Hemingway* (Oxford and New York: Basil Blackwell, 1986), 25–6.

3. Michael S. Reynolds, *Hemingway's Reading, 1910–1940* (Princeton: Princeton University Press, 1981).

4. Gertrude Stein, *The Autobiography of Alice B. Toklas* (New York: Random House, 1933), 216.

5. Ernest Hemingway, *Death in the Afternoon* (New York: Scribner's, 1932), 487.

6. Reynolds, *The Young Hemingway*, 73–4.

7. Ernest Hemingway, *Dateline: Toronto, The Complete Toronto Star Dispatches, 1920–1924*, ed. William White (New York: Scribner's, 1985), 359.

8. Ernest Hemingway, *By-Line: Ernest Hemingway, Selected Articles and Dispatches of Four Decades*, ed. William White (New York: Scribner's, 1967), 166.

9. Reynolds, *Hemingway's Reading*, 132.

10. Carlos Baker, *Ernest Hemingway: A Life Story* (New York: Scribner's, 1969), 244, 271.

11. Reynolds, *Hemingway's Reading*, 168.

12. Patrick Hemingway's edited version of the African manuscript has just been published by the Scribner division of Simon & Schuster under the title *True at First Light* (1999).

13. Ernest Hemingway, "Fathers and Sons," *The Short Stories of Ernest Hemingway* (New York: Scribner's, 1966), 499.

"Hemingway and the Natural World" Keynote Address, Seventh International Hemingway Conference

TERRY TEMPEST WILLIAMS

My first memory of Ernest Hemingway is his death: July 2, 1961. Our family was driving to California on vacation. We heard it announced on the radio. "Hemingway was a great writer," my father said. "He was also a great hunter, loved the outdoors," I recall my mother turning the radio off and saying, "What a tragedy." Our parents tried delicately to explain how he died. It was the first time we had ever heard the word, "suicide."

What loosely followed was "with his shotgun" and the word "complicated."

In 1962 Marilyn Monroe died. As children, we heard the same word, "suicide." Only this time it was with pills and alcohol. I could never fully separate Monroe and Hemingway from my imagination. They would remain intrinsically linked like star-crossed lovers in my young impressionable mind. And they both mattered in my family. My father loved Hemingway. My mother loved Monroe. Marilyn Monroe loved John F. Kennedy, and the next year, President Kennedy was dead. Another gun. Another tragedy. The world was not a safe place.

Thirty-three years later, I found myself sitting at a table in the Hemingway Room at the JFK Library with a bronze head of Ernest Hemingway staring through me as I looked out windows facing Boston Harbor.

Boston Harbor. I think of my Uncle Richard Tempest who served as Mission President for the Mormon Church a few years ago in Boston. In 1964, he went on a hunting safari to Bechuanaland, now known as Botswana. He loved Hemingway too and carried a copy of *Green Hills of Africa* with him. "Hemingway got the character of the kudu exactly right," my uncle recently told me. "I knew kudu before I ever saw one because of that book."

"Did you ever shoot one?" I asked.

"Sure I did," he replied, "but I blew the shot at a sixty-inch trophy."

Another word returns to me, "complicated."

Men. Women. The Hunt.

A return to origins, that's what my uncle tells me when he talks about hunting. I want to understand. He quotes René Dubos. "Even though he lived by hunting, primitive man worshipped animals and modern man, also. The desire to hunt is paradoxically compatible with love of wildlife. Hunting is a highly satisfying occupation for many persons because it calls into play a multiplicity of physical and mental attributes that appear to be woven in the human fabric."

The word I hear is "love."

Hemingway. *A Farewell to Arms*. Lieutenant Henry speaking to a priest.

> "I don't love much."
>
> "Yes," he said. "You do. What you tell about in the nights. That is not love. That is only passion and lust. When you love you wish to do things for. You wish to sacrifice for. You wish to serve."
>
> "I don't love."
>
> "You will. I know you will. Then you will be happy." (72)

A few paragraphs later as the lieutenant begins to fall asleep:

> There were trout in the stream below the town. . . . For a foreigner to hunt he must present a certificate that he had never been arrested. There were bears on the Gran Sasso D'Italia but it was a long way. Aquila was a fine town. . . . But what was lovely was the fall to go hunting through the chestnut woods. The birds were all good because they fed on grapes. . . . (73)

Feeding on grapes. Drunk with pleasure. Hemingway knew love and he knew it most deeply in his relationship to landscape. And it was physical, sensual, call it "an erotics of place."

"Big Two-Hearted River":

> He stepped into the stream. It was a shock. His trousers clung tight to his legs. His shoes felt the gravel. The water was a rising cold shock.
>
> Rushing, the current sucked against his legs. Where he stepped in, the water was over his knees. He waded with the current. The gravel slid under his shoes. He looked down at the swirl of water below each leg and tipped up the bottle to get a grasshopper.
>
> The first grasshopper gave a jump in the neck of the bottle and went out into the water. He was sucked under in the whirl by Nick's right leg and came to the surface a little way down stream. He floated rapidly, kicking. In a quick circle, breaking the smooth surface of the water, he disappeared. A trout had taken him. (224)

A few paragraphs later. . .

> He had wet his hand before he touched the trout, so he would not
> disturb the delicate mucus that covered him. If a trout was touched
> with a dry hand, a white fungus attacked the unprotected spot. (225)

Again, a few pages later,

> Nick climbed out onto the meadow and stood, water running down
> his trousers and out of his shoes, his shoes squlchy [sic]. He went over
> and sat on the logs. He did not want to rush his sensations any. (227)

Body. His body, the body of fish and grasshopper. The taking of life is
the giving of life. Offerings left for mink. The body of Hemingway's text is
the body of love.

We read. We eat his words as sacrament.

The Sun Also Rises: Jake is fishing in Spain, the Irati River, with his
buddy Bill Gorton. He has just wrapped the trout he caught in ferns and
put them in his bag. They sit down for lunch. Bill is wet from the waist
down from wading the stream.

> "Gentlemen," he said, and unwrapped a drumstick from a piece of
> newspaper. "I reverse the order. . . . As a tribute to the Great
> Commoner. First the chicken; then the egg."
>
> "Wonder what day God created the chicken?"
>
> "Oh," said Bill, sucking the drumstick, "how should we know?
> We should not question. Our stay on earth is not for long. Let us
> rejoice and believe and give thanks."
>
> "Eat an egg."
>
> Bill gestured with the drumstick in one hand and the bottle of
> wine in the other.
>
> "Let us rejoice in our blessings. Let us utilize the fowls of the air.
> Let us utilize the product of the vine. Will you utilize a little,
> brother?" (121–22)

The ritual continues. Bill again pointing a drumstick at Jake.

> "Let me tell you. We will say, and I for one am proud to say—and I
> want you to say with me, on your knees, brother. Let no man be
> ashamed to kneel here in the great out-of-doors. Remember the
> woods were God's first temples. . . ." (122)

Eros. Nature. Even our own as we touch, eat, feel, holy ground.

But Hemingway writes, "I do not love."

And Hemingway writes, to a Mr. Hall, that he is a man of no religion
(16 October 1933).

What are we to believe?

What are we to believe of a writer who creates a character like Santiago in *The Old Man and the Sea* who says to a warbler which has strayed out to sea, weary and resting on his line, "I am sorry I cannot hoist the sail and take you in"?

What are we to believe in, Mr. Hemingway? Perhaps in the Gulf Stream?

From *Green Hills of Africa*:

> "When, on the sea, you are alone with it and know that this Gulf Stream you are living with, knowing, learning about, and loving, has moved, as it moves, since before man, and that it has gone by the shoreline of that long, beautiful, unhappy island since before Columbus sighted it and that the things you find out about it, and those that have always lived in it are permanent and of value because that stream will flow, as it has flowed . . . it is as clear and blue and unimpressed as it was ever before the tug hauled out the scow; and the palm fronds of our victories, the worn light bulbs of our discoveries and the empty condoms of our great loves float with no significance against one single, lasting thing—the stream." (149–150)

"I have not loved. I am not a religious man," Hemingway tells us. And then we read a sentence like, "It's damn strange how you can love a country" (*Green Hills* 15).

I believe Ernest Hemingway was a lover of country, a patriot and a naturalist, at once, and I believe he was a deeply spiritual man in his attachments to place. Perhaps the pain he had to endure was in feeling too much. He had to create a mask to his own vulnerable nature. He could move. He could dodge. He could drink the blood of Spanish bulls. But the memories of wild nature, the knowledge of wild nature, his need for wild nature never left him. That was his gulf stream, in his blood, on the land, on the page.

In the last chapter, unpublished, of *Death in the Afternoon*, Hemingway writes that if one cares for an undeveloped country, it will seem to change its appearance as a loved woman changes in the eyes of her lover. If the changes are for the worse, the lover moves on. The acceptance of an old established country is a vain attempt to gain security, a security that is impossible to attain. Historical change is inevitable and one's only choice is whether to accept it or reject it and move on to another country.

And what changes did Hemingway see?

Again, in the unpublished chapter of *Death in the Afternoon*, Hemingway writes that in his boyhood, all of northern Michigan was forested, and clear streams abounded. The clear-cutting of the forests and the building of highways, along with the increased fishing of the streams, changed the character of the land. Family farms were lost as young men went into the cities for jobs. The real "heart" vanished from a land Hemingway had loved as a boy. Nobody who did not know that original "heart" can comprehend it once it is gone.

Alfred Kazin writes, "No nature writer in all American literature save Thoreau has had Hemingway's sensitiveness to color, to climate, to the knowledge of physical energy under heat or cold, that knowledge of the body thinking and moving through a landscape that Edmund Wilson, in another connection, has called Hemingway's 'barometric accuracy.' That accuracy was the joy of the huntsman and the artist" (*On Native Grounds* 334).

"Can no branch of Natural History be studied without increasing that faith, love and hope, which we also, every one of us, need in our own journey through the wilderness of life," writes Hemingway.

What I can tell you as a writer of natural history, a storyteller of the American West, is that Ernest Hemingway has been a powerful mentor, in terms of what it means to create a landscape impressionistically on the page, to make it come alive, pulse, breathe, to "make the country so that you could walk into it" (*A Moveable Feast* 91). Hemingway studied Cezanne. We study Hemingway.

And Hemingway's characters in context with the land itself inspire me. Think of Pilar in *For Whom the Bell Tolls* with her earthy sensuality, her bedrock wisdom. And Santiago in *The Old Man and the Sea* with his revolutionary patience. David's story of the elephant hunt in *The Garden of Eden* is another tale of love and loss. We witness the shattering of a young man's innocence. I think of Aldo Leopold's account in *A Sand County Almanac* when he shoots one of the last remaining wolves in the continental United States and watches "the green fire die" (130). Likewise, David sees the vacant eyes of the elephant, once a vital force, now a grey withered body. Hemingway, hunter of hunters, introduces through his characters the idea that betrayal may be inherent in the hunt.

Ernest Hemingway reminds me not that we are conquerors of nature, but rather that we can be lovers. That the primordial forest does still exist and can offer us sustenance and safety, that death must be embraced daily, eye to eye, matador, bull, engaged in a conversation of death.

Ritual. Sacrament. Blood. Body. Earth.

Much has been said and written about "the Hemingway Code," the hero holding himself together in a world without meaning. What would happen if we reversed it, turned it inside out, the hero is held together by the physical world he or she inhabits. Key West. Paris. Spain. Africa.

[11]

Cuba. Idaho. The sea. The city. The bullring. The savannah. The river. The mountains. We are literally held in place. Nature is our nature.

I was not surprised to find a complete set of field guides on the shelves of Hemingway's home here in Ketchum. Peterson's field guides to butterflies, birds, mammals, reptiles, amphibians, insects, ferns, wildflowers, trees, rocks and minerals, stars and planets.

Hemingway's rapacious appetite for the facts of nature supports his apprenticeship as a child, a naturalist. He was mentored by his paternal grandmother Adelaide who was a botanist and his father, Clarence Hemingway, an amateur naturalist himself, who gave young Ernest an "ethic of place," not only a love of hunting but a reverence and respect for the hunted, beginning with "eat what you kill."

It is a well-known story that one day young Hemingway and his friend shot a porcupine. His father made them eat it. A lesson not easily forgotten.

The fact that Hemingway learned, knew, over 250 genus and species, the Latin names of the plants and animals of the Upper Peninsula in Michigan and the midwestern United States, cannot be underestimated in terms of the natural aura and influence of wildlands that coursed through his veins.

"A real writer is studying everything all the time," Hemingway writes. No doubt this kind of bedrock knowledge contributed to his specificity, his insistence on accurate as well as impressionistic representation of landscape.

For Ernest Hemingway, landscape, nature, may be the primary character throughout his work.

There is another facet, chamber, if you will, inside a naturalist's heart and Hemingway possessed it—a preoccupation with death. "Bullfighting is not a sport," he writes. "It is a tragedy, and it symbolizes the struggle between man and beasts."

The first bullfight I ever witnessed was in Valencia, Spain. It was during the celebration of St. Joseph's Day. The country's finest matadors were present, Enriche Ponce among them. My husband and I bought tickets in full sun. As the first bull charged into the arena, every hair on my arm raised. I recognized wildness. And then the carefully orchestrated ritual began. I watched intently aware of the role the crowd played in this drama. My husband, Brooke, was repulsed by what he saw. Sick. He wanted to leave. I wanted to stay, completely caught up in the emotion I saw before us. Our reactions could not have been further apart.

Later that night at dinner, we had one of the most embattled conversations of our marriage. He wanted to know how I could call myself a conservationist with any semblance of conscience, how I could actually enjoy the slaughtering of animals in the name of machismo. I tried to explain myself, that my reaction went beyond thought, I felt something, something old and deep and archaic, right down to my bones. I saw an ancient story of love and loss, life and death, the paradoxical nature of both. I understood on some basic level the need to witness death over and over again. I felt like the roles in the *corrida* were actually reversed. We were the bull. Death was the matador. The importance of our lives is to face death with grace.

What I didn't articulate because it was too vague was that I also felt some remote connection to a Spanish bullfight and what I was witnessing in the American West.

I think about the men in my family, similar to Hemingway in many ways. Sensitive, dark, driven by deep masculine mythologies of hunting, love, and war. When engaged in these activities they tell me they are somehow more alive, alert, spiritually awake. Life is infused with meaning and import. You react, you respond, they tell me. You don't have time to think or feel—that comes later—maybe. When adrenaline flows, ironically it numbs. Drama is its own addictive drug that stays the pain of living.

For Hemingway, perhaps the pain begins when the pen is picked up. This is the terror of reflection that a writer cannot escape if he or she is committed to the truth. But the pain of not writing is worse. Memory, a writer's greatest tool, is a way back to the heart of our collective healing. Art saves our souls.

Do I dare say, in these moments Hemingway embodied the *wild feminine*?

My mind returns once again to Santiago,

> He always thought of the sea as *la mar* which is what people call her in Spanish when they love her. . . . The old man always thought of her as feminine and as something that gave or withheld great favours, and if she did wild or wicked things it was because she could not help them. The moon affects her as it does a woman, he thought. (32–3)

La mar. Hemingway's beloved sea. Jung's collective unconscious.

The story of *The Old Man and the Sea* possesses great significance for me as a writer. Fishing becomes a wonderful metaphor for writing: the patience required, the distance one must travel, the darkness one inhabits. You throw your line into the depths and wait for the great fish to bite. You wait and wait. It asks everything of you. Finally, a strike. The fish has taken the bait. Now the hard work begins. You try to bring the fish to the surface. It demands a muscularity of both body and soul. Cut hands. Torn ligaments. Sore back. Santiago, exhausted, lashes the marlin to his boat. It is the most beautiful animal he has ever seen. They are one, the man and the fish; the artist and his work. The sharks circle him, tear at the fish he has risked his life for. I recognize these sharks as the editing process, tearing into the language, what we must let go of—so painful, until only the bones remain. The architecture of bones. Santiago returns to the village with the skeleton tied to his boat. His great gift to the community is the story. More important than meat to feed the village is the tale to lift their spirits. It is the story that inspires collective courage. He rests. His art, the story, survives him.

"Prose is architecture, not interior decoration." Hemingway writes.

Bones. Bare-boned sentences. Spare, scalding sentences.

The burden of restraint. What we remove is as potent as what remains. This is Hemingway's religion of omission. Less is more. Perhaps because he was a man, an individual of excesses, he economized the page. With all his unbridled passions, perhaps the only thing he could control were his sentences.

This was his survival, his mask, his secret.

Consider one of his titles for *The Sun Also Rises*. "For in much wisdom is much grief. He that increases knowledge increases sorrow." What do you do with this much feeling?

Hemingway—this complicated man with a hunter's eye and a naturalist's heart. A patriot's soul. His insatiable hunger, desire for freedom, for the land.

Let us listen to the opening sentence of *The Spanish Earth*: "This Spanish Earth is dry and hard and the faces of the men who work on that Earth are hard and dry from the sun."

We see the clenched fist of Republican Spain.

We feel the clenched fist of the writer.

Hemingway's fingers wrapped around his pen were his freedom. The clenched fist opens—what do we hold on to, what do we let go?

I often wonder if Ernest Hemingway were alive, what would he have held on to and what would he have let go. I'll bet you an eland dinner, he would have let go of the killing, that his naturalist's heart in the end would have beat the loudest.

Spain.

Africa.

Key West.

The American West—the changes, the heartbreaking changes.

A few months before he died, Hemingway told an interviewer, "To know and love nature is a simpler and higher thing than to know the geology of the rocks and the chemistry of trees."

One returns to origins, wilderness, after walking through the slashing. Remember this passage in "The Last Good Country"?

The slashings had run up to the top of a ridge and over and then the forest began. They were walking on the brown forest floor now and it was springy and cool under their feet. There was no underbrush and the trunks of the trees rose sixty feet high before there were any branches. It was cool in the shade of the trees and high up in them Nick could hear the breeze that was rising. No sun came through as they walked and Nick knew there could be no sun through the high top branches until nearly noon. His sister put her hand in his and walked close to him.

"I'm not scared, Nickie. But it makes me feel very strange."

"Me, too," Nick said. "Always."

"I never was in woods like these."

"This is all the virgin timber left around here."

"Do we go through it very long?"

"Quite a way."

"I'd be afraid if we were alone."

"It makes me feel strange. But I'm not afraid."

"I said that first."

"I know. Maybe we say it because we are afraid."

"No. I'm not afraid because I'm here with you. But I know I'd be afraid alone. Did you ever come here with anyone else?"

"No. Only by myself."

"And you weren't afraid?"

"No. But I always feel strange. Like the way I ought to feel in church. . . ."

"This is the way forests were in the olden days. This is about the last good country." (*The Nick Adams Stories* 73–4)

I feel these things about wild, open country in the American West, "cathedrals" Hemingway writes.

Hemingway was a war correspondent. He saw plenty of wounding. Perhaps it intensified his own.

As a writer who concerns herself with landscape and as a woman deeply rooted in the American West, I have to tell you there are times I feel like a war correspondent as well.

I resist the metaphor. I resist the metaphor of war believing it can only create and add to the hurtful and simplistic oppositions we manufacture for ourselves. But just this once, I am going to allow myself to give in, to let this metaphor run.

Yes. A war correspondent witnessing, chronicling road cuts, road kills, clear-cuts, even the peeled bodies of our elders, Douglas firs and cedars chained to the flatbeds of trucks and hauled away on our highways.

Dammed rivers: Glen Canyon. Cathedral in the desert: Davis Gulch. Remember their names. Toxic waste. Toxic deserts—bombed, battered, and betrayed in the name of national security. The Nevada Test Site in the Mojave. Rocky Flats. Hanford. Alamogordo. Dugway. INEL, even in Idaho. The nuclear west is simmering. Coyote watches with burning eyes. There is a war raging within our own nation.

Breyten Breytenbach says, "The real revolutionary question is, 'What about the Other?'" Salmon. Grizzly. Curlew. Tortoise. Call their names. Remember their names. Wildness disappearing before our eyes.

As a species, we are slowly committing a collective suicide.

Strip mines. Strip search. Gold-blooded murders. Remember Hemingway's story, "A Natural History of the Dead"? In an unpublished coda to the story there is a tale of watching a sergeant during World War I investigate the teeth of the dead. He would open their mouths, pry out their gold fillings with a trench knife, then use a piece of pipe to break out other filled teeth, putting them in a German gas mask tin for later. Describing the sergeant's efforts as "research," Hemingway ironically suggests that we learn from this "industrious" man and extract gold from the dead.

Last night, I stayed at Hemingway's home in Ketchum. I can tell you, I didn't get much sleep. First of all, I thought I heard a heart beating inside the house. I was terrified and did what any sensible person would do. After dinner I asked the distinguished professors I was with if they would check out the noise with me. They graciously agreed and after a good thorough investigation, ears on walls, hands on refrigerators and furnaces, they concluded it was simply a water pump. They left. I tried to read and could not. Finally, I walked up the stairs to the room where I was to sleep, the room Hemingway wrote in (the little he did there), and climbed into bed. Of course, I lay awake. Scared to death about today's talk, my mind racing back and forth, I sat up and without any hesitation and a fair amount of humor, I said, "Mr. Hemingway, if any part of you is still here, certainly you have to see how funny this is, how pitiful this is, trying to speak about you in front of all these academicians. If you really believe as you write in 'The Snows of Kilimanjaro,' that you are a writer and not carrion, could you please help me out. Just give me a clue as to what is the most important thing about your work, your writing, your life. What can I say?" I paused. "Thank you, Mr. Hemingway. Good night."

I fell asleep and had wild dreams all night long.

When I awoke, my eyes still closed, mindful of what I had asked, I listened. I felt at peace. I sat up, opened my eyes, and through the large picture window facing east, I watched the sun rise over the Wood River.

One generation passeth away, and another generation cometh; but the earth abideth forever. . . .The sun also ariseth . . . all the rivers run into the sea; yet the sea is not full; unto the place whence the rivers come, thither they return again.

ECCLESIASTES.

How can we begin to understand the writing of Ernest Hemingway if we only focus on his work inside, on the page, in the academy? Hemingway showed us through the passion, electricity, and physicality of his life that the marrow of life is to be found and lived outside. His language has its roots in place. His nature is nature. We need not look further than the ground beneath our feet and the overarching sky.

"We are born with an eye toward the heavens," Hemingway writes, "Thank heavens we don't have to kill the stars . . . but we die with our head bowed toward the earth."

May I close with the first paragraph from *For Whom the Bell Tolls*:

He lay flat on the brown, pine-needled floor of the forest, his chin on his folded arms, and high overhead the wind blew in the tops of the pine trees. (1)

And the last:

Robert Jordan lay behind the tree, holding onto himself very carefully delicately to keep his hands steady. He was waiting until the officer reached the sunlit place where the first trees of the pine forest joined the green slope of the meadow. He could feel his heart beating against the pine needle floor of the forest. (471)

Whose Nature?: Differing Narrative Perspectives in Hemingway's "Big Two-Hearted River"

FREDRIK CHR. BRØGGER

Reading Hemingway criticism can sometimes turn the most committed contextual scholar into a New Critic. The critical interpretations of Hemingway's "Big Two-Hearted River" are a case in point. One critic after the other seems bent on basing his or her interpretation on extra- rather than intratextual evidence—no matter whether such extratextual evidence is taken from Hemingway's life, from other Hemingway stories, or from the original nine-page interior monologue that Hemingway most emphatically decided *not* to use as conclusion to his story.[1]

Although Malcolm Cowley suggested in his 1944 introduction to *The Portable Hemingway* that Nick's fishing trip in "Big Two-Hearted River" represented "an escape" probably propelled by his war experiences,[2] the true founder of the biography-and-war business of Hemingway criticism was of course Philip Young, who saw Nick as a young man on the run from the memories of the horrors of the First World War. Young asserts that Nick is afraid of the swamp in "Big Two-Hearted River" because it evokes "the geography of the place where he was blown up. . . ."[3] Hemingway's later observation in *A Moveable Feast* that the story "was about coming back from the war but there was no mention of the war in it"[4] lends authority to Young's interpretation, although some see this evidence as somewhat tainted by its belatedness. In any case, it is one thing to see shellshock as a possible explanatory motif in the story; it is quite another to make—as Young does—Nick's childhood and war experiences into the "whole 'point' of an otherwise pointless story."[5] Its so-called pointlessness, then, is projected by its main subject matter, namely that of hiking, camping, and fishing. Is the description of a man seeking solace through interaction with nature pointless? Emerson and Thoreau might have been inclined to object.

Later critics, however, have proceeded further on the basis of scant textual evidence. Kenneth Lynn refers to Hemingway's relationship with his mother prior to the writing of the story and therefore suggests that the "other needs" Nick "feels he has put behind him include a need to please his mother, while his talk of his tent as his home may represent a reaction to being thrown out of his parents' summer cottage."[6] Debra A. Moddelmog refers to the original conclusion to the story and to the context of the other stories of *In Our Time* and argues that the fishing trip in "Big Two-Hearted River" is a result of Nick's worries about marriage and his fear of fatherhood.[7] The urge to provide some extratextual "explanations" of Nick's state of mind seems irresistible for readers of "Big Two-Hearted River."

Hemingway critics thus rival novice literary students in their desire to provide fictional characters with motives when such motives are deliberately left out in the text itself. By doing so, such scholars have constructed a text different from the one we actually read. By deliberately eschewing rational explanations of Nick's state of mind, "Big Two-Hearted River" evokes in modernist fashion an indefinite but pervasive sense of alienation and insecurity. Its possible sociocultural causes—mortars, mothers, marriage—are a nonsubject; what is emphasized is the indeterminacy of Nick's angst. The central subject of the story is Nick's attempt to overcome his mental imbalance and his fears by escaping from culture into nature. Thus the description of nature becomes itself a basic feature in the story.

Indeed I can still remember my own reaction at the age of seventeen when first reading "Big Two-Hearted River" in Norwegian translation. To me it represented a remarkably vivid celebration, something akin to a eulogy, of outdoor life. This initial response to the story may be closer to its core meaning than a great many critical views. What Philip Young regarded as pointless in "Big Two-Hearted River" may in fact be regarded as its basic point, and Paul Smith loses a great deal of the text when he observes that the content of Hemingway's story is "at the end not much more than two fish, while the form is everything."[8] "Big Two-Hearted River" is first and foremost a fishing story. As with most great stories of outdoor life, its ultimate theme is linked to the relationship between man and nature. The central interpretive questions are therefore: What kind of vision of outdoor life does the world of "Big Two-Hearted River" project? What is the significance that the story ultimately ascribes to nature?

Part of the answer to these questions has to do with the character of Nick. From the outset of the story Nick is presented as a man attempting to recover a sense of control in his interaction with nature. He needs to reexperience this control in order to regain his mental balance. It is the tale of a man who needs his challenges to be simple and manageable, as they indeed are when one is hiking in such "long undulating country."[9] Repeatedly in the course of the story we discover that the relationship between Nick and nature is that between subject and object. Nature, to Nick, is something that must be mastered and controlled; it is defined not in terms of itself but in terms of Nick's needs.

But the significance ascribed to nature in Hemingway's story depends not only on Nick's vision of it. This fishing story may be refracted through Nick's consciousness, but it is nonetheless told by an anonymous narrator who is not Nick. The issue of the narrative point of view in "Big Two-Hearted River" is therefore important. Again, Hemingway critics have often obfuscated rather than clarified the essential nature of this short story. Referring to the original nine-page conclusion to the story that Hemingway omitted, Moddelmog argues that Nick should be considered the implied author of the story and of *In Our Time* as a whole.[10] This introduction of an implied author "Nick" who writes about a made-up character named Nick in the voice of a third-person (fictionalized?) narrator is a distortion of the simple narrative character of Hemingway's final version. As Moddelmog herself acknowledges, it runs up against Hemingway's explicit reason, stated in a mid-November 1924 letter to Robert McAlmon, for omitting the original concluding monologue: "I have decided that all that mental conversation in the long fishing story is the shit and have cut it all out. The last nine pages. . . . I've finished it off the way it ought to have been all along. Just the straight fishing."[11] In its final form, the story presents straight telling as well as straight fishing.

In traditional narratological terms, "Big Two-Hearted River" is a narrative restricted in its focus to the *character* Nick; it employs what Wayne C. Booth in *The Rhetoric of Fiction* calls a third-person "reflector" or "center of consciousness."[12] It is often assumed in older narrative theory that the use of a third-person restricted focus marks—like first-person narration—an exclusively subjective perspective. Thus Carl Ficken in his essay "Point of View in the Nick Adams Stories" argues that "Big Two-Hearted River" "represents Nick totally as a Center of Consciousness. . . . At no point in the story does the focus come from any observer other than Nick, at every point first person would work. . . . There is nothing else to feel and see except what Nick feels and sees."[13] This total disregard of the *narrator* of "Big Two-Hearted River" needs some modification. Employing Gérard Genette's narrative theory helps distinguish between *narration* and *focalization*, between *who tells* and *who sees* (perceives). "Big Two-Hearted River" may thus be designated a *heterodiegetic* narrative (where the narrator is absent from the story he tells) with *internal focalization* (where things are perceived through a character in the story).[14] Although the story is predominantly filled with Nick's viewpoints and feelings, Genette's scheme allows us better to note its interplay of narration and focalization. This is no trifling quarrel over literary terms. Whereas traditional narrative theory only allows for *one* point of view and thus *one* view of nature in Hemingway's story, namely that of Nick, more recent theories of narratology would admit two perspectives, namely that of the narrator as well as that of Nick.

A closer analysis of "Big Two-Hearted River" reveals that even the focalization varies considerably, spanning the entire spectrum of what Dorrit Cohn in *Transparent Minds* calls "quoted (interior) monologue," "narrated monologue," and "psycho-narration."[15] Quoted monologue, in which the narrator's presence is obliterated by a character's direct thoughts, occurs only once in Nick's story, when he thinks: "By God, he [the trout] was the biggest one I ever heard of" (151). Narrated monologue, in which the presence of the narrator is almost eclipsed except for the markers of person and tense, occurs more often, revealing Nick's thoughts directly: "Still, it [the pack] was too heavy. It was much too heavy" (134). Psycho-narration—what Cohn terms "the narrator's discourse about a character's consciousness"[16]—is, however, a relatively frequent technique in Hemingway's story, in which the narrator is a mediator of Nick's perceptions and feelings: "Nick felt awkward and professionally happy with all his equipment hanging from him" (147).

Nick's thoughts and feelings are less often portrayed, however, than are his *actions* and his *sensations*. Quite often when the latter are presented, the narrator envisions the scene together with him: "Now as he looked down the river, the insects must be settling on the surface, for the trout were feeding steadily all down the stream. As far down the long stretch as he could see, the trout were rising, making circles all down the surface of the water, as though it were starting to rain" (138). In such descriptions, Nick's perspective and the narrator's voice merge and cannot be distinguished from each other; is for instance the image of raindrops that of the main character or the anonymous narrator? In many descriptive passages of Hemingway's story it is uncertain how much of the language reflects the narrator's own perceptions and how much of it springs from his *vision with* Nick. In other passages, however, the language seems definitely slanted toward Nick's perspective, as in the descriptive repetitions at the outset of the story about the trout "holding themselves" and "keeping themselves steady" in the current (133), which seem to express Nick's obsession with control and balance. There are other passages in the story, however, in which perception cannot be primarily attributed to Nick, for instance when the narrator himself seems to describe the scene directly from a more detached perspective: "The river was clear and smoothly fast in the early morning" (145).

There are many fluid transitions between the narrator's and Nick's discourses, but these variations in perspective can be boiled down to two basic views in "Big Two-Hearted River," a "narratorial" view of the landscape and an "actorial" one.[17] The former is that of the anonymous narrator (rare but significant) and the latter is that of Nick. This combination of heterodiegetic narration and an extended use of internal focalization allows for interesting contrasts in perspective between that of the narrator on the one hand, however unobtrusive and unintrusive it may be, and that of the character-actor on the other.

When the narrator of Hemingway's story seems to speak directly to the reader, he appears to be a detached, precise, and keen observer. Sometimes his summaries break through in descriptions primarily devoted to Nick's view of the landscape. At the end of the opening paragraph of the story, for instance, it seems to be the narrator who sums up the scene of the town in ruins in a strikingly straightforward manner: "It was all that was left of the town of Seney. Even the surface had been burned off the ground" (133). The forthrightness is an indication of the narrator's voice: Although the burnt landscape comes as a pure surprise to Nick, the summary contains nothing of the discomfort or fear that emerges in the unstable Nick when later confronted with the swamp.

Similarly, the lens through which we look at the hike seems sometimes to pull back from Nick and allow the narrator to form a carefully described overview of the scene. One such instance occurs when Nick strikes out toward the river away from the road: "Two hundred yards down the hillside the fire line stopped. Then it was sweet fern, growing ankle high, to walk through, and clumps of jack pines; a long undulating country with frequent rises and descents, sandy underfoot and the country alive again" (136). Here again is a narratorial summing-up whose voice, as it emerges intermittently in the story, reveals a mind generously open and yet meticulously precise in its recording of the natural environment. This may also be seen in the depiction of the pine grove in which Nick takes a rest. This passage is not an internalization of Nick's observations; it bears the marks of a narrator concerned with accuracy and explanation:

> Around the grove of trees was a bare space. It was brown and soft underfoot as Nick walked on it. This was the overlapping of the pine needle floor, extending out beyond the width of the high branches. The trees had grown tall and the branches moved high, leaving in the sun this bare space they had once covered with shadow. Sharp at

the edge of this extension of the forest floor commenced the sweet
fern. (137)

Here is a desire to record the tallness of the trees, the elevation of their
branches, the brown color of the fallen needles—a narrator's exegesis
complete with identification ("This was the overlapping of the pine needle floor") and explanation ("The trees had grown tall . . . leaving in the
sun this bare space they had once covered with shadow"). In the unfolding of the story of "Big Two-Hearted River," the reader becomes aware of
an anonymous narrator who tries to describe nature as directly and accurately as possible. The narrator's relationship to nature is marked by a
refusal to impose meaning on it; his literary reticence when evoking the
landscape through language seems to reflect a respect for the factuality
and many-facetedness of nature itself.

Nick's relationship to nature is different. This, however, is not usually
revealed in the general descriptions of the landscape; here narration
often merges with internal focalization to the extent that it is impossible
to distinguish between narratorial and actorial discourse. Nonetheless,
the reader often suspects that even in the many passages where the narrator's voice and Nick's perspective merge, the vivid and accurate impressions of the landscape are indicative of the narrator's mentality: "On the
left, where the meadow ended and the woods began, a great elm tree was
uprooted. Gone over in a storm, it lay back into the woods, its roots clot-
ted with dirt, grass growing in them, rising a solid bank beside the
stream" (151). In passages that express Nick's thoughts and feelings
directly, however, it becomes obvious that Nick does not share in the narrator's disinterested openness vis-à-vis nature. As Don Summerhayes
observes in a recent article, in "Big Two-Hearted River" we hear "a narrator's voice that produces images that persistently dissolve their metaphorical suggestiveness into metonymy, and a character's voice we can identify
by its insistence on spotting metaphorical connections with his own 'case'
everywhere he looks."[18] Nick's viewpoint is unabashedly anthropocentric;
he is first and foremost concerned with what nature means to *him*.

It does not take the reader long to see that Nick seeks the river less as
an explorer than as a fugitive. As Nick attempts to escape the problems he
is struggling with, hiking and fishing are, as critics have pointed out, primarily a means to keep his worries simple—to keep him preoccupied with
the heaviness of his pack and camping arrangements. The basic exigencies
of outdoor life make it possible to him to leave "everything behind, the
need for thinking, the need to write, other needs" (134). His reflections on
the landscape are goal-directed and limited. If he may be said to have an
eye for detail, it is a narrow one guided by his obsession with the tasks at

hand, which embody his need for predictability and order. As Sheldon Norman Grebstein has suggested, in "Big Two-Hearted River" "limited omniscience functions perfectly to connote both the geographical isolation of the protagonist and his emotional insularity."[19]

Nick's consciousness reveals that he is fundamentally out to recapture "all the old feeling" (134) he used to have. Time and again Nick's thoughts reveal that to him nature exists to fulfil his expectations, to affirm what he is already cognizant of: He "knew" the hills "could not all be burned" (135); he does not need the map because he "knew where he was from the position of the river" (135); guided by the sun he "knew where he wanted to strike the river" (136); as he leaves the pines for the river, he "knew it could not be more than a mile" (137); while fishing he "was certain he could catch small trout in the shallows" (149). Having his expectations confirmed gives Nick a sense of control—a satisfaction similar to the one he gets from mastering his simple camping-and-fishing rituals, including pitching the tent, making buckwheat cakes, or tidying up camp. Nick's need to have everything come out as he has expected and planned it to takes the form of pure compulsion: "Nick was happy as he crawled inside the tent. He had not been unhappy all day. This was different though. Now things were done. There had been this to do. Now it was done. It had been a hard trip. He was very tired. That was done" (139).

Happiness to Nick is a matter of control, control is a matter of competence, and competence is a matter of being familiar with the simple tasks of outdoor life. The cultural environment, be it the war or the city, is a complex one, often beset by the unexpected. Nature's advantage over the society in the first part of the story resides precisely in its predictability. Nick's preoccupation with the familiar and the expected on his camping-and-fishing expedition is obvious as early as the second paragraph of the story: "Nick looked at the burned-over stretch of hillside, where he had expected to find the scattered houses of the town and then walked down the railroad track to the bridge over the river. *The river was there*. It swirled against the log piles of the bridge" (133, my emphasis). The narrated monologue of "The river was there" seems to embody *Nick's* immediate reaction. The river's living presence comes as a relief in the wake of the description of the unforeseen wasteland of the town: Here things finally turn out as expected—the river proves full of trout and the trout are "very satisfactory" (134). A major point in the story is quite simply that the subject, Nick, appreciates the object, nature, only insofar as it satisfies his expectations. The first part of "Big Two-Hearted River" opens with the "satisfactory" trout and ends with Nick moving his match quickly to the canvas over his head: "The mosquito made a satisfactory hiss in the flame" (142).

The next morning Nick is certainly "excited" to be near the river (145), but to him the river has value predominantly in terms of its promise of fish: "The trees of the left bank made short shadows on the current in the forenoon sun. Nick knew there were trout in each shadow. In the afternoon, after the sun had crossed toward the hills, the trout would be in the cool shadows on the other side of the stream" (152). Most of Nick's descriptions of nature are concerned with the riverscape's usefulness for trout-catching. Nick views the landscape as a fisherman, not a naturalist.

Indeed the narrated monologues of "Big Two-Hearted River" usually serve as expressions of Nick's self-absorbed need for ritual rather than any desire on his part to be open to the surrounding nature. Nick's desire to avoid instances when fishing is too difficult is a case in point; angling is fundamentally a matter of gaining control. Nick's fear of the swamp is connected precisely with the fact that fishing will prove impossible there: It is a place where "the big cedars came together overhead," where the sun shines through only "in patches," where fishing "in the fast deep water, in the half light . . . would be tragic" (155). In the swamp Nick's competence will no longer suffice; the result of his fishing ceases to be predictable. Nick fears complication and disorder, projected here by deepening water, the lack of landing sites, the overgrowth, and the scarcity of light. Complexity equals uncertainty, which equals tragedy; Nick still needs nature to be something he can master.

Yet there is considerable hope for the mentally unbalanced Nick. He is attempting to extend the limits of his tolerance, and he has moments where nature appeals to more than his desire to have expectations fulfilled or mastery confirmed. The first part of "Big Two-Hearted River" portrays a Nick who needs to affirm what he used to know and who wants to avoid any risks of pain (including that of burning his tongue on his dinner), but the second part presents a man who several times tests his self-imposed limits. He initially does not want to try to flop the buckwheat cake, but does (146). He may feel "shaky" and "a little sick" (150) after losing the battle with the big trout, but he is at the same time able to laugh at a tiny trout rising at the match he throws into the current (151). He does "not care about fishing that hole" by the beech tree, but he does anyway, hooking *and* losing a "heavily" thrashing trout (153). Thus "Big Two-Hearted River" is a tale not only of a man who needs to feel in control of his environment; it is at the same time the story of a man who tries to challenge that need. Thus, when Nick observes at the story's end that "There were plenty of days coming when he could fish the swamp" (156), the reader tends to believe that he will continue to test his own ability to tolerate complications.

At the end Nick consequently gives voice to his desire to continue to expose himself to the two-heartedness of the river. To Nick, mastering the simple tasks of camping and fishing certainly evokes a sense of harmony, but enjoying nature is not a matter of competence only; it is a matter of accepting and tolerating the other side of its pulsating heart, its unexpected snarls and entanglements, as represented by the swamp. The challenges of nature, after all, are not different from those of culture, except that they may be tackled more piecemeal and approached when one is more prepared to face them; one has, in a sense, the *choice* of tackling the difficulties or not, which is less possible in a cultural environment. Ultimately, however, appreciating nature for itself involves respecting its separateness. In time, Nick's attitude toward outdoor life approaches the openness of the narrator, who is free and disinterested enough to note in accurate detail the variety of his natural environment. Indeed, after having been shook up by the battle with the big trout, Nick's appreciation of nature is for once quite unrestricted and undirected, with little of the discipline that he so tenaciously clings to:

> He sat on the logs, smoking, drying in the sun, the sun warm on his back, the river shallow ahead entering the woods, curving into the woods, shallows, light glittering, big water-smooth rocks, cedars along the bank and white birches, the logs warm in the sun, smooth to sit on, without bark, gray to the touch; slowly the feeling of disappointment left him. (151)

The tone of the passage reflects the impressionability of Nick's emotional state, combined with the narrator's appreciation of the many-faceted landscape's beauty. Multiple-sense impressions seem to flow over Nick, visual as well as tactile, and their attractiveness seems to reside not least in their variety—the combination of the heat of the sun, the curve and movement of the river, the glitter of light, the varieties of trees, the smoothness of the rocks and logs. Here is something close to an eroticism of landscape. Here Nick for once succumbs to nature rather than forcing nature to succumb to him. And if the openness and accuracy of Cezanne may first and foremost characterize the style of the narrator himself, Nick is here shown to have the potential, at least, of becoming a kindred spirit.

Thus Hemingway's tale is not necessarily and certainly not primarily about a man fleeing from war or women. It is a narrative about Nick's development and progression, presented in terms of his interaction with the natural environment through hiking, camping, and fishing. The two-heartedness of the river is analogous with the two-heartedness of the narrative itself, projecting two differing views of nature—on the one hand Nick's anthropocentric need to master the natural environment and on the other hand the narrator's non-anthropocentric openness and respect for whatever nature may represent. This ambivalence is quite typical of American attitudes toward nature in the inter-war years. However pleasant it is for Nick to master the simpler tasks of outdoor life, his mental health ultimately depends on his capacity to move beyond this impasse, to relinquish his need for control, to be able to lose fish and laugh about it, to test his tolerance of intricacy, and to learn to accept and appreciate the variety of nature—which is to say the complexity of life.

NOTES

1. The original nine-page ending is reprinted with the title "On Writing" in Ernest Hemingway, *The Nick Adams Stories* (New York: Scribner's, 1972), 233–41. For an extended discussion of "Big Two-Hearted River" in relation to this piece, see Robert Paul Lamb, "Fishing for Stories: What 'Big Two-Hearted River' Is Really About," *Modern Fiction Studies* 37 (Summer 1991): 161–81.

2. Malcolm Cowley, Introduction to *Hemingway* (New York: Viking, 1944), ix.

3. Philip Young, *Ernest Hemingway: A Reconsideration* (University Park: Pennsylvania State University Press, 1966), 53. Based on his original volume *Ernest Hemingway* (1952).

4. Ernest Hemingway, *A Moveable Feast* (New York: Scribner's, 1964), 76.

5. Young, *Ernest Hemingway: A Reconsideration*, 47. For a recent discussion of Young's psychographic criticism, see Wayne C. Holcombe, "Philip Young or Youngerdunger?" *Hemingway Review* 5 (Spring 1986): 24–33.

6. Kenneth Lynn, "The Troubled Fisherman," in *New Critical Approaches to the Short Stories of Ernest Hemingway*, ed. Jackson J. Benson (Durham, N.C.: Duke University Press, 1990), 151.

7. Debra A. Moddelmog, "The Unifying Consciousness of a Divided Conscience: Nick Adams as Author of *In Our Time*," in *New Critical Approaches to the Short Stories of Ernest Hemingway*, 24–30.

8. Paul Smith, *A Reader's Guide to the Short Stories of Ernest Hemingway* (Boston: G.K. Hall, 1989), 98.

9. Ernest Hemingway, "Big Two-Hearted River," in *In Our Time* (New York: Scribner's, 1930), 136. Subsequent references to "Big Two-Hearted River" will be given as page numbers in the text.

10. Moddelmog, "The Unifying Consciousness," 17–32.

11. Carlos Baker, ed., *Ernest Hemingway: Selected Letters, 1917–1961* (New York: Scribner's, 1981), 133.

12. Wayne C. Booth, *The Rhetoric of Fiction* (Chicago: University of Chicago Press, 1961), 153.

13. Carl Ficken, "Point of View in the Nick Adams Stories," in *The Short Stories of Ernest Hemingway: Critical Essays*, ed. Jackson J. Benson (Durham, N.C.: Duke University Press, 1975), 106.

14. Gérard Genette, *Narrative Discourse* (Oxford: Basil Blackwell, 1980), 244–45, 189.

15. Dorrit Cohn, *Transparent Minds: Narrative Modes for Presenting Consciousness in Fiction* (Princeton, N.J.: Princeton University Press, 1978), 58–98 (quoted monologue), 99–140 (narrated monologue), and 21–57 (psycho-narration).

16. Ibid., 14.

17. For a discussion of these terms, see Gérard Genette's *Narrative Discourse Revisited* (Ithaca, N.Y.: Cornell University Press, 1988), 114–129, particularly 118, 120.

18. Don Summerhayes, "Fish Story: Ways of Telling in 'Big Two-Hearted River,'" *Hemingway Review* 15 (Fall 1995): 24.

19. Sheldon Norman Grebstein, *Hemingway's Craft* (Carbondale: Southern Illinois University Press, 1974), 83.

Man Cannot Live by Dry Flies Alone: Fly Rods, Grasshoppers, and an Adaptive Catholicity in Hemingway's "Big Two-Hearted River"

DAVID N. CREMEAN

Perhaps Ernest Hemingway's greatest achievement in writing with a major focus on the natural world is the two-part story, "Big Two-Hearted River." One curious and seemingly insignificant nature-related detail in the story appears in Part II: To catch trout Nick employs bait—a grasshopper—with a fly rod.[1] Like many others ranging from the story's title to its bipartite structure, this detail actually bears great dualistic weight that gathers mass from elements of Hemingway's life and other writings to support a religious, predominantly (but by no means solely) Catholic reading of the text. In angling with this line of thought, my casts are made from the solid ground established by "In the Nominal Country of the Bogus: Hemingway's Catholicism and the Biographies," H. R. Stoneback's extensively researched argument leading to his conclusion that Catholicism "is everywhere in [Hemingway's] work. . . . it is in the fiction that we must undertake the pilgrimage with Hemingway."[2] To join the pilgrimage, my reading primarily depends on the confluence of symbolism, some relevant biographical matters, and intertextuality within selected works of the Hemingway canon.

As alluded to above, the word "two" in the title underscores the numerous dualisms at the center of the story. Hemingway's hyphenation of "two-hearted" adds to that duality. Most relevant here is the fact that, given Western civilization's typical associations of heart with both the physical and the spiritual sides of the human condition, Hemingway's title strongly leads readers to examine the story from these two vantage points. The hyphenation additionally underscores the ultimate unity of these two seemingly disparate elements.

The two-part structure of the story further bulwarks this claim, with Part I tracing Nick Adams' movement through the fire-ravaged area around Seney and into the edenic natural environs where he later sets up camp. Most of Nick's work in this section, such as the hiking and camp craft, can be viewed as predominantly physical activities. I do not, however, mean to suggest that any of Nick's activities in Part I are without ritualistic overtones; rather, the rituals here strike me as inherently primitive. In contrast, the activities of Part II center on concerns that are, on the surface, nonessential to practical daily living, concerns thus arguably primarily "spiritual." In particular, Nick's fishing transforms into more strongly ritualistic, even sacramental, behavior. Moreover, the rituals become primarily Christian, mostly Catholic, especially because of an emphasis on sacrifice revolving around the fish, one of Christianity's principle symbols, particularly as a historical symbol for Christ. Yet the rituals in Part II maintain links to the primitive not only because of their relationship to Part I but also because, similar to Christian rituals, they parallel or grow out of primitive rituals. In addition, at least to some extent, they therefore continue these more primitive rituals.[3] The ultimate unity of the physical-spiritual, primitivistic-Catholic dualisms is in turn vital to understanding the union of the grasshopper and fly rod.

Before I directly pursue this argument, however, a few details about fly fishing supply important background that further extends the physical-spiritual and thus the primitivistic-Catholic dualisms. To those largely unfamiliar with the codes of fly fishing, combining a fly rod with a grasshopper may seem unexceptional, but to the purist fly fisher, bait fishing at all is blasphemous, bait fishing with a fly rod the unpardonable sin. For the purist, the fly rod and fly are inviolable icons in what amounts to a sacramental ritual; to neglect using either or both in fishing for trout is to risk raising a purist's hackles. These attitudes—common knowledge even among fly fishers not subscribing to the faith at a zealous purist level—permeate much of the writing about fly fishing.

Some particularly illustrative examples of such fishing fundamentalism occur in Norman Maclean's novella "A River Runs Through It." Maclean writes that he, his Presbyterian minister father, and his brother Paul held to the purist creed, since "In our family, there was no clear line between religion and fly fishing."[4] Therefore the Reverend disparages Izaak Walton as follows: "not a respectable writer. . . . an Episcopalian and a bait fisherman."[5] Later, Paul curses the very thought of fishing with Norman's brother-in-law Neal, a Montana expatriate moved to California, arguing

> I won't fish with him. He comes from the West Coast and he fishes with worms. . . . he's a bait fisherman. All those Montana boys on the West Coast. . . . when they come back home they don't even kiss their mothers on the front porch before they're in the back garden with a red Hills Bros. coffee can digging for angleworms.[6]

In fact, though in writings about fly fishing an occasional brave author maintains a fly rod can be used with bait, for the most part these writers are viewed by purists as heretics.[7] Yet in "Big Two-Hearted River" Hemingway, often grouped with Maclean and a handful of others as patron saints of fly fishing, has Nick use what purist eschatology, to echo biblical language, could well term "the abomination of combination" to pursue the most high and holy trout. The question remains, "Why?"—certainly Hemingway, ever-conscious craftsman and long-time fly fisher even when he wrote the story in 1924–25, knew what he was doing and chose to do so for several reasons.

In an essay unpublished until 1991, "On Fly Fishing," Hemingway opens by reminiscing about his youthful trout fishing: "When we first fished, as boys, we did not believe in flies. . . . We used a long cane pole . . . [and] bait." Though this bait was "angleworms" and not grasshoppers, the important detail is that it was still of course bait, not a fly.[8] Coupled with a cane pole rather than a fly rod, the bait places the boys in a purely primitive relationship with fishing instead of a more ethereal one relying on crafted flies, designed rods, and specialized lines, leaders, and hooks. Now, years later, Hemingway looks back on that time and remarks about how he has changed with age:

> This way of fishing [with cane pole and bait] I learned to look down on and it was not until long afterward that I knew that it is not the duration of a sensation but its intensity that counts. If it is of enough intensity it lasts forever no matter what the actual time was and then I knew why it was that I had loved fishing so.[9]

Years of what purists view as more sophisticated fishing have come and gone, but only recently has he realized that for him the more elemental, physically-based boyhood angling held greater intensity and romance than the seemingly more refined, delicate, time-involved fly fishing of his adult years. The primitive form has a spiritual side, too, but it is an appeal more sensed than consciously known, more related to the physical than the metaphysical. Only from the perspective of having participated in and having understood the "institutionalized" form could the primitive one be properly appreciated. Logically, the opposite is also true. Thus a variety of dualistic syncretism is essential to arriving at the truth of experience, with each type informing the other.

This quality is part of the spirituality my reading of "Big Two-Hearted River" reflects, including as it does a major feature of the intense boyhood experience, bait in the form of grasshoppers. Of course, the frequent critical identifications of Nick as an autobiographical character would help reinforce the notion that Hemingway's brief essay relates to the fictional character. But one need not force biographical parallels to argue that the boys in Hemingway's essay correspond to Nick. For instance, Adams uses items from Hemingway's boyhood and adult fishing experiences: a fly rod and bait. In this way, the detail reflects a dichotomy in Nick's life: He is caught somewhere between his disappearing youth, symbolized by his employing the more romantic and elemental grasshopper as bait, and his oncoming manhood, symbolized by the more artistic and refined fly rod. On the symbolic level, the combination is necessary to the holistic spirituality Nick seeks. For Nick as for Hemingway, the bait—like primitivism— is primarily physical and of the earth, while the fly rod is essentially spiritual and airborne. Thus this combination reflects the major dualistic elements inherent in the human condition.

A letter from Hemingway—often noted in other writings about "Big Two-Hearted River," though in different contexts than this one—also sheds some light on a spiritual reading of the short story. The letter, written circa 15 September 1919 to Howell Jenkins (or "Shittle"), details a trout fishing trip Hemingway had recently taken with a couple of friends to the Black and Fox Rivers of Michigan's Upper Peninsula.[10] This trip occurred shortly after the end of World War I, when Hemingway was approximately Nick's age in the story. Hemingway was also in need of similar purgation after suffering trauma from the war, one of "the things left out" in "Big Two-Hearted River," as Hemingway later stressed in "The Art of the Short Story."[11] Carlos Baker wrote of Hemingway, "He later recalled that he was still badly hurt in body, mind, spirit, and morals at this time."[12] The letter reveals a number of other parallels between Nick's and Hemingway's experiences there, as does Baker's account of the trip the letter deals with.[13] But only a couple of these parallels relate directly to my subject here: In the letter Hemingway writes that he and his companions caught some smaller trout on flies, and he mentions "Hoppers" (grasshoppers) as well.[14]

In the story Nick has his fly book along (175). Yet he still chooses to fish live grasshoppers rather than artificial flies. One practical reason for his selection is that after leaving the train, his hike to the vegetated river area takes him through the burnt town of Seney and through the scorched *terra damnata* surrounding it, where he sees a large number of black grasshoppers. The next day he seeks live grasshoppers to fish with and finds that with the verdant landscape, the grasshoppers have changed to "brown ones" (173). Likely he chooses the live grasshoppers because he either lacks dry patterns to imitate these insects or at least lacks any that match those he sees, since by fly fishing conventions he would normally use patterns of the area's species, not bait, with the fly rod. Ironically, in his often-cited essay on the Fox, its locale, and the story, Sheridan Baker notes (perhaps out of season?) that on the Fox "You find no grasshoppers."[15] At the very least, however, Hemingway's choice of these insects for the story is another example of what he termed the "poetry" involved in his substituting the neighboring Two Hearted River's name for the Fox, a choice employed "not from ignorance nor carelessness."[16]

Hemingway's classic novel *The Sun Also Rises* (1926) is also relevant to this discussion. Written in the same general time period as "Big Two-Hearted River," the novel includes an idyllic scene in which Jake Barnes and friend Bill Gorton go fishing on Spain's Fabrica.[17] The two men are apparently armed with fly rods: They "jointed up the rods, put on reels, tied on leaders"; the use of the term "leaders" suggests fly rods. Bill says that "If [the fish] don't take a fly I'll just flick it around." Flicking is an action far more likely with a fly rod than with another type. But Jake, like Nick Adams wounded in the war, further mirrors Nick by electing to use bait with his rod. By bait fishing, Jake can more easily remain dry, since much bait fishing does not demand wading, in contrast to most fly fishing. So he casts from a dam.[18] Jake seems afraid of fighting current, of entering the water, even more than Nick, who wades but nonetheless fishes "down the stream" (176), which resembles common bait fishing strategy and thus violates another code sacred to many fly fishing purists. The point is driven home when Bill returns and good-naturedly calls Jake a "lazy bum" for using worms, at which point Jake notes that Bill "was wet from the waist down and I knew he must have been wading the stream."[19] In other words, by fishing the worms or hoppers and by not entering the water or not resisting its flow, both Jake and Nick refuse to fully engage either the rivers or the sport they are practicing, just as each is currently unable to engage fully life itself. Each of them thus seems spiritually impoverished at first glance, unable or unwilling to appropriately ritualize their behavior.

Both men at these points are probably physically and psychologically unable to engage the river or life fully, and their methods may be viewed as adaptive and individualized rather than cowardly or lazy. They follow flexible personal codes rather than rigid, social ones. As Stoneback has argued, "Hemingway was not, Jake is not, a 'mere wormer'; they were bait *and* fly fishermen, sportsman [*sic*] of the highest order, aficionados with a disciplined and passionate code. . . ."[20] Granted, however, the personalized ritual must include elements of the traditional type, must be connected to the past and some sort of enduring form. At the same time, however, the ritual cannot be frozen in mere tradition; it must also be efficacious across time, to different people and personalities.

So ritual at once fixed and adaptive is particularly vital in understanding Nick's spiritual journey in "Big Two-Hearted River," since as Paul

Smith claims, "He fishes the stream with no premises other than those inferred from the terrain and the surface of the stream."[21] Applying Smith's principles to the reading I am pursuing here, Nick at least in part, if not to a large degree, is himself open to a religious relationship to nature that is at once partly primitivistic but essentially Catholic in Thomistic, even modified Franciscan, senses. For instance, the young Nick in Hemingway's fragmentary "The Last Good Country" associates nature with religion. As an outlaw youth in the Michigan woods, Nick remarks to his sister that this "last good country" makes him feel "the way I ought to feel in church." She follows up this statement by asking, "Nickie, do you believe in God?" His answer, "I don't know" is reflected in Nick Adams stories set later, some of which I discuss below. Yet his connection of God and nature, a connection important to my reading of "Big Two-Hearted River," is further affirmed in the fragment. His sister soon remarks that "this kind of woods makes me feel awfully religious." Nick responds, "That's why they build cathedrals to be like this."[22] Through Nick's lens here, then, we again see the union of the primitive and the institutional, the natural and supernatural.

Additionally, Smith's position and ultimately my own are further supported by part of the original ending Hemingway excised in revising "Big Two-Hearted River," entitled "On Writing" in *The Nick Adams Stories*. Early in this deleted segment, Nick ponders how books on fishing always stress fishing upstream, which is "no fun . . . although all the books said it was the only way." He also ponders how the books "all started with a fake premise."[23] For him, then, natural or spiritual discovery comes from finding one's own rituals naturally—and in nature itself. What is set down in writing or institutionalized must correspond to nature or it is "fake." Consequently, the union of fly rod and grasshopper employed by Nick can be seen as reflecting his belief in the need for a connection between truth and experience.

Of greater importance to my argument are two other Nick Adams stories, both written after but set prior to "Big Two-Hearted River" and published soon after it in *Men Without Women* (1927) and *Winner Take Nothing* (1933). Significantly, these two stories, like "Big Two-Hearted River" and *The Sun Also Rises*, were written during what Stoneback establishes as Hemingway's "[p]eriod of bitter rejection of Protestantism and discovery of Catholicism, and awakening to an aesthetic sense centered on ritual and ceremony . . . and deepening engagement with the sacramental sense of experience and the incarnational patterns of the Catholic church" (which Stoneback dates as 1917–25) and his "[p]eriod of rather intense Catholicity, formalized at the time of the marriage to Pauline but intellectually and emotionally arrived at pre-Pauline" (which

Stoneback identifies as running from 1925–37).[24] Each of these two stories at once both underscores and adds to the significance of Nick's choosing to fish with grasshoppers in "Big Two-Hearted River." The composition and publication dates of all three works, along with Hemingway's use of grasshoppers and fishing in each of them, also suggest they are intended to inform each other.

In "Now I Lay Me," Nick's first method for "occupying" himself during bouts of insomnia is imaginary trout fishing. Along with numerous other details closely corresponding to those in "Big Two-Hearted River" is the following material dealing with grasshoppers:

> Sometimes the stream ran through an open meadow, and in the dry grass I would catch grasshoppers and use them for bait and sometimes I would catch grasshoppers and toss them into the stream and watch them float along swimming on the stream and circling on the surface as the current took them and then disappear as a trout rose.[25]

For Nick Adams, then, fishing with grasshoppers was an obsession as he lay awake: The prayer-like image of fishing served to occupy his sleepless mind, to bring it a touch of peace and tranquility associated with such natural activity.

Nick's nocturnal daydreaming is a ritual in its own right; in fact, in this story it is directly connected to prayer. It also obviously intersects with parallel ritualized behavior in "Big Two-Hearted River," in which Sheridan Baker observes, "Fishing . . . becomes something ritualistic, something symbolic of a larger endeavor."[26] And as Stoneback notes, "Sport as a redemptive ritual is central to Hemingway's life and work."[27] In fact, fishing's ritualization with grasshoppers, which occurs in "Big Two-Hearted River," "Now I Lay Me," and "A Way You'll Never Be," causes the three works to become a significant part of a larger ritual, a religious one reaching its consummation in "Big Two-Hearted River," incarnating and thus controlling Nick's obsessions.

"Now I Lay Me" adds bulk to a Catholic reading of "Big Two-Hearted River" and the other two short works currently under discussion. This story's title is of course the name of the well-known children's prayer requesting God to protect the children's souls, taking them to heaven if they die.[28] Nick cannot sleep for fear of death, and he opens the story listening to silk worms eating "in racks of mulberry leaves."[29] He next brings up how he imagines fishing with bait, then moves to fishing with grasshoppers specifically.[30] So Nick's mind associatively connects the two insects, each of which is destructive but also produces something useful: silk or trout. But the religious connections in the story go deeper than the grasshopper element, which admittedly would be shaky alone. On occasional nights when Nick "could not fish," he filled the time by repeating the Catholic prayers of his adult religion: "I . . . said my prayers over and over and tried to pray for all the people I had ever known. . . . If you prayed for all of them, saying a Hail Mary and an Our Father for each one, it took a long time and finally it would be light, and then you could go to sleep. . . . "[31] By here juxtaposing fishing with prayer, Hemingway stresses a close connection between the two. Last, the prayer leads to other important principles relating to my reading of "Big Two-Hearted River": Prayer takes Nick to light and light brings him rest.

Furthermore, "A Way You'll Never Be" supports this line of thought both by continuing parallels found in the other two stories and by adding important aspects to the grasshopper/fishing/Nick Adams triangle. In this story the unhealthy, more visibly obsessive side of Nick's preoccupation with grasshoppers and fishing becomes apparent. Several pages into the story, Nick begins a "spell" by equating grasshoppers with soldiers and with the locusts that the American "hoppers" actually are: "[S]oon you will see untold millions wearing this uniform swarming like locusts. The grasshopper, you know, what we call the grasshopper in America, is really a locust. The true grasshopper is small and green and comparatively feeble."[32] The grasshopper thread that runs through all three stories clearly drives home that the war is at least one "thing left out" in "Big Two-Hearted River," regardless of protestations by Kenneth S. Lynn and others.[33] In addition, this connection stresses the destructive nature of the American insects, since plagues of locusts have long marauded many regions of the world, including the western United States. Metaphors comparing invading, destructive armies to locusts and grasshoppers are frequent biblical images as well. Thus Nick's employment of grasshoppers in his daydreams, his preoccupations, and his fishing both imaginary and actual is, at least on one level, a method for destroying a destroyer, since the fish consume them.

Slightly later in "A Way You'll Never Be," Nick says of grasshoppers, "These insects at one time played a very important part in my life" (312). At first this claim would seem to refer to Nick's prior love of fishing, much like Hemingway's in his "On Fly Fishing." Certainly we know from other Nick Adams stories that Nick fished a great deal as a youth. But Nick's monologue following his above words indicates a different context altogether: He goes into great detail to discuss how to catch the hoppers, but never into fishing with them. This crucial missing detail, coupled with how Nick stresses the importance of grasshoppers in his past, suggests that he is in fact referring to a destructive, even evil past. The elements of this past would most likely consist not merely of all war-related experiences, but also of every major traumatic aspect of his entire life. As a result, these three stories combine to show that at some primal symbolic and ritualistic level, Nick needs to fish again with the grasshoppers to regain his physical, mental, emotional, moral, and spiritual equilibrium, all of which inseparably intertwine. He does both in "Big Two-Hearted River."

In fact, as Robert M. Slabey notes, in "Big Two-Hearted River," "[F]ishing is more than recreation as relaxation, it is a search for something permanent. (The fish is an ancient symbol of faith and water a symbol of regeneration.)"[34] In short, then, in one context, Nick is the agent by which the good—the rarely-glimpsed, mysterious, water-dwelling fish—consumes the destructive—the grasshoppers and locusts that often symbolize evil in the Bible. In Hemingway's hands, however, an essentially Jungian symbolism operates: The grasshoppers are transformed into personal rather than literal demons. These symbolic associations are further strengthened by Hemingway's evangelical upbringing and ongoing interest in Catholicism, an interest particularly centered on Christ, who again is frequently symbolized by a fish. In the process, unlike Jake Barnes, who confesses to being at best a bad Catholic, Nick at least wades in the stream. Wading for Nick here serves as a renewal of his baptism, reidentifying him with the death, burial, and resurrection of Christ.[35] In contrast to the outcome of "Big Two-Hearted River," Nick in "Now I Lay Me" can only dream-pray about victory over the evils the grasshopper represents, and the apparently insane Nick in "A Way You'll Never Be" can only rant against these evils like one of Shakespeare's prophetic fools.

However, in the dualistic world of "Big Two-Hearted River," the grasshoppers represent more than evil on a spiritual level; in fact, they also metaphorically suggest suffering creation as a whole, including humanity, on a physical level.[36] The black grasshoppers furnish only one example of this situation. In addition, after Nick's first grasshopper escapes him only to plop into the water and be eaten by a trout, Nick takes another out and runs "the slim hook under his chin, down through his thorax and into the last segments of his abdomen. The grasshopper [takes] hold of the hook with his front feet, spitting tobacco juice on it" (175).[37] Through this description, we see the grasshopper undergo a crucifixion of sorts and thus gain identification with Christ. This same identification is further reinforced by the fact that the same hook with which Nick impales the grasshoppers leads to his landing three trout, of which he actually kills two. As a result, the trout represent suffering creation. But they are also commonly associated with Christ on a spiritual level. At this level, consumed by Christ, the grasshoppers represent both those humans ultimately damned (by merely being consumed) and those ultimately redeemed (by becoming part of the body of Christ). Like Nick himself, the grasshoppers are also extremely adaptive, as further symbolized by the black grasshoppers in the burnt-out land near Seney.[38]

It should be noted that in "Big Two-Hearted River" Nick, like Hemingway on his trip to the Fox in 1919, loses the "biggest" trout.[39] This detail too is overlaid with religious terminology, as the narrator exclaims about the trout, "By God, he was a big one. By God, he was the biggest one I ever heard of" (177). Both the direct association of God with the fish, repeated twice for emphasis, and the intrusion of the "I" add to the mystery Hemingway is conveying here. This is the only point in the story utilizing the first person: Some scholars view it as a mistake left over from earlier drafts; others have speculated the "I" is Nick or Hemingway. Given Hemingway's painstaking work and revisions of the story, it is highly unlikely that he unknowingly left the "I." And it seems highly unlikely that the "I" is necessarily Nick or Hemingway by intent, since inserting either of them in this fashion would break drastically with the narrative voice and thus the unity of the story. In itself, this startling invocation of God calls for the reader's consideration.

It also must be stressed again that in "Big Two-Hearted River" Nick releases one trout and kills two others caught on the grasshoppers. These details support a religious reading as well. As not all of Christ or God in any of His forms can be captured, kept, or even held, neither can the fish which represent them. Thus not only does the big one get away, but also the other small fish is released, with Nick taking great care in wetting his hand to protect the sacred life he has held and is returning to the stream (176). Yet both this small and the large trout consume the grasshoppers they strike. On the level that the grasshoppers represent evil, Christ swallows that evil. Similarly, on the level where they are identifiable with suffering creation and humanity, Christ takes on their suffering and makes it His own.

Furthermore, and perhaps most important to my argument here, Nick will eat the two fish he keeps; by doing so he will engage in a Eucharistic act on the symbolic level at which the fish symbolize Christ. Without their deaths, Nick could not consume the fish, and the Eucharistic overtones would be lost. Significantly, after slaying and cleaning the two trout he keeps, Nick "throws the offal ashore for the minks to find" (180). Consequently, creation itself shares in this figurative Eucharist. As for the fish that escape, are released, or never caught to begin with, they also suggest the recurring nature of the Eucharist—as well as renewal to the point of resurrection itself. Moreover, trout further connect to renewal because they spawn in streams with "pebbly bottom[s]" like Hemingway's Big Two-Hearted.[40]

Nevertheless, the swamp (not unlike the Protestant Bunyan's Slough of Despond) still looms for Nick: There, he believes, the fishing will be "a tragic adventure" (180). The swamp and the trout it holds suggest mystery, the great unknown about God, the disturbing philosophical and theological questions about and implications of the Christian God's existence, the dark night of the soul. In the swamp, it is "impossible to land" the trout (180). Only particles of Christ, of God, can be apprehended, consumed, whether Eucharistically, intellectually, or experientially. To begin pondering these additional mysteries, attaining what he can of them, is more than Nick is currently capable of. And as the narrator states, "There were plenty of days coming when he could fish the swamp" (180). So Nick's renewal is not unequivocal; neither is it necessarily permanent. In the Eucharist's Catholic form, it must be repeatedly engaged in to remain efficacious for grace. Faith and belief are far from easy, as Hemingway's own relationship with Catholicism illustrates.

Nonetheless, what Stoneback points out regarding Hemingway appears to be confirmed by "Big Two-Hearted River": despite his very human fluctuations in relationship to his chosen religion, he is

> very Catholic, the writer who, if we come to him free of the Protestant baggage packed with the myths of progress and perfectability [sic], the gnostic denial of inexplicable evil and suffering and therefore grace and joy, we might truly discern to be one of our most "hopeful," whose vision is fundamentally redemptive.[41]

So in the end this timeless short story flows into a previously unexplored flood plain of meaning, making it on the whole a hopeful finale to *In Our Time* as it reveals the "specifically Catholic tension" that Stoneback argues "informs [Hemingway's] books and life."[42] Nick Adams, still part Old Nick and part New Adam himself, has begun to float the rough waters back toward the request of the Evening Prayer which the short story collection takes its title from: "Grant us peace in our time, O Lord."[43] By following brown grasshoppers cast by a fly rod down the rivers running through Hemingway's prose, a reader can see that Nick has arguably attained more of that peace than either Baker or most readers previously imagined.

NOTES

1. Ernest Hemingway, "Big Two-Hearted River," in *The Complete Short Stories of Ernest Hemingway* (New York: Scribner's, 1987), 174–75. Subsequent references to "Big Two-Hearted River" will be given as page numbers in the text.

2. H. R. Stoneback, "In the Nominal Country of the Bogus: Hemingway's Catholicism and the Biographies," in *Hemingway: Essays of Reassessment,* ed. Frank Scafella (New York: Oxford University Press, 1991), 122.

3. An overall piece of criticism concerning primitivism and "Big Two-Hearted River" is Paul Civello, "Hemingway's 'Primitivism': Archetypal Patterns in 'Big Two-Hearted River,'" *Hemingway Review* 13.1 (Fall 1993): 1–16. Civello, however, makes an error akin to the one made by the biographers and criticized by Stoneback in "In the Nominal" when maintaining that "Nick . . . 'returns' to a time before the war and to a time when ritual sacrifice effectively controlled man's violent nature—something Christianity, apparently, could not do" (6). Thus summarily dismissing Hemingway's Catholicism, particularly at a time in life when Hemingway was intensely interested in it, is problematic at best, particularly since much of Civello's earlier argument in his essay stresses Christian elements in the story.

4. Norman Maclean, "A River Runs Through It," in *A River Runs Through It and Other Stories* (Chicago: University of Chicago Press, 1976), 1.

5. Ibid., 5.

6. Ibid., 10–11.

7. For a refreshing and well-made argument against purist fly fishing mentality and on the "art" and refinement actually involved in "clear-water worming," see H. R. Stoneback, "'You Sure This Thing Has Trout in It?' Fishing and Fabrication, Omission and 'Vermification' in *The Sun Also Rises,*" in *Hemingway Repossessed,* ed. Kenneth Rosen (Westport, Conn.: Praeger, 1994), 123.

8. Ernest Hemingway, "Epilogue: On Fly Fishing," in *Hemingway: Essays of Reassessment,* ed. Frank Scafella (New York: Oxford University Press, 1991), 257.

9. Ibid., 258.

10. The Fox, not the Upper Peninsula's Two Hearted River, has of course long been established as the "true" stream in the story. Hemingway in fact took poetic license with descriptive aspects of the Fox as well as with its name. See, for examples of this license, Sheridan Baker, "Hemingway's Two-Hearted River," in *The Short Stories of Ernest Hemingway: Critical Essays,* ed. Jackson J. Benson (Durham, N.C.: Duke University Press, 1975).

11. Ernest Hemingway, "The Art of the Short Story," *Paris Review* 89 (Spring 1981): 88. While as Civello notes, the poorly named "war-wound" theory (I prefer simply war theory, since the wound is only part of the horror) is unfashionable in certain critical circles, it remains a powerful presence in writings about "Big Two-Hearted River," including in Civello's own essay ("Hemingway's 'Primitivism,'" 6, 8, 14–15). Moreover, it seems to remain by far the best interpretation for Nick's main problem in the story, both intertextually and textually. This position, however, does not necessarily demand that the war be the only

psychological trauma Nick is battling at the time of the camping-fishing trip; in fact, most psychological problems are composites. But the war does appear to be Nick's major problem. Finally, though it is true that Hemingway's own words often cannot be trusted, to dismiss them out of hand is a mistake, especially if the text supports his statements.

12. Carlos Baker, *Ernest Hemingway: A Life Story* (New York: Scribner's, 1969), 63.

13. Ibid., 63–64.

14. Ernest Hemingway, *Ernest Hemingway: Selected Letters, 1917–1961*, ed. Carlos Baker (New York: Scribner's, 1981), 28.

15. S. Baker, "Hemingway's Two-Hearted River," 158.

16. C. Baker, *Life,* 127. Given the focus of this essay, it should also be noted that the Two Hearted River of reality includes neither "Big" nor a hyphen in its name, making Hemingway's title all the more poetic.

17. Stoneback, "'You Sure,'" 115–28. In this article, Stoneback also convincingly argues that the stream is indeed the Fabrica, not the Irati as has been commonly believed.

18. Ernest Hemingway, *The Sun Also Rises* (New York: Scribner's, 1926), 118–19.

19. Ibid., 120–21.

20. Stoneback, "'You Sure,'" 125.

21. Paul Smith, "Hemingway's Early Manuscripts: The Theory and Practice of Omission," *Journal of Modern Literature* 10.2 (1983): 285.

22. Ernest Hemingway, "The Last Good Country," in *The Complete Short Stories of Ernest Hemingway* (New York: Scribner's, 1987), 516–17.

23. Ernest Hemingway, "On Writing," in *The Nick Adams Stories* (New York: Bantam, 1972), 213.

24. Stoneback, "In the Nominal," 117.

25. Ernest Hemingway, "Now I Lay Me," in *The Complete Short Stories of Ernest Hemingway* (New York: Scribner's, 1987), 277.

26. S. Baker, "Hemingway's Two-Hearted River," 153.

27. Stoneback, "In the Nominal," 136.

28. Although a Protestant prayer, "Now I Lay Me Down to Sleep" provides a link to Nick's and Hemingway's Protestant upbringing. The prayers in the story, dealt with below, are Catholic.

29. Hemingway, "Now I Lay Me," 276.

30. Ibid., 276–77.

31. Ibid., 277.

32. Ernest Hemingway, "A Way You'll Never Be," in *The Complete Short Stories of Ernest Hemingway* (New York: Scribner's, 1987), 312. Subsequent references will be given as page numbers in the text.

33. Kenneth S. Lynn, *Hemingway* (New York: Simon and Schuster, 1987), 102–8, 258.

34. Robert M. Slabey, "The Structure of *In Our Time*," in *Ernest Hemingway: Six Decades of Criticism*, ed. Linda W. Wagner[-Martin] (East Lansing: Michigan State University Press, 1987), 71.

35. River dousings are commonly used as baptismal symbols in a multitude of literatures, including much that can be labeled Catholic writing.

36. On the whole, Civello's Girardian treatment of this material in "Hemingway's Primitivism" is very solid, though again I find his movement to an exclusively primitivistic reading problematic.

37. Civello's discussion of sacrificial surrogacy and Hemingway's "anthropomorphic" language in describing the grasshopper is excellent and fits my reading here (8–9).

38. These black grasshoppers may be more of Hemingway's "poetry." Black ones like these are "highly unlikely," orthopterists told Sheridan Baker ("Hemingway's Two-Hearted River," 157).

39. Hemingway, *Selected Letters*, 29.

40. The "pebbly bottom" may well be more of Hemingway's "poetry," since my two nonfishing visits to the Fox near Seney show, as Sheridan Baker maintains, it is not really a pebbly stream ("Hemingway's Two-Hearted River," 150).

41. Stoneback, "In the Nominal," 114.

42. Ibid., 116.

43. The phrase "in our time" is used in Catholic as well as Anglican/ Episcopalian prayer. It also bears remembering that this phrase and much of the *Book of Common Prayer* came directly from Catholicism.

Hemingway's Use of
a Natural Resource: Indians

PETER L. HAYS

Hemingway's opening story in his *Collected Stories* is "Indian Camp."
The author claimed to be part Cheyenne, and in his infamous *New
Yorker* interview with Lillian Ross, he spoke pidgin, like a movie Indian.
Exactly how does Hemingway use American Indians in his fiction? In
Jackson Benson's 1990 volume, *New Critical Approaches to the Short
Stories of Ernest Hemingway*, Robert W. Lewis contributed an article on
the subject which I would like to expand upon.[1]

First, as Lewis noticed, Indians occur primarily in Hemingway's short
stories; except for occasional allusions and one special instance, they are
never in the novels. This is not surprising, since most of the novels and
non-fiction works are set in Europe or Africa; only *Torrents of Spring, To
Have and Have Not, Old Man and the Sea*, and *Islands in the Stream* take
place in this hemisphere, and none of them have central characters who
are Indians. Thus, Native Americans are never major characters, but
rather serve as foils to increase our understanding of the nature of the
protagonist, or, in the special instance of *Torrents*, to act as vehicles of
satire.

It would be nice to believe that Hemingway was ahead of his time in
anticipating the present ecological movement, in spite of the evidence of
Green Hills where he writes of immigrants to America:

> Our people went to America because that was the place to go then.
> It had been a good country and we had made a bloody mess of it and
> I would go, now, somewhere else as we had always had the right to
> go somewhere else and as we had always gone. . . . Let the others
> come to America who did not know that they had come too late.[2]

In the same passage in *Green Hills* Hemingway states, "A continent ages
quickly once we come. The natives live in harmony with it."[3] That's the
extent of the writings published during his lifetime praising Indians for
their wise and conservation-minded use of the land. In his own behavior,
he and his family participated in a jack rabbit shoot that killed 400 hares

in one day near Sun Valley, Idaho.⁴ And while it would be pretty to think
that he had anticipated *Dances with Wolves*, especially since he often
claimed to be part Cheyenne (201), I don't think the evidence of the stories supports such a reading.

In northern Michigan, where many of Hemingway's stories are set,
Indians are a part of the landscape, like the hemlock forests and lakes.
Describing the country as a background to Nick's adventures,
Hemingway includes the Native Americans as indeed indigenous. But as
Ezra Pound said in "A Retrospect," "The natural object is always the *ade-
quate* symbol."⁵ So the Indians are there, like the trout in "Big Two-
Hearted River," not as protagonists, but appropriate to the scene and
symbolic within it. And as Lewis says of *Green Hills*, Hemingway's
"extensive treatment of [Africans] would confirm his refusal to stereotype
them as either noble or ignoble savages. Like the portrait of Bugs in 'The
Battler,' they would be individuated" (206–7). The same is largely true of
his use of Native Americans in his works. I am interested in, however,
two consistent uses that Hemingway makes of Indians.

Hemingway first published a work about Indians in *Tabula*, the Oak
Park High School literary magazine. In "The Judgment of Manitou"
(Feb. 1916), a Cree trapper named Pierre believes that his white partner
has stolen from him. Pierre catches the partner in a trap that leaves him
as wolf-bait, only to discover too late that he (Pierre) was wrong in his
judgment. Trying to rectify his fatal error, the Indian is caught in his own
bear trap and reaches for his rifle to commit suicide as the wolves close
in. The story is bloody and melodramatic, a mixture of Poe and Jack
London, heightened by connotations of the cold, cruel Arctic north and
featuring a bloodthirsty savage.

The second Indian story in *Tabula* is "Sepi Jingan," the name of a Jack
London-inspired dog that protects his master, an Ojibway Indian named
Billy Tabeshaw. Sepi Jingan tears the throat out of Paul Black Bird,
another Indian about to kill Billy, and Billy lays Paul Black Bird on the
Pere Marquette Railroad tracks, where the train wheels erase evidence of
the dog's violence—our first of several meetings in Hemingway's writings
with a Tabeshaw and with Indians on the road or tracks. Again, dime-
novel savagery, but Billy Tabeshaw is also a connoisseur of pipe tobacco,
and as high-school age Hemingway says, "Bill is not the redskin of popular magazine. He never says 'ugh.' I have yet to hear him grunt or speak
of the Great White father in Washington."⁶ The violence in the story
appeals to the high school author, but he presents his fanciful tale of
revenge with a portrait of his protagonist that undermines and satirizes
stereotypes, here both racial and cultural, as he will do later in *Torrents of
Spring*.

Hemingway, of course, knew a real Billy Tabeshaw from his summer residence on Walloon Lake, close to the Indian camp farther east on the same lake. Billy would later appear, knowing no English, in "The Doctor and the Doctor's Wife," and by name only in "The Last Good Country." Other early Hemingway portraits of real Indians include this sketch unpublished during the author's lifetime:

> There were no successful Indians. Formerly there had been—old Indians who owned farms and worked them and grew old and fat with many children and grandchildren. Indians like Simon Green who lived on Hortons Creek and had a big farm. Simon Green was dead, though, and his children had sold the farm to divide the money and had gone off somewhere. . . . It did not bring one half as much as everyone expected.[7]

Another neighboring Indian family, the Gilberts, lend their name to Billy Gilbert,[8] the Indian who appears in a "Cross Roads" sketch, a predecessor to the *In Our Time* characterizations. This fictional character went to Canada, enlisted for the First World War in the Scots Black Watch, and returned unappreciated for his medals and wound stripes, laughed at for his kilts. Gilbert also finds that his wife has sold their property in his absence and run off with one of Simon Green's sons. His response is to reshoulder his pack and stoically march down the road, whistling "It's a Long Way to Tipperary."

Still another early portrayal occurs in the poem "Oklahoma,"[9] which appeared in *Three Stories and Ten Poems* (1923). In the poem, the life of Indians close to the land in an earlier time and without most of the "benefits" of white civilization is characterized in ways that have now become stereotypical in describing Native Americans. Thus, "The prairies are long, / The moon rises, Ponies / Drag at their pickets. / The grass has gone brown in the summer." These lines are juxtaposed with clichés of ignorant whites, such as "A good Indian is a dead Indian" and "the oil lands, you know, they're all rich."[10] Two of the benefits of white civilization mentioned are myopic trachoma and gonorrhea.

These early sketches introduce the two categories that Hemingway uses most consistently with Indians: 1) then-common stereotypes of Indians as promiscuous, unfaithful in relationships, and lazy; and 2) loss. Promiscuity and infidelity occur repeatedly. We see them in Billy Gilbert's wife's desertion, in Prudie's betrayal of Nick in "Ten Indians," and again (though she is unnamed [*NAS*, 84]) in "The Last Good Country." Promiscuity is present in "Indian Camp" for those who believe that George in the story is passing out cigars because he is the father of the Indian infant. Uninhibited indulgence in sex occurs with Trudy and

[47]

Nick—while her younger brother observes—in "Fathers and Sons." "Oklahoma" also hints of promiscuity with mention of gonorrhea. Promiscuity and infidelity are also evident at the end of *Torrents* with the departure of the naked squaw, who leaves her husband to go off with Yogi Johnson. Conforming also to the common stereotypes of the period is the laziness of the Fontans' daughter-in-law in "Wine of Wyoming." This Indian woman is described as weighing 225 pounds, staying in bed constantly, neither working nor cooking; her kitchen is described as "dirty and sloppy."[11] But she is not an exceptional American in Fontans' eyes. Here the Native American is representative of the larger, nonindigenous population, which the Fontans see as mannerless and cultureless. In the story Americans outlaw alcohol and then drink to get drunk, they pour whiskey into their beer and wine, and they vomit on their tables. Similarly stereotypical is the laziness of Mrs. Tabeshaw, an Indian woman in "The Last Good Country" who would rather sell her handmade baskets to John Packard for a lower price than walk to the hotel to sell them. But the Anglos in Hemingway's story are not universally admirable either: Evans and Porter are mean and vindictive, and Porter is even implied to be a treacherous murderer.

The losses of the character from "Cross Roads," Scots Watch veteran Billy Gilbert, are obvious: his wife, his property, even his sense of accomplishment as a decorated veteran of a world-famous fighting unit. As Hemingway had said, "There were no successful Indians." But loss in Hemingway's fiction, of course, is not limited to Indians: it's pandemic. His protagonists are a catalog of losers: Jake Barnes, Frederic Henry, Harry Morgan, Francis Macomber, Santiago, Thomas Hudson, etc. By using Indians, who have lost their lands, much of their culture, and their health, Hemingway has a historical objective correlative for man's fate as he saw it.[12] The line from "Fathers and Sons" with which Lewis titles his essay, "Long time ago good. Now no good," not only points to chronological primitivism, as Lewis states, but also to a common pattern in Hemingway's fiction—of initiation from relatively Romantic youth and happy innocence into painful awareness and scarred adulthood, starting with "Up in Michigan" and "Indian Camp." And certainly the Indians in America do represent loss, actually and in Hemingway's fiction.

In "Indian Camp" the Indians live in shanties; the one described in the story "smelled very bad" (*NAS*, 7). They make their living as bark peelers, stripping the landscape of hemlock trees. As Hemingway describes it in "The Last Good Country," they slash the trees and waste the wood merely for the tannin in the bark to be shipped to Boyne City tanneries. Their poverty is suggested by the shanties they live in, the pungent smell pervading them, the absence of medical care, and the lack of cleanliness (Dr. Adams' request to his brother George to turn back the quilt covering the woman in labor protects his just-washed hands but still suggests revulsion at the bed linen). Except for the vacationing doctor, who has no medical equipment with him, the nearest source of regular care is in St. Ignace.[13]

These Indians are deprived of a remunerative livelihood, a clean lifestyle, free use of their former lands, control of their health, and many aspects of their dignity. These deprivations are all objectified in the impotence of the wounded and suicidal husband, who cannot care for his wife or shield her from pain, or the wife who cannot give birth without a white doctor's aid. The Indian artifacts Dr. Adams collects in "Now I Lay Me" represent a lost culture, possibly a masculine one, as the phallic arrow points suggest, artifacts which his wife burns, signalling her lack of respect for them or for him, his interests, and his possessions.

As I pointed out earlier, the Indians in *Torrents of Spring* are a special case, their role largely dictated by Hemingway's satire of Sherwood Anderson's fiction, particularly *Dark Laughter*, in which Anderson juxtaposes the laughter and freedom of emotion of African-Americans against the inhibitions and joylessness of Caucasians:

> Slow lazy laughter of niggers. Bruce remembered a line he had once seen written by a negro. "Would white poet ever know why my people walk so softly and laugh at sunrise?"[14]
>
> From the throats of the ragged black men . . . strange haunting notes. Words were caught up, tossed about, held in the throat. Word-lovers, sound-lovers—the blacks seemed to hold a tone in some warm place, under their red tongues perhaps. . . . Unconscious love of inanimate things lost to whites (106).
>
> The older negro woman tried to quiet the younger, blacker woman, but she kept laughing, the high shrill laughter of the negress (318).

Anderson in fact echoed the complaint of many whites during the Twenties that Anglo-Saxons were repressed, inhibited, out of touch with nature and their own feelings.[15] He echoed the sentiments of cultural Primitivists that other races were more in touch with their feelings and led lives of greater spontaneity and joy, a cultural movement pointing to Rousseau's "noble savage," who was unspoiled by civilization's corruption. Though most notably an eighteenth-century movement, Primitivism experienced a revival with late nineteenth-century uneasiness against increasing urbanization and industrialism and can be seen in such disparate literary works as those of Jack London, Kipling, Edgar Rice Burroughs, and in the art of Gauguin (who is mentioned in Anderson's

Dark Laughter) as well as in Picasso's incorporation of African and Iberian elements in his painting.

In his satire of Anderson, Hemingway portrays the sterility of his white characters, Scripps O'Neill and Yogi Johnson, who look for love, meaning, and purpose in their lives, but Hemingway punctuates his narrative, not with African-American laughter, but instead with Indian war whoops. Once, though, when Brown's Beanery cook (who is black) laughs at him, Scripps wonders, "Could that be the laughter of the Negro?"[16] He further satirizes his characters and national stereotypes by having Yogi meet Indians, who, despite the fact that both had been at Carlisle Indian School, speak pidgin. Yogi delivers a rambling disquisition on World War I, only to learn that the taller of the pidgin-speaking Natives was a major in the South African Fourth Cape Mounted Rifles during the war and earned the Distinguished Service Order and the Military Cross;[17] the shorter Indian lost both arms and legs at Ypres and earned the Victoria Cross and prosthetic limbs—but still beats Yogi in a game of pool.

The two Indians take Yogi to a private club and speakeasy, run by Indians, with a laughing Negro bartender, "high-pitched uncontrolled laughter. The dark laughter of the Negro" (68). The Indian club (pun, no doubt, intended) is decorated with autographed portraits of Longfellow (author of *Hiawatha*, a poem Hemingway saw performed as a play by Indians near his Michigan summer home), D. H. Lawrence, Mabel Dodge (whose last husband was an Indian), Mary Austin, Jim Thorpe, and General Custer. Only the black bartender speaks in dialect. The club members, despite names like Running Skunk-Backwards, speak precise and perfect standard English in contrast to the Indians who had brought Yogi. Explains the "tall refined Indian to whom Yogi was talking . . . , 'They're woods Indians. . . . We're most of us town Indians here'" (67), a satirical allusion to the class distinction between black field slaves and house servants. When the Indians discover that Yogi isn't one of them, is of Swedish descent and not Indian, they throw him and the two woods Indians out of the speakeasy at gunpoint. Everyone has prejudices, but the contrast between superficial appearance and actual reality is a point that the author of iceberg fiction appreciated.

At the end of the short book, Yogi sets out along the railroad track following a nude squaw, who is married to an Indian with artificial limbs. Yogi takes off his clothes to be like her—presumably a free spirit in touch with nature, which at the time, is freezing cold. The woman's husband and the ex-major, who are thrifty in addition to being primitive, collect Yogi's clothes to sell to the Salvation Army.

Because Hemingway's main intent is to have fun, particularly at Anderson's expense, he both uses and overturns stereotypes. Both imperfectly speaking, impoverished Indians are courageous—one was a regimental leader; the Indians with refined diction are snobs. Hemingway similarly used stereotypes with the Jewish outsider Cohn in *The Sun Also Rises*, lazy black Wesley in *To Have and Have Not* and the cruel Spaniards in *For Whom the Bell Tolls*. He was not above doing so. But like any great author, when he fleshed out a character, he invested that character with individuality, as he does with Cohn and Billy Gilbert. Unfortunately, he has no major Indian characters who illustrate this characterization working at length.

Thus I am left with my original statement: Hemingway frequently uses stereotypes to depict Indians, and they usually portray one of two things in his writing, promiscuity or loss. Perhaps the promiscuity puts them, in line with Primitivism, more in touch with their feelings and a natural lifestyle, however much pain it causes others; certainly it contrasts radically with the repressed sexuality of Dr. Adams and the lessons on sexuality given Nick by his father. Loss, of course, had become theirs through history, and a perfect symbol for Hemingway of all the losses flesh is heir to. The poem "Oklahoma" begins "All of the Indians are dead." But Paul Smith directs our attention to another appearance by Indians in Hemingway's "The Art of the Short Story."[18] In that long-unpublished introduction to his short stories, Hemingway writes:

> If you leave out important things or events that you know about, the story is strengthened. . . . "Big Two-Hearted River" is about a boy coming home beat to the wide from a war. . . . So the war, all mention of war . . . is omitted. . . . There were many Indians in the story, just as the war was in the story, and none of the Indians nor the war appeared.[19]

We have, at least most of us, long figured that the war was in the story: The waste land description of Seney and the burnt-over landscape Nick is fleeing from were solid clues. But where were the Indians? I think they are in all that Nick has lost: youth, health, innocence, and confidence. "Long time ago good, now no good" applies not just to Indians, but to Nick's fishing and much of his history.[20] As the capstone story in *In Our Time*, "Big Two-Hearted River" takes us back to "Indian Camp," where thoughts of mortality first dented Nick's innocent unawareness, and where cracks first showed in his father's omnipotence, cracks that widened in the subsequent stories.[21]

Indians, for Hemingway, meant carefree youth at Walloon Lake, freedom of the out-of-doors, and open, unrestrained sexuality, whether real or imagined. As Peter Messent says, "The loss of his first boyhood American world resonates throughout Hemingway's fiction. . . . The romantic celebration of a return to nature and to the 'primitive' . . . disappears here in a sense of lost origins that can never be recovered."[22] That freedom, that innocence, those carefree days died when Simon Green died and Billy Gilbert went to war, with Ernest Hemingway soon following.

NOTES

1. The claim to be part Cheyenne is quoted by Lewis in his article, "'Long Time Ago Good, Now No Good': Hemingway's Indian Stories," in *New Critical Approaches to the Short Stories of Ernest Hemingway*, ed. Jackson J. Benson (Durham, N.C.: Duke University Press, 1990), 201. Subsequent references to this article will be given as page numbers in the text. Lillian Ross's interview with Hemingway was originally published in *The New Yorker*, 13 May 1950, and then reprinted in book form as *Portrait of Hemingway* (New York: Simon and Schuster, 1961).

2. Ernest Hemingway, *Green Hills of Africa* (New York: Scribner's, 1935), 285.

3. Ibid., 284.

4. Carlos Baker, *Ernest Hemingway: A Life Story* (New York: Scribner's, 1969), 352.

5. Ezra Pound, *Literary Essays*, ed. T. S. Eliot (London: Faber & Faber, 1954), 5. The added emphasis is Pound's.

6. Ernest Hemingway, "Sepi Jingan" (Nov. 1916), reprinted by Constance Cappel Montgomery, *Hemingway in Michigan* (New York: Fleet Publishing, 1966), 51. Also reprinted in *Hemingway at Oak Park High*, ed. Cynthia Maziarka and Donald Vogle, Jr. (Oak Park: Oak Park and River Forest High School, 1993), 98.

7. Ernest Hemingway, "The Indians Moved Away," *The Nick Adams Stories* (New York: Bantam, 1973), 23. This same story carries a repeat of Paul Black Bird's apparent death by train and an anticipation of "Ten Indians": An Indian "who had gone into Petoskey to get drunk on the Fourth of July and, coming back, had lain down to go to sleep on the Pere Marquette Railroad tracks and been run over by the midnight train" (22–23). Subsequent references to *The Nick Adams Stories* will be given as page numbers in the text preceded by *NAS*.

8. Constance Cappel Montgomery mentions the Gilberts as neighbors (*Hemingway in Michigan*, 62) but doesn't name the children. Billy Gilbert is named, however, in a letter Hemingway wrote: "My Ojibway Pal and woodcraft teacher, Billy Gilbert" (letter to Emily Goetsmann, 15 July 1915, published in Peter Griffin's *Along With Youth* [New York: Oxford University Press, 1985], 23). Billy Gilbert's sister in Hemingway's sketch is Prudence, whom we know as Prudence Boulton from history, Prudence Mitchell from "Ten Indians," and Trudy Gilby—a variant of Gilbert?—from "Fathers and Sons." (Griffin also publishes the Billy Gilbert vignette, 126–27.)

9. I am indebted to Fern Kory for pointing this poem out to me.

10. Ernest Hemingway, *Three Stories and Ten Poems* (n. p.: Contact Press, 1977), 50.

11. Ernest Hemingway, "Wine of Wyoming,"in *The Short Stories of Ernest Hemingway* (New York: Scribner's, 1938), 464. Subsequent references to Hemingway's short stories will refer to this edition and will be given as page numbers in the text.

12. Mary O'Neal comes to a similar conclusion in her recent "Romantic Betrayal in 'Ten Indians,'" in *Ernest Hemingway: The Oak Park Legacy*, ed. James Nagel (Tuscaloosa: University of Alabama Press, 1996): "Hemingway shows the wilderness being destroyed and, with the loss of the trees, the end of the Indian way of life" (108).

13. Although it was based on the Indians and logging camp of Walloon Lake, Hemingway has moved the site of the story to the Upper Peninsula of Michigan.

14. Sherwood Anderson, *Dark Laughter* (New York: Liveright, 1970), 79. Subsequent quotations from this novel will refer to this edition and be inserted in the text.

15. Eugene O'Neill makes a distinction in *All God's Chillun Got Wings* similar to that of Anderson's novel by dissociating whites from African Americans. A stage direction stresses that "the Negroes frankly participate in the spirit of spring, the whites laughing constrainedly, awkward in natural emotion." (Eugene O'Neill, *Nine Plays* [New York: Modern Library, 1993], 85).

16. Ernest Hemingway, "The Torrents of Spring," in *The Hemingway Reader*, ed. Charles Poore (New York: Scribner's, 1953), 53. Subsequent quotations from "Torrents of Spring" will refer to this edition and will be given as page numbers in the text.

17. The Cape Mounted Rifles was a white South African military unit (Eric A. Walker, *A History of Southern Africa* [London: Longmans, 1965], 369, 371), whose participation in the war, as nearly as I can determine, was only in German colonies in Southwest or East Africa, only white infantry serving in Egypt and Europe, and African and Coloured units serving primarily in support roles. Making an American Indian a major in a white South African unit heightens Hemingway's satire on race and racial assumptions.

18. Paul Smith, *A Reader's Guide to the Short Stories of Ernest Hemingway* (Boston: G. K. Hall, 1989), 99.

19. Ernest Hemingway, "The Art of the Short Story," in *New Critical Approaches to the Short Stories of Ernest Hemingway*, ed. Jackson J. Benson (Durham, N.C.: Duke University Press, 1990), 3.

20. O'Neal, "Romantic Betrayal": "Though 'Ten Indians' is about Nick's adulthood, it is also a commemoration of a lost world: of childhood, the wilderness, and the Indian way of life" (120).

21. Perhaps significantly, in the original ending to "Big Two-Hearted River," now published separately as "On Writing" in *The Nick Adams Stories*, "lost" is reiterated four times on the story's second page (214).

22. Peter Messent, *Ernest Hemingway* (New York: St. Martin's Press, 1992), 128. Cf. Jackson J. Benson, *Hemingway: The Writer's Art of Self-Defense* (Minneapolis: University of Minnesota Press, 1969): "All the basic aspects of living—birth, sex, and death—are discovered in the Michigan woods by Nick, the young, semi-autobiographical protagonist of the Hemingway short stories. . . " (5).

Roosevelt and Hemingway:
Natural History, Manliness, and
the Rhetoric of the Strenuous Life

SUZANNE CLARK

Thinking about Ernest Hemingway together with Theodore Roosevelt, as Michael Reynolds in particular does in *The Young Hemingway*, elucidates both Hemingway's situation in cultural history and his more radical situation in literary tradition.[1] For Hemingway is not like Roosevelt in his advocacy of a nationalistic manliness that would value the right stuff so much as he is like Roosevelt in continuing a rhetorical tradition of natural history writing that is connected to the literature of the West—a pursuit of accurate description that would record an act of discovery, the frontier of writing.

Theodore Roosevelt was the hero of the generation before World War I, of Oak Park, and of Hemingway's childhood: advocate of the strenuous life and of the strong middle-class family. Teddy had also—like Hemingway—been taken up by the adventures of natural history from an early age.[2] As a child, Roosevelt specialized in writing a natural history journal, collecting specimens to describe as Audubon had done, by shooting them. The Roosevelt family was closely connected to the establishment of the American Museum of Natural History. Young Hemingway had his own connections to natural history in the Field Museum in Chicago, where Dr. Hemingway sometimes took his children on weekends. Michael Reynolds tells us that Hemingway was assistant curator of the Agassiz Club at the age of ten.[3] And is it entirely irrelevant that Hemingway wanted to disguise the Pilar, in 1942, as a vessel belonging to the American Museum of Natural History in order to search out the German submarines?[4] Hemingway owned a large number of natural history and travel books, including Teddy Roosevelt's 1902 *The Deer Family* and his 1910 *African Game Trails*.[5]

Hemingway's *Green Hills of Africa* recaptures for the 1930s the 1909 safari taken by Roosevelt, this time with the writer, not the politician, emerging as the key cultural icon.[6] If Hemingway never wrote about Oak

Park, he clearly wrote about the dreams he had as a little boy who dressed in safari khaki in 1909. But after World War I, when he served with the Red Cross in Italy and was wounded, Hemingway came to doubt the warrior ethics he associated with Roosevelt. Neither Roosevelt nor the generation of Hemingway's parents who idolized him foresaw the difference between the strenuous life of courage and the life of the soldier in World War I, and on that pivot the century turned.

I am especially interested in comparing Roosevelt's western writing to material drawn from several of Hemingway's publications in the 1920s, materials written before a certain self-definition with respect to Roosevelt occurred in the 1930s relationship to Africa, before Hemingway broke with Owen Wister over Wister's critique of *A Farewell to Arms*—and before Hemingway read (and critiqued) Wister's biography of Roosevelt. In these early years of his career, Hemingway rejected the optimistic attitudes toward war. Hemingway's 1923 poem, "Roosevelt," which appeared in *Poetry*, immediately established a certain skeptical distance from the heroic figure. The poem points out with characteristic Hemingway skepticism that even though workingmen said "What he'd have done in France!", he died in bed. "Roosevelt" ends with the lines: "and all the legends that he started in his life / Live on and prosper, / Unhampered now by his existence."[7]

If Hemingway was disaffected with Roosevelt the legend and the figure of cultural history, he was not—far from it—to lose faith in the writing method endorsed by Roosevelt and grounded in the methods of natural history. The true reporting of experience, of the active life carefully observed—that was a moral basis for writing itself that Hemingway translated into the literary tradition. Hemingway's early interest in natural history locates him within the epistemology of discovery connected to Louis Agassiz. It was a method well known to Roosevelt, but also a method that influenced other modernist writers than Hemingway, though he most clearly united stylistic and scientific frontiers. Agassiz's approach to natural history was famously described by Ezra Pound, who advocated that writers take up the practice of careful observation that Agassiz exacted. The student was required to return again and again to look at his specimen in order to accurately describe a fish. This method does not privilege the untutored eye, however. In "Is There a Fish in This Text?" Robert Scholes has looked carefully at this story to show how the very narrative presumes that the experience of repeated looking can get at the truth. But the anecdote itself depends upon prior texts, so that it is also a moment in a textual tradition.[8] In *ABC of Reading*, Ezra Pound means to present a scientific approach to studying poetry: "The proper METHOD for studying poetry and good letters is the method of contemporary biologists, that

is careful first-hand examination of the matter, and continual COMPARI-
SON of one 'slide' or specimen with another."9 Pound gives as his model
the storied pedagogical method of Louis Agassiz, the legendary scientist
of natural history:

> A post-graduate student equipped with honours and diplomas went
> to Agassiz to receive the final and finishing touches. The great man
> offered him a small fish and told him to describe it.
>
> Post-Graduate Student: 'That's only a sunfish.'
>
> Agassiz: 'I know that. Write a description of it.'
>
> After a few minutes the student returned with the description of
> the Ichthus Heliodiplodokus, or whatever term is used to conceal
> the common sunfish from vulgar knowledge, family of
> Heliichtherinkus, etc., as found in textbooks of the subject. Agassiz
> again told the student to describe the fish.
>
> The student produced a four-page essay. Agassiz then told him to
> look at the fish. At the end of three weeks the fish was in an
> advanced state of decomposition, but the student knew something
> about it.[10]

This story featuring the intensity of prolonged close attention was an
oft-repeated Harvard tale of initiation into apprenticeship under Agassiz.
Men who studied with Agassiz recorded their accounts of the experience,
and the same tale was told by many prominent scientists who had appren-
ticed under Agassiz: Nathaniel Southgate Shaler, Samuel H. Scudder,
Henry Blake, David Starr Jordan, Addison Emory Verrill, Burt G.
Wilder.[11] As the scene of an initiation, the call to close observation became
the guarantor of a certain reliance on individual experience that might be
coupled with claims of scientific objectivity. The initiation into close
observation relied not on a specific text but on the whole metaphor of the
world as text.

Both Nathaniel Shaler and William James were Theodore Roosevelt's
professors at Harvard. And, of course, James was also the most significant
influence in the academic career of Gertrude Stein, engaging her in
experiments on writing and attention. Theodore Roosevelt entered
Harvard an ardent naturalist; he not only studied with Agassiz's student,
Shaler, but visited him in his home. Natural history encompasses a textual
tradition with a specific syntax of method that is thus traceable in stories
of personal apprenticeships as well, including perhaps not only
Hemingway's youthful encounter with Agassiz's method and Roosevelt's
model, but his early exchanges with Gertrude Stein. In this respect he
might also be connected to Roosevelt's friend, Owen Wister, who wrote
The Virginian and then Roosevelt's biography to describe the American

hero of the active life—and, moreover, to locate it not in Roosevelt's native New York, but on the frontier, in the narratives of the West.[12] Hemingway's use of the methods of observation associated with natural history represents a hidden confluence of realist and modernist traditions in American literature.

Natural history is a method distinguished from literary writing that advocates the powers of the imagination and the resources of fantasy, dream, and the unconscious. Natural history writing aims to bring together practical knowledge, scientific nomenclature, the experience of the senses, and a style that draws upon precise and concrete naming. Writing a modernist prose that resonated with the discourse of natural history, Hemingway represented a difference from the European symbolist and surrealist modernisms with their advocacy of a derangement of the senses. But the distinction takes a new form in Hemingway, who read Baudelaire and understood very well Mallarmé's principle of painting not the thing, but the effect it produces. Nietzsche might call empiricism metaphorical, but Pound first called his own poetics "imagism" in order to emphasize the close, *realistic* articulation with the senses of an Agassiz-influenced concrete style. Hemingway causes us to bring the disjunction of modernism and realism into question. Was literature not a discourse of truth?

A significant attribute of natural history writing for Roosevelt was its truth. While he was president of the United States, Theodore Roosevelt found time not only to go to Yellowstone with John Burroughs and to Yosemite with John Muir, but also to enter with Burroughs into the "nature fakers" debate over the veracity of stories about animals. By that time, in the first decade of the twentieth century, nature studies had achieved the status of a social movement, there was a tremendous market for nature books, and reviewers began to complain about "goody-goody books of the natural history kind" and "mawkish sentimentalism."[13] Is it too much to suppose that Roosevelt feared not only for the veracity of nature stories, but also for their manliness? In an article in the *Atlantic*, Burroughs defined the danger as "putting in too much sentiment, too much literature." Roosevelt encouraged the opposition to the "nature fakers" behind the scenes. There ensued a vigorous debate, in the course of which Roosevelt went public in an interview. The *New York Times* and the *Washington Post* carried stories that promptly lambasted TR as a "gamekiller."[14] After more violent debate, Roosevelt assembled a panel of naturalists whose testimony could appear in print. The naturalists wrote that "all who know the truth and who care for the honest nature study or for literary honesty should raise their voices against such writings." And TR's own article appeared together with the writings of that panel, asserting the danger to the schools of propagating misinformation in nature stories: "we abhor deliberate or reckless untruth in this study."[15]

Perhaps the young Hemingway, himself involved in nature study, took such a lesson to heart. The fakers were not scientists, and their manhood was in doubt besides. Hemingway's obsessive concern with a truth that many thought he regularly distorted may be thought about in the context of this debate. In the painful father-son story, "I Guess Everything Reminds You of Something," the father's admonition to the son to "Write about something that you know" means, specifically, that he should know about the type of gull in the story he wrote, and it is the fact that the boy could not have known such a gull that first arouses the father's suspicion about plagiarism (597).[16]

Natural history writing is also connected to a history of exploration that had intimate connections to nationalism and power. The great naturalists and travel writers of the nineteenth century were prompted by colonialism and the seductions of empire. In the United States, Lewis and Clark wrote their daily journals under the imperative of another American president, Thomas Jefferson, who like Roosevelt saw the interests of exploration coincide with the scientific techniques of natural history. In particular, those Lewis and Clark descriptions had objectivity and botanical precision because they conveyed a vivid sense of interest. What plants might have value as food? Which might be poisonous? Which might have medicinal qualities? Roosevelt not only wrote natural history himself, but together with his friends Owen Wister and Frederic Remington might be said to have made western natural history the discourse of the eastern elite.[17] After Jefferson and Roosevelt, Hemingway: his interest in the world he explores has that same desire for precision, objectivity, and purposefulness. If Hemingway takes up the discourse of the American frontier, however, he does so with a difference, without the confident faith of the legendary Teddy in the righteousness of war or the power of the strenuous life to protect the hero from harm.

Lewis and Clark may have been the first, as Stephen Ambrose claims, to have combined a military and a scientific purpose; Teddy Roosevelt clearly brought his interests in natural history together with his interests in rough rider imperialism. The "frontier" operated like the other spaces of imperialism and colonialism, but the proof of its virtue was in the production of a manly life. Progress was not equated with more and more civilized behavior, but rather with strenuous effort. The narrative of modernity equates evolutionary progress with *fitness*. The Roosevelt/American version of progress thought not in terms of reproduction of the species but in terms of the manly striving that reproduced an American individual.

[59]

For Roosevelt, the "arena" corresponded to both physical and episte-
mological action. The narrative of the hunter overlapped with the narrative of the scientist: The great scientists of the nineteenth century
gathered their specimens for collections by killing them. As Donna
Haraway tells us in her analysis of the institution of natural history, the
struggle for life depends upon death.[18] This hunter of scientific discovery
who proves himself in the act is the subject of the heroic American nation
in its moment of ascendancy to world domination, taken up in its imper-
ial aspect. It is too easy to read Hemingway as appropriated by this manly
imperialism, even though Hemingway's reading of Roosevelt is characterized by resistance. Hemingway, however, has a complex and often critical
relationship to the entanglements of natural history discourse with
national history.

Viewed from the perspective of a writing tradition intimately bound
up with the history of nationalism and associated with the frontier,
Hemingway's work represents both a continuation of certain principles
and a significant questioning of the national project. Masculinity is thus
split. As Reynolds argues, the moral values of "courage, love, honor, self-
reliance, work, and duty" continue to ground Hemingway's version of the
strenuous life; they also frame the authenticity of a writing that avoids
faking it. The rhetoric of honest observation does not take place in an
ethical vacuum.

On the other hand, Hemingway diverges from Roosevelt's association
of manliness with the victorious nation. Roosevelt responded to difficulty
by extending himself. His asthma and bad eyesight were frailties he was
able to overcome, for in fact Roosevelt as a small child was not only, at
intervals, asthmatic, but also already strenuously energetic, as David
McCullough tells us. It was that same principle of energetic action that led
him to the ranch in North Dakota, perhaps—but not from an uncomplicated pursuit of manliness. Hemingway's disillusionment with Roosevelt
has to do with the myth more than with the complexities of the man.

What Hemingway took from Roosevelt might be found in the ethos of
Roosevelt's own writing. In *Ranch Life and the Hunting Trail*, Roosevelt
reported his experiences with life among the cowboys in the Badlands of
North Dakota.[19] It isn't one of the books in Hemingway's own collection,
but it is an earlier work related to other Roosevelt books that Hemingway
owned: *The Deer Family* and the *African Game Trails* that followed
Roosevelt's safari in 1910. More importantly, it shows Roosevelt in the
lineage of natural history, environmental writing, and the literature of the
frontier that is taken up by Owen Wister, whose book on Roosevelt
Hemingway did read. I argue that that tradition probably influenced the
way Hemingway wrote. It surely influenced the way he has been read.

Roosevelt's descriptions are embedded in a human narrative of discovery. For Roosevelt, in fact, as for Hemingway, the encounter with nature might provide a way to regain health after trauma. Hemingway's Nick Adams represses the experience of war by his concentration on fishing in "Big Two-Hearted River." Roosevelt went to Medora, North Dakota, after his mother and his wife died in the same day, and he took up life on a most remote western ranchland, recording his experiences there. The detail of his observation suggests a connection between sublimation and writing, but not because he adds fantasy or untruthfulness—rather because of the feminine life that is not there. His descriptions are not for the domestic reader but for the hunter. He makes the assumption still common in the West that appreciation of natural beauty is not at odds with killing the animal. His objectivity, or lack of feeling, is in the tradition of natural history writing.

> Sometimes strings of sandhill cranes fly along the river, their guttural clangor being heard very far off. They usually light on a plateau, where sometimes they form rings and go through a series of queer antics, dancing and posturing to each other. They are exceedingly wide-awake birds, and more shy and wary than antelope, so that they are rarely shot; yet once I succeeded in stalking up to a group in the early morning, and firing into them rather at random, my bullet killed a full-grown female. Its breast, when roasted, proved to be very good eating.
>
> Sometimes we vary our diet with fish—wall-eyed pike, ugly, slimy catfish, and other uncouth finny things, looking very fit denizens of the mud-choked water; but they are good eating withal, in spite of their uncanny appearance. We usually catch them with set lines, left out overnight in the deeper pools.[20]

After his experience ranching in North Dakota, Roosevelt made famous his association with the "rough riders" who worked with unbroken horses. His descriptions of them record the violence of bronco-busting at length, if not with an aura of endorsement.

> A first-class flash rider or bronco-buster receives high wages, and deserves them, for he follows a most dangerous trade, at which no man can hope to grow old; his work being infinitely harder than that of an Eastern horse-breaker or rough-rider. . . . one of the first lessons the newly-caught animal has to learn is not to 'run on a rope'; and he is taught this by being violently nubbed up, probably turning a somersault, the first two or three times that he feels the noose settle round his neck, and makes a mad rush for liberty. The snubbing-post

is the usual adjunct in teaching such a lesson; but a skillful man can do without any help and throw a horse clean over by holding the rope tight against the left haunch, at the same time leaning so far back, with the legs straight in front, that the heels dig deep into the ground when the strain comes, and the horse, running out with the slack of the rope, is brought up standing, or even turned head over heels by the shock.

A bronco-buster has to work by such violent methods in consequence of the short amount of time at his command. . . . The average bronco-buster, however, handles horses so very rudely that we prefer, aside from motives of economy, to break our own. . . . The best and quietest horses on the ranch are far from being those broken by the best riders; on the contrary. They are those that have been handled most gently, although firmly, and that have had the greatest number of days devoted to their education.[21]

In spite of his conclusion, Roosevelt's mode of writing conveys the intensity of the violence more strikingly than his reservations. He describes a western culture far from eastern influence, where gender is invisible because it is only male.

Hemingway emphasizes doubleness and ambivalence more than Roosevelt, whose prose is overwhelmed by interest in the novelty of the West. Similarly, Hemingway writes within a doubleness about the Roosevelt advocacy of manliness so often associated with his work, but which he also critiques. In "The End of Something," Nick has taught Marjorie her considerable knowledge about fishing. On this trip along the lake to the site of a ruined lumber mill, however, he declares that "It isn't fun any more," not even the love, and she goes away without a scene (81). Bill then appears: It is apparently the end of love and the beginning of a male bonding. Not fishing trips, however, but the scenes of war (in the brief "Chapter III" and "Chapter IV" that precede and follow "The End of Something") frame its significance, with its turn to a purely masculine relationship. The scenes of war enable the slightly nostalgic aura of fishing trips with Marjorie to function as critique. If it is *self*-criticism, in that too Hemingway diverges from the self-certainty of Roosevelt's textual persona, both out West and at war.

Hemingway describes the natural world with great care, as does Roosevelt, and like Roosevelt when he went to ranch in Medora, North Dakota, Hemingway turns to the good place for healing. But only Hemingway is able to write with accurate intensity both of the good place and of the pain that needs a refuge. "Big Two-Hearted River" shows the method. The wonderful, careful detail gains another resonance through repetition: "the trout keeping themselves steady in the current with wavering fins"; "many trout in deep, fast moving water, slightly distorted as he watched far down through the glassy convex surface of the pool, its surface pushing and swelling smooth against the resistance of the log-driven piles of the bridge. . . . big trout looking to hold themselves on the gravel bottom"(163); the grasshoppers in the fire zone "all turned black from living in the burned-over land"(165). Like Thoreau, Hemingway uses the description of nature as a means of thinking about larger issues, with Thoreau's critical view of the human community. One can read the descriptive passages, as one can read Thoreau, two ways. First, the report needs no other purpose than to approach as near as possible to the objective accuracy of natural history. The intrinsic value of the natural world requires nothing of Nick's observation and attentiveness, thus displacing the question of value away from the self. But like Thoreau, Hemingway subjectively selects the details of nature for their resonance with other levels of significance. This is true as well in his nonfiction, even though Hemingway distances himself from the too literary versions of nature writing, including Thoreau.[22]

Thus Hemingway returns to the *locus amoenus* of American pastoral. But it is a place where the town has burned down, the forest has been reduced to stumps, and the grasshoppers match the charred landscape. It is not just a mirror of Nick's postwar depression, however. Even though this is fiction, the description works as true nature writing to prompt an environmental sensibility. The unspoken trauma has not just damaged Nick. The war, indeed, comes to seem part of the industrial juggernaut that has cut down the pines. The restorative power of the North Dakota ranch for Teddy Roosevelt only thirty-five years earlier rested on the assumption that the wildlife and the river he described so attentively were more permanent than the person in pain who escaped through his engagement in those narratives of discovery. Hemingway's nature is more vulnerable, though he is not sentimental about the vulnerability. He uses grasshoppers for bait, after catching them early while they were still too cold and wet with the dew to jump: "Nick took him by the head and held him while he threaded the slim hook under his chin, down through his thorax and into the last segments of his abdomen" (175). The truthful representation of nature holds a significance for the man by the very placing and repetition of the words, just as the landscape holds him.

Other stories give further information about Hemingway's nature writing. In "Now I Lay Me," Hemingway tells the trick of remembering the trout streams and fishing them to make it through the night during the war in Italy. All the stories that seem, then, at first like the vivid description of experience might also, from this perspective, take on the aura of vividly remembered experience, imagined so realistically not just in pursuit of accuracy but also as respite for the imagination from the real sounds of war. In "A Natural History of the Dead," descriptive writing serves with almost surreal irony to undermine the reassuring tone of some writers in the naturalist tradition. Hemingway will resist the tendency toward denial. He sets out to write "a few rational and interesting facts about the dead" as if he will write a bitter reply to his paradoxically sentimental question: "can any branch of Natural History be studied without increasing that faith, love and hope which we also, every one of us, need in our journey through the wilderness of life?" (335). The story also challenges the "Humanist" elevation of human culture: "hit badly enough, they died like animals. . . . from little wounds as rabbits die. . . . Others . . . lie alive two days like cats that crawl into the coal bin with a bullet in the brain" (338). The tone in the story goes from satire to horror to eloquence. Hemingway does indeed use the methods of natural history to describe the dead, we see. This story, which appeared also as part of *Death in the Afternoon*, includes a number of terrible scenes portrayed with terrible accuracy—a genre that appears widely elsewhere in Hemingway's fiction: the mules drowning in the water at Smyrna, the explosion of a munitions factory, a recaptured battlefield in Italy, a death from influenza, a still-live man consigned by the doctor to a cave with the dead—and a catalogue of burials. The mixed genres of this story overlap natural history as fiction and nonfiction, while Hemingway's critique of earlier naturalists suggests his revision of earlier sentiment about reading the text of nature.[23]

In Hemingway's text, the "true sentence" of natural history writing becomes not an optimistic completion, mastery, or truth-telling but a delay, tact, and reserve which, precisely, does *not* wholly name its object. So it is an unmaking of positivism; the detail of contact swerves away from the narrative of closure with nature and mastery over it. The "symbiosis with the natural world" associated romantically with Native Americans is at once true and not describable. Glen Love has charged that Hemingway represents a Darwinian individualism implicated in survival of the fittest, and that he imposes tragedy on nature.[24] But Hemingway records "truly" what even some of us as environmentalists would like to disavow, that the contact zone between twentieth-century individualism's narcissistic economy and a wider ecology resonates with violence and death.

Other Hemingway scholars have noted a connection to Roosevelt. I would like to emphasize that the connection is double: one of emulation but also of disillusionment. Jeffrey Meyers lists "striking similarities" between Hemingway and Roosevelt, but without qualification, as if

Hemingway simply continued the legend of the strenuous life.[25] And this is precisely the legendary trap that would reduce Hemingway's work to a much less complex and less historically-significant intervention than it was. Kenneth Lynn says that Hemingway "tapped into the twentieth century's enormous nostalgia for the manly virtues of earlier times, as defined in America by the pathfinders of Fenimore Cooper, the foretopmen of Herman Melville and the cowboys extolled by Theodore Roosevelt, Owen Wister, and Frederic Remington."[26] This is to say that Hemingway is a western writer, but I want to be careful about the sense in which this is meant: The association of the western with nostalgia may be misleading. Modernism's nostalgia for a lost innocence is neither specific to Hemingway nor central to his path-breaking style. Instead, I might argue that Hemingway renovates virtue where he can find it rather than adopting the antiheroism of modernist narrative; if innocence is lost, nostalgia does not replace the sense of writing as a powerful act, and a remedy to nostalgia. Roger Whitlow argues that Hemingway exemplified the "man in the arena" that Roosevelt admired, and shared with Roosevelt the sentiment that "It is not the critic who counts."[27] However, even Hemingway's resistance to academic criticism was more modernist than Roosevelt's. Taking Hemingway as representative of his times may be valid; to some extent he helped produce the modern cultural history he is taken to represent. However, to take him as representative of a particular link to Roosevelt, a certain kind of male subject, risks confounding cultural, natural, and personal histories. The comparison reported by Denis Brian between the manic-depressive personality of Roosevelt and Hemingway may be misleadingly specific: Among other things, it ignores the widespread association of so-called manic-depression with modernist writers—Hart Crane, Robert Lowell, Louise Bogan, Theodore Roethke, Sylvia Plath.[28]

There is, in other words, a sense in which we ought to think of Hemingway in a tradition associated with Roosevelt, as a western writer of natural history, and yet it's not the sense that would identify him as yet another cowboy or worse, yet another famous myth whose legend would do better without the realities of his existence. The comparison with Roosevelt ought to alert us as well to the ways Hemingway diverged from the Roosevelt legend. Perhaps it should even alert us to take another look at Roosevelt himself, a more complex man than the myth he produced: Thus Hemingway's case could suggest a rereading of Roosevelt, in the light of natural history traditions. Hemingway's West and Hemingway's Africa are invested neither with innocence nor with the escape from death. The danger was, and is, that a legendary manliness first promulgated by Teddy Roosevelt might overwrite the more complex history of Hemingway.

[65]

NOTES

1. Michael Reynolds, *The Young Hemingway* (New York and Oxford: Basil Blackwell, 1986).

2. For the story of Roosevelt's early years and his extraordinary involvement in natural history, I draw from David McCullough, *Mornings on Horseback* (New York: Simon and Schuster, 1981).

3. Reynolds, *Young Hemingway,* 30.

4. Kenneth Lynn, *Hemingway* (New York: Simon and Schuster, 1987), 503.

5. Michael S. Reynolds, *Hemingway's Reading, 1910–1940* (Princeton, N.J.: Princeton University Press, 1981), 177: items #1805 and #1806. James D. Brasch and Joseph Sigman, *Hemingway's Library: A Composite Record* (New York: Garland, 1981), 318.

6. Ernest Hemingway, *Green Hills of Africa* (New York: Scribner's, 1935).

7. Ernest Hemingway, "Roosevelt," *Poetry* 21.4 (January 1923): 193–94. The other poems in the group, entitled "Wanderings," are mostly about the war. Hemingway is identified as "a young Chicago poet now abroad" (231).

8. Robert Scholes, "Is There a Fish in This Text?" *Textual Power: Literary Theory and the Teaching of English* (New Haven: Yale University Press, 1985).

9. Ezra Pound, *ABC of Reading* (1934; reprint, New York: New Directions, 1960), 17.

10. Ibid., 17–18.

11. James David Teller gives an account drawn on Shaler and cites the others in *Louis Agassiz, Scientist and Teacher* (Columbus, Ohio: Ohio State University press, 1947), 74ff; the stories have been widely published.

12. See Darwin Payne, *Owen Wister: Chronicler of the West, Gentleman of the East* (Dallas, Tex.: Southern Methodist University Press, 1985).

13. Ralph H. Lutts, *Nature Fakers: Wildlife, Science & Sentiment* (Golden, Col.: Fulcrum, 1990), 37.

14. Ibid., 108.

15. Ibid., 129.

16. This and other Hemingway stories I consider in this essay are from *The Complete Short Stories of Ernest Hemingway: The Finca Vigía Edition* (New York: Scribner's, 1987). Subsequent references will be given as page numbers in the text.

17. Roosevelt, Wister, and Remington had varying experiences and interpretations of the West, of course, but they shared the view that inserted the West into a larger history—the progressive, evolutionary development of civilization. Thus they were responsible for interpreting the West in a way that made it politically

responsive to the concerns of the eastern establishment, at the same time that it reinforced a certain version of the story of capitalism—particularly the version that dramatized the role of the United States. They "saw the West as a stage in the history of American civilization," G. Edward White writes in *The Eastern Establishment and the Western Experience* (New Haven and London: Yale University Press, 1968), 78.

18. Haraway's analysis of the Natural History Museum and its confluence of interests leads her to characterize the institution as a "Teddy Bear Patriarchy," the title of her essay in *Cultures of United States Imperialism* (Durham: Duke University Press, 1993), 241: The "central moral truth" is "the effective truth of manhood, the state conferred on the visitor who successfully passes through the trial of the museum. The body can be transcended."

19. Theodore Roosevelt, *Ranch Life and the Hunting Trail*. Illustrated by Frederic Remington (1888; reprint, New York: Century, 1920).

20. Ibid., 42–43.

21. Ibid., 31–33.

22. Ronald Weber, in *Hemingway's Art of Non–Fiction* (London: Macmillan, 1990), makes the comparison with the doubleness in Thoreau that, according to F. O. Matthiessen, gave him a literary dimension beyond the reportage of other naturalists and travelers.

23. For an insightful discussion of "A Natural History of the Dead," see Susan F. Beegel, *Hemingway's Craft of Omission: Four Manuscript Examples* (Ann Arbor, Mich.: UMI Research Press, 1988). She examines in particular the ramifications of Hemingway's cutting four manuscript pages that ended the story with a return to satire.

24. Glen Love, "Hemingway's Indian Virtues: An Ecological Reconsideration," *Western American Literature* 22.3 (November 1987): 201, 205.

25. Jeffrey Meyers, *Hemingway: A Biography* (New York: Harper & Row, 1985).

26. Lynn, *Hemingway*, 9.

27. Roger Whitlow, *Cassandra's Daughters: The Women in Hemingway* (Westport, Conn.: Greenwood Press, 1984).

28. Denis Brian, *The True Gen: An Intimate Portrait of Ernest Hemingway by Those Who Knew Him* (New York: Grove Press, 1988), 314–15.

Shadow Rider: The Hemingway Hero
as Western Archetype

JAMES PLATH

Ever since Western writer Owen Wister praised Ernest Hemingway in a publicity blurb for *A Farewell to Arms*, noting especially "the unmuted resonance of a masculine voice,"[1] a number of critics have observed similarities between Hemingway's fictional world and the rugged American West. Among the earliest was Leslie Fiedler, who concluded that "For Hemingway there are many Wests, from Switzerland to Africa, but the mountains of Spain are inextricably associated in his mind with the authentic American West, with Montana whose very name is the Spanish word for the mountains that make of both isolated vastnesses holy places." By "holy places," Fiedler meant that "Great Good Place" apart from the "busy world of women"—in other words, an outdoor arena where a man can do what a man's gotta do.[2]

Although Fiedler stopped short on that trail, John J. Teunissen wrote at length about the Custer legend which serves as the mythic underpinning to *For Whom the Bell Tolls*, while a number of scholars have since explored the Hemingway-Wister relationship, focusing on the latter's criticism and Hemingway's response.[3] In one of the more recent studies, Dean Rehberger notes that elements of the Western showdown are present in *For Whom the Bell Tolls* and characteristics of the Western hero appear in Robert Jordan. Rehberger states, "it is possible to read the standard definitions of the Hemingway 'code' as a rewriting of the adventure ethos: the taciturn character of stoic reserve who faces the presence of death in life and who always exhibits grace under pressure. Who better exemplifies this code than the stereotype of the cowboy?" Yet Rehberger, quickly shifting to a discussion of the Custer myth and Western rhetoric, claims that "we need to go beyond simply listing the conventions and stereotypes of the Western formula that can be matched up with Hemingway works" because such "elementary comparisons lead to a reductive reading of both Hemingway and the popular Western."[4]

I would argue, however, that if the Custer myth is recognized as an important underpinning, then the Western formula that shapes the novel's infrastructure also deserves a closer look, especially since, as Michael Reynolds reminds us, Owen Wister was the only American fiction writer available to students at Oak Park High School, where the curriculum was largely British literature.[5] *The Virginian*, Wister's 1902 novel about knights on horseback, was almost as romantic as Sir Walter Scott and was required as outside reading.[6] *The Virginian* is also widely regarded as the novel that established what would become the "formula" in all Western genre fiction to follow. Then there's the Wister-Hemingway correspondence from 1928–36, where Frank Scafella reports that "the main burden of Wister's letters was to identify and instruct Hemingway in the treatment of 'garbage,'" which the older author found in Hemingway's depiction of "foul and violent" elements.[7] Though Hemingway's responses never indicate whether he took any of Wister's advice to heart, his fiction grows increasingly more romantic after *The Sun Also Rises*. At the very least, the lengthy correspondence shows the respect Hemingway apparently had for Wister as a writer, just as copies of *The Virginian* and a nine-volume set of Wister's works included in the author's Key West inventory indicate Hemingway's familiarity with Wister's sense of the American West.[8] Likewise, as Rehberger noted, whether Carlos Baker was correct that young Hemingway's first complete sentence was "I don't know Buffalo Bill" is "not as important as the fact that Hemingway was exposed at an early age to the perpetuation of the frontier myth."[9]

After a century of pulps, dime novels, literary and popular Westerns, and a cinematic celebration that dominated television and movie marquees during the Fifties, the genre is as familiar as Stetsons and Colt .45s. Will Wright summarizes the classic Western structure as a system of primary oppositions: inside versus outside society, good versus bad, strong versus weak, and wilderness versus civilization, with an uncomplicated plot that revolves around the moral character of the hero[10]—all elements of Hemingway's various fictions as well. Although revisionists have since challenged the notion of the Western as grand metaphor for westward expansion—Jane Tompkins, for example, posits that the Western "isn't about the encounter between civilization and the frontier. It is about men's fear of losing their mastery, and hence their identity, both of which the Western tirelessly reinvents"—most nonetheless acknowledge what Tompkins termed "the classic oppositions from which all Westerns derive their meaning: parlor versus mesa, East versus West, woman versus man, illusion versus truth, words versus things." Even if "Westerns strive to depict a world of clear alternatives" but are "just as compulsively driven to destroying these opposites and making them contain each other," or if the Western is "a reaction against a female-dominated tradition of popular culture,"[11] it's still the man's world that Wister described and Fiedler observed. Cynthia Hamilton sees the classic Western as being set in "an idealized environment which allows competitive individualism free reign. The two crucial attributes of the formula's setting are lawlessness and the maximum opportunity for personal enrichment. . . . Women and the aged are particularly at risk."[12] And as Tompkins so succinctly puts it, "When life itself is at stake, everything else seems trivial by comparison."[13]

In the world of men always on guard, where justice is dispensed at the end of a gun's barrel or rope, the archetypal Western hero knows the rules and abides by them, skillful at everything that could be perceived as a test of his manhood. In the American West, card playing was never only a game, but an arena for displaying and judging character, just as the corral gave men a chance to showcase their cowboy skills, while the mountains and chaparral gave them an open field in which to demonstrate their knowledge of the wilderness. In such a society, the Western hero is the quintessential Man among men whose "code" reinforces his superior position: Strong and silent, he's slow to anger, cool under fire, and more duty-bound than the common citizen or the most stoic settler. In the lawless West, the hero has a heightened sense of personal morality which goes beyond simple knowledge of the unwritten laws that govern other men's behavior. His code requires him to act, even when action could result in a quick trip to the cemetery. As Wright observes, society recognizes the hero's special nature, yet it never fully accepts him because he *is* so different—literally, the odd man out.

The rest, Wright reminds us, is equally familiar. Villains stronger than society, or who somehow break the unwritten code of the West, threaten the stability of that society. The hero, like the country whose mythic code he embodies, is never the aggressor and always acts to dispense justice on behalf of others, sacrificing his own happiness to do so—or at least causing conflict between his love interest and himself. His horse, of course, doesn't mind. Eventually he wins because he knows the territory, knows the rules, knows human nature, and knows himself. *The Virginian*, for example, suggests that "Every good man in this world has convictions about right and wrong. They are his soul's riches, his spiritual gold. When his conduct is at variance with these, he knows that it is a departure, a falling; and this is a simple and clear matter."[14] The code, which sets him and a select group of others apart from everyone else, lies at the center of every Western novel and film, shaping and defining the genre. But I'm suggesting that it may also have shaped and defined the code by which Hemingway's heroes aspire to live—even more than Rehberger would have us believe—for the Western hero and the Hemingway "code" hero bear a striking resemblance to one another. Both privilege experiential over book knowledge, action over talk, and precision and skill over sloppiness or mediocrity. Both value stoicism and self-control, and both respect coolness under fire and confronting death bravely.

Wister's description of the cowboy's character and proclivities could just as easily describe the typical Hemingway code hero's: "Adventure, to be out-of-doors, to find some new place far away from the postman, to enjoy independence of spirit or mind or body (according to his high or low standards)—this is the cardinal surviving fittest instinct."[15] The Western hero lives on the edge, his survival skills are constantly tested, his manhood challenged every day. Among cardplayers, gunfighters, brawlers, trackers, hunters, cowboys, drinkers, and sagebrush philosophers, he's the best because he *has* to be. Wister thought cowboys "the manly, simple, humorous American type" and "the bravest we possess. . . . They work hard, they play hard."[16] As Wister explained, the cowboy "fought his way with knife and gun and any hour of the twenty-four might see him flattened behind the rocks among the whizz of bullets and the flight of arrows, or dragged bloody and folded together from some adobe hovel. . . . Among these perils the cow-puncher took wild pleasure in existing"[17]—experiencing as heightened a sense of what it meant to be alive as Hemingway's bullfighters felt.[18]

All this, of course, sounds remarkably like the fictional world which Robert Penn Warren described and Philip Young and Jackson Benson detailed in the early years of Hemingway scholarship, save linking Hemingway to the Old West except through metaphorical language and undeveloped comparisons. Perhaps the notion of a code hero dominated early Hemingway scholarship because it *was* such a deeply enculturated and familiar archetype. Writing in the Fifties, Warren noticed that Hemingway's was a showdown-style world of violence, where the "typical character faces defeat or death." As Warren observed, Hemingway's characters are usually

> tough men, experienced in the hard worlds they inhabit, and not obviously given to emotional display or sensitive shrinking. . . . His heroes are not squealers, welchers, compromisers, or cowards, and when they confront defeat they realize that the stance they take, the stoic endurance, the stiff upper lip mean a kind of victory. . . . They represent some notion of a code, some notion of honor, that makes a man a man, and that distinguishes him from people who merely follow their random impulses and who are, by consequence, "messy."[19]

Despite the long shadow cast by the Hemingway code hero on the American literary horizon, there's nothing uniquely Hemingwayesque about it if one considers it alongside the archetypal Western hero. In *The*

Virginian, as with subsequent formulary Westerns—including the serial-ized Westerns by Ernest Haycox that Hemingway enjoyed as late as 1950[20]—that which sets the hero apart is immediately noticeable, even before his heightened moral sense becomes clear: His skills are honed to a fine precision. When the tenderfoot narrator, a code-hero "wannabe," first lays eyes on the man known as *The Virginian,* the cowboy is trying his hand at what others have repeatedly failed to accomplish: to rope a pony so "rapid of limb" and watchful of eye that he resembles "a skillful boxer" (1). But, of course, the animal is no match for the hero, who moves with "the undulations of a tiger, smooth and easy" (1). Unlike other wranglers, the Virginian holds his rope so that the pony can't see it until it's too late, and "like a sudden snake [the tenderfoot] saw the noose go out its length and fall true," causing a fellow train passenger to remark, "That man knows his business" (2).

One can't read such a passage without thinking of the white hunter in "The Short Happy Life of Francis Macomber," who also wears a Stetson and whose skill level has made him a professional,[21] or of Santiago from *The Old Man and the Sea,* who kept his lines "straighter than anyone did, so that at each level in the darkness of the stream there would be a bait waiting exactly where he wished it to be for any fish that swam there,"[22] or Robert Jordan, who "knew from experience how simple it was to move behind the enemy lines in all this country" and "knew how to blow any sort of bridge that you could name and he had blown them of all sizes and constructions."[23]

Jordan, who hails from Montana and whose grandfather was an Indian fighter during the Custer era (336–38), comes closest among Hemingway's characters to the consummate Western hero. Like the Virginian, he is even called by a referential nickname, "the Inglés" (199). As much an outsider as the typical Western hero, Jordan risks his life to help a community of rebels to which he will never truly belong—the blowing of the bridge constituting Jordan's high noon, his moment of truth. His code of honor is stronger than that of the strongest man in the brigade, and where even the bravest among them fears something, Jordan is outwardly fearless, confining any display of weakness or insecu-rity to his private thoughts, as the Virginian does.[24] Code-bound, the only fear Jordan voices is "of not doing my duty as I should" (91).

Like Wister's hero, Jordan works with almost exaggerated ease, prefer-ring action to inaction. For him, "the problem of [the bridge's] demolition was not difficult. . . . He sketched quickly and happily; glad at last to have the problem under his hand; glad at last to be actually engaged upon it"—this wartime showdown (35). It's the same relief that the Virginian feels when the time finally comes for him to face the rustler and murderer

Trampas in a confrontation that had been brewing since the beginning of the novel. Finally, "It had come to that point where there was no way out, save only the ancient, eternal way between man and man. It is only the great mediocrity that goes to law in these personal matters" (291).

Just as the Western hero is set apart from others in the community by his outsider status and his skill at gunplay, in war Jordan is an expatriate weapons expert among patriot amateurs. He knows guns as well as explosives, and his knowledge seems even more superior when juxtaposed against the limited experience and perception of those around him. When a machine gun is captured and Jordan asks what kind of a gun it is, a gypsy vaguely replies, "A very rare name." Jordan asks how many rounds of ammunition they have for it, and the gypsy says, "An infinity. One whole case of an unbelievable heaviness," and Jordan thinks, "Sounds like about five hundred rounds." After another question and response he thinks, "Hell, it's a Lewis gun" (26–27)—identification complete. But the Inglés, like the Virginian, never wears his knowledge like a pair of shiny new spurs. His observations stay largely in his mind, and when spoken they're voiced in quiet tones or with near self-effacing casualness. That's because action is more important to the Western hero than talk. Bragging is for tenderfoots and tinhorns.

In *The Virginian*, when a train full of starving passengers pulls into a beefless cow town where the residents are also starving, the cowboy notices a swamp and remembers a frog farm where he once lived and recalls having frog legs at Delmonico's. He and sidekick Scipio head into the swamp with empty sacks and return with them full to cook for all of the passengers. But like Santiago, who "was too simple to wonder when he had attained humility" (13), the Virginian shrugs off their praise of his resourcefulness and superior knowledge, chalking it up to experience: "I've been where there was big money in frawgs, and they ain't been," he explains. "They're all cattle here. Talk cattle, think cattle, and they're bankrupt in consequence" (117–19).

Likewise, when a stagecoach driver attempts to pull his stalled rig from the riverbed in which it was mired, the stranded heroine aboard "saw the tall one delaying beside the driver, and speaking. He spoke so quietly that not a word reached her, until of a sudden the driver protested loudly. The man had thrown something, which turned out to be a bottle. This twisted loftily and dived into the stream." After showing the driver the safe spot for crossing, the Virginian "dropped his grave eyes from hers, and swinging upon his horse, was gone just as the passenger opened her mouth and with inefficient voice murmured, 'Oh, thank you!' at his departing back." The driver, meanwhile, was humbled not by the Virginian's superior attitude, but by his superior knowledge. He held his head "meek as his own drenched horses" and drove out of the riverbed "a chastened creature" (63).

All of Hemingway's code heroes, despite their superior knowledge and skill, similarly value modesty and humility. Even the oldest among them, the venerable Santiago, thinks, "I am a strange old man," though he knows "many tricks" (14). Hemingway code heroes are schooled early in the importance of silence and humility. When Frederic Henry is in the hospital, Catherine pleads, "Don't brag, darling. Please don't brag. You're so sweet and you don't have to brag."[25] This part of the code is best illustrated, perhaps, by Jake Barnes' running commentary on the very unheroic Robert Cohn in *The Sun Also Rises*. Cohn's attitude is instantly offensive to everyone: "The publishers had praised his novel pretty highly and it went to his head. Then several women had put themselves out to be nice to him" and *that* went to his head. "Also," Barnes recalls, "playing for higher stakes than [Cohn] could afford in some rather steep bridge games with his New York connections, he had held cards and won several hundred dollars. It made him rather vain of his bridge game, and he talked several times of how a man could always make a living at bridge if he were ever forced to" (8–9). The problem, of course, is that Cohn is most emphatically *not* a man by code standards. He talks about feelings that "real men" would keep to themselves, and even cries in public—as Joaquin, the self-confessed "failed bullfighter" (140) does in *For Whom the Bell Tolls* (106, 139). For Cohn, talk replaces action. Even in the bedroom, where a man's man would spring into action (and Catherine reminds her young lover, "Come on. Don't talk. Please come on") (92), Cohn talks too much (13), and one quickly surmises that his talk about going to South America is just that—talk. In Hemingway's novelistic meditation on manhood, Cohn fares no better than he would have had he lived in the Old West.

Proper conduct for a man is almost always on the Western hero's mind. In a humorous section where the Virginian's love interest tries to engage him in a discussion of literature, the cowboy turns it instead into a discussion of manhood, revealing how his world is governed by this simple principle. Molly reads him a Browning poem about "the need of a world of men for me," which causes the Virginian to say, almost reverently, "That is very, very true" (219). Asked his opinion on *Romeo and Juliet*, the Virginian says simply that Romeo was "no man. I like his friend Mercutio that gets killed. He is a man. If he had got Juliet there would have been no foolishness and trouble" (174). Likewise, the Virginian thinks the prince in *Henry the Fourth* a man because "He killed a big fighter on the other side who was another jim-dandy—and he was sorry for having to do it" (217). When Molly reads more Browning to him, the

Virginian recoils from lines spoken by a dying soldier: "Touched to the quick, he said, / 'I'm killed, sire!' And, his chief beside, / Smiling, the boy fell dead." The Virginian tells Molly in his laconic drawl, "Now a man who was man enough to act like he did, yu' see, would fall dead without mentioning it" (218). For the Virginian—and "real" men—death isn't worth making a fuss over. At the end of *For Whom the Bell Tolls*, when Robert Jordan and his gray horse are shot down by a tank, Jordan, not the horse, pulls up lame with a broken leg. Agustín casually, but seriously, offers to shoot him, but Jordan just as matter-of-factly responds, "*No hace falta* . . . . Get along. I am very well here" (465) and only hopes to "last" until the enemy comes upon him (471). Significantly, during Jordan's last stand he thinks of his grandfather, comparing his own tale and his own heroics against the Indian fighter's (469).

In the Western hero, skill and experience combine to produce an individual who is so exceptional and knowledgeable of all aspects of life—death included—that he is supremely confident and therefore gracious. He's also seldom afraid, since fear stems partly from uncertainty and partly from not having the dedication to an ideal that would override any self-protective impulse. By the tender age of twenty-four the Virginian had seen nine states, and "Everywhere he had taken care of himself and survived; nor had his strong heart yet waked up to any hunger for a home." He was "one of thousands drifting and living thus, but . . . one in a thousand" (33). Skills honed over time and experiential knowledge make the Western hero as much a fearless survivor as Santiago, who, as an accomplished navigator, never worried when a hooked fish carried him far from the safety of daylight and land. It's the same supreme confidence that sends Wilson walking casually into tall grass to finish off a wounded animal, or allows Jordan to coolly focus on blowing a bridge without demolition caps.

The Virginian puts the philosophy clearly into perspective for his tenderfoot protégé, explaining how skill is important for both bad men and good:

> Now back East you can be middling and get along. But if you go to try a thing on in this Western country, you've got to do it *well*. You've got to deal cards *well*; you've got to steal *well*; and if you claim to be quick with your gun, you must be quick, for you're a public temptation, and some man will not resist trying to prove he is the quicker. You must break all the Commandments *well* in this Western country. (250–51)

The tenderfoot is the first to admit that "[the Virginian] invariably saw game before I did, and was off his horse and crouched among the sage while I was still getting my left foot clear of the stirrup" (47). Robert Jordan, likewise, is a better tracker and spotter than the old man who accompanies him. When he and Anselmo see "three monoplanes in V-formation" and the old man proclaims "They are *Moscas*," Jordan can tell by the profile of the planes that instead "It was a Fascist Patrol coming home" (38). Despite his status as an outsider, Jordan knows the country so well that he astounds El Sordo with his knowledge and is able to offer attack advice that native Spaniards cannot provide (147).

Often, the Western hero is depicted alongside someone with two left feet—a pupil, a tenderfoot, or a not-as-skilled sidekick—to further highlight his near-mythic prowess. Here too, Young's distinction between the Hemingway code hero and the young Hemingway hero who aspires to learn the code sounds a lot like the accomplished cowboy tutor and his spunky protégé: The Virginian has his tenderfoot, Santiago has the boy, Wilson has Macomber, Harry Morgan has his rummy mate in *To Have and Have Not*, the bullfighter has Jake Barnes, and a succession of men whose knowledge was derived from experience, not books, are there to informally instruct Nick Adams.

Just as the Western hero has mastered his professional skills, more importantly he has mastered himself. He won't be provoked, and he won't tolerate being perceived as weak or imperceptive. He drinks—since that's part of the game, part of male bonding—but never to excess, because that leads to a loss of control, a loss of poise. He gets emotionally involved, at times, with women, but keeps his true feelings inside except on rare occasions when he speaks of them to his lady, but never around witnesses. In all situations, his actions are informed more by reason than emotion. The Virginian knows when to back down and he knows when to back others down. His calm response to being called a son of a bitch during a card game has since become a Western cliché: "When you call me that, *smile!*" (18). In other words, you'd better be joking. It's the same poker-style response the Inglés has when he enters the stronghold and a man with a scar asks in Western fashion what he is looking at, Jordan's response is a single word: "Thee" (57). And that response disarms his would-be opponents. When pressed by the gypsy about his reason for not killing Pablo, since he would "have to kill him sooner or later," Jordan tells the gypsy that he opted against violence because "I thought it might molest you others or the woman" (61). Besides, Jordan knows that to kill before being pushed to the brink of necessity is not to kill, but "to assassinate" (61). While those around him would follow their emotions, Jordan remains reasonable.

Similarly, the Virginian is cool in situations where other men are noticeably more nervous, and his calm demeanor disarms his opponents at times, while at other times it unsettles them. When his archrival Trampas utters for the first time another cliché, "I'll give you till sundown to leave town," the Virginian says, somewhat tongue-in-cheek, "Trampas, are yu' sure yu' really mean that?", which drives his opponent to a bottle-throwing rage. That kind of Western slap-leather tension is reflected in Hemingway's description of Jordan's first encounters with Pablo and the freedom fighters (50–53). At several points gunplay seems likely, and Jordan, the consummate professional, senses potential danger and casually readies himself. While smiling at Maria,

> At the same time he sucked in on his stomach muscles and swung a little to the left on his stool so that his pistol slipped around on his belt closer to where he wanted it. He reached his hand down toward his hip pocket and Pablo watched him. . . . His hand came up from the hip pocket with the leather-covered flask and he unscrewed the top and then, lifting the cup, drank half the water and poured very slowly from the flask into the cup. (50)

Later, Jordan was "watching Pablo, and as he watched, letting his right hand hang lower and lower, ready if it should be necessary, half hoping it would be" (53).

Interestingly, however, the tension between Pablo and the Inglés never turns into a showdown in *For Whom the Bell Tolls*, though Pablo, like Trampas, grows drunk and belligerent later, and the cave becomes for a moment tense as a barroom. "I am drunk," Pablo announces, adding that "To drink is nothing. It is to be drunk that is important." Jordan, with a coolness equal to the Virginian, says, "I doubt it. Cowardly, yes," after which it became "so quiet in the cave, suddenly, that he could hear the hissing noise the wood made burning on the hearth where Pilar cooked" (211–13). Jordan thinks, "I'd like to kill him and have it over with. . . . Come on. Let us get it over with" (212). But he remains cool, and Pablo reacts as Trampas did when the dealer in the barroom chided all who would disrupt the fragile silence with shifting chairs or sudden movements: "Sit quiet. Can't you see he don't want to push trouble? He has handed Trampas the choice to back down or draw his steel" (19), and Trampas wisely elected to back down. As the tenderfoot narrator put it, "In no company would [the Virginian] be rated a novice at the cool art of self-preservation" (19).

Throughout Wister's novel this early Western hero displays a coolness under fire that anticipates the Hemingway hero's ability to conduct himself with what Hemingway termed "grace under pressure"[26]—the secret of which, as big-game guide Wilson explains, is an acceptance of death: "That's it," he tells Macomber. "Worst [a lion] can do is kill you." After speaking this part of the hero's code, "He was very embarrassed, having brought out this thing he had lived by, but he had seen men come of age before and it always moved him" (32). Yet, one senses that Wilson is far less embarrassed by the vocalization of this maxim than he was by Macomber's earlier flight from danger. Clearly, the code hero is moved that his protégé has learned the most difficult part of the code, that which makes them stand taller than others: facing death bravely and gracefully as the bullfighters do in *The Sun Also Rises* (10).

The same emotion is stirred in the Virginian when he recalls how bravely his friend faced the hangman's noose, tightened around his neck by order of the Virginian himself, because the man had broken one of the unwritten but understood rules of conduct: He had been caught rustling cattle. The Virginian's view "was simple enough: you must die brave. Failure is a sort of treason to the brotherhood, and forfeits pity. It was [his friend's] perfect bearing [at the moment of his execution] that had caught his heart so that he forgot even his scorn of the other man" (247). The key, of course, is that killing and exercising force is never relished by the hero, who at one point exclaims, "I have been fearing he would force it on me" (103). When the hanging was accomplished, and the tenderfoot remarks how the Virginian "never did this before," the tall man responds, "No, I never had it to do" (246). But his code and sense of duty demanded that he execute his friend in order to enforce the unwritten laws of the West.

In a Godless and lawless land, the responsibility for administering justice ultimately rests with those Western heroes whose moral codes are as superior as their skills. But to be heroic, they must be reluctant, rather than eager enforcers. Speaking of the last "nervous" dynamiter, Jordan says matter-of-factly, "I shot him. . . . He was too badly wounded to travel and I shot him" (149). Once again, what Young observed of the Hemingway code hero sounds similar to the typical Western hero:

> he represents a code according to which the hero, if he could attain it, would be able to live properly in the world of violence, disorder, and misery to which he has been introduced and which he inhabits. The code hero, then, offers up and exemplifies certain principles of honor, courage, and endurance which in a life of tension and pain make a man a man . . . and enable him to conduct himself well in the losing battle that is life.[27]

Life, to the Western hero, is a game to be played, and played well— especially in the arena of men only, where playing it well *extends* one's life. When the Virginian and Molly read Browning's poem about a world of men, the Virginian tells her that he was sure the man would come back "afteh he had played some more of the game." When she asks what he means, he replies, "Life, ma'am. Whatever he was a-doin' in the world of men" (219). When the Virginian's friend, Steve, gets involved with rustlers and only he and another get caught, the narrator thinks how "he stayed game" throughout his unfortunate capture (247) and remarks, "Yes, the joke, as they put it, was on Steve. He had lost one point in the game to them" (243). When the Virginian hangs his friend, he thinks, "I would do it all over again. The whole thing just the same. He knowed the customs of the country, and he played the game" (258). In *For Whom the Bell Tolls*, when Pablo executes four *guardia civiles*, Pilar vividly remembers how each member of the losing side faced death (101–2)—two more "gamely" than the others. For the rest of the fascists, Pablo constructs an elaborate gauntlet that the men must run, a game that turns the crowd cruel only because of "the insults" of one fascist and "the cowardice" of a second (114)—both violations of unwritten rules of proper conduct.

Talk may be cheap, but banter is a necessary part of the game, an important way for the hero and others to deal with injuries, indignities, and the ever-present possibility of dying. But there are rules here, too. Even the tenderfoot narrator of *The Virginian* quickly learns this part of the code, for at a boardinghouse dinner he notices that his "strict silence and attention to the corned beef made [him] in the eyes of the cow-boys at table compare well with the over-talkative commercial travellers" (11). Later, after he had seen the Virginian "wildly disporting himself" in a moment of revelry, the tenderfoot discovered that "those were matters which he chose not to discuss with me" (26). Riding together proved just as conversationally fruitless, since five or ten miles would pass before the Virginian would speak a word. Yet, while "The Virginian was grave in bearing and of infrequent speech . . . he kept a song going—a matter of some seventy-nine verses. Seventy-eight were quite unprintable, and rejoiced his brother cow-punchers monstrously" (59). Joking and idle talk are not the same thing.

When Jordan meets brigade leader Golz, they verbally spar. And when a staff person complains "in the language Robert Jordan did not understand," Golz tells him to "Shut up. . . . I am so serious is why I can joke" (8). If life is a game, then verbal sparring is a round-one form of character assessment as well as a stress reliever. "How otherwise can we divert ourselves?" Pilar asks Jordan (98). Such is the case both in the classic Western and in Hemingway's fictional world. One can't read the bunkhouse banter in *The Virginian* without thinking of the priest-baiting section from *A Farewell to Arms* (6–9), or the banter at the cave where Pilar takes on all comers (92–93, 155–56). Pilar even bests Jordan in the verbal duel that takes place before their big offensive. "I begin to think thou art afraid to see the bull come out," she teases, to which Jordan responds, "Thy mother." But Pilar, who "would have made a good man" (92), whispers, "Thou never hadst one" (405). Those who fail to understand what constitutes appropriate verbal jousting are denigrated. Anselmo, for example, criticizes the gypsy for the latter's exaggerated talk: "He is a gypsy, so if he catches rabbits he says it is foxes. If he catches a fox he would say it is an elephant. . . . Gypsies talk much and kill little" (19). Those who cannot hold their own in a war of words are as poorly thought of as those who fail to act and act well.

Game references and metaphors in Hemingway's fiction have been well documented, most extensively by Benson. Santiago is likened to a baseball player, and the men in *The Sun Also Rises* are compared to matadors, bulls, and steers. Catherine Barkley says to her young patient-lover, Frederic Henry, "This is a rotten game we play, isn't it?" (*Farewell*, 31). Frederic realizes that "This was a game, like bridge, in which you said things instead of playing cards," though "Nobody had mentioned what the stakes were" (30–31). Jordan, meanwhile, is engaged in his own form of gamesmanship. He runs his demolition wire from the bridge "as an outfielder goes backwards for a long fly ball" (445). Earlier, upon hearing that some of the band have killed two members of the *guardia civil*, he responds, "That is big game" (21). "It is like a merry-go-round, Robert Jordan thought. . . . But this is another wheel. This is like a wheel that goes up and around. . . . There are no prizes either, he thought, and no one would choose to ride this wheel" (225). The game, of course, is the same one of which the Virginian spoke: Life itself. And, as Benson notes, "In the game of life you lose by playing, and the harder you play the more you lose."[28]

How one plays the game—abiding by the rules or the code, and acting with style—therefore becomes most important, for both the Western hero and the Hemingway hero. Ironically, those who have a heightened sense of the code risk losing more so and more often than those who would play it safe—and therefore develop the heightened sense of living that characterizes both heroes. As the Virginian warned his beloved Molly, "Cow-punchers do not live long enough to get old" (209). He may have a way with horses and women, but his code makes him put duty first, because "a man goes through with his responsibilities" (258). Jordan, likewise, tells Pilar that he will not let drink or women interfere with his work. Duty comes first (91). The call of duty also makes the Virginian forestall his courtship to tend his herd and track rustlers, and it draws him into a gunfight with Trampas on the day of his wedding—even as coming up short on the wheel of fortune causes the Inglés to send Maria away with the others after his broken leg dooms him to stay behind and face death alone.

Although Rehberger suggests that in *For Whom the Bell Tolls* Hemingway equally embraces and subverts the myths of the Old West,[29] I would argue that the complicated network of formulaic elements indicates a considerably stronger embrace—which, nonetheless, makes the Custer underpinning all the more ironic. For one thing, there's Hemingway's own propensity for romance, not just in his adventurous life, but in documented episodes. Gertrude Stein sensed it when she wrote that he "looks like a Modern and he smells of the museums,"[30] and as Reynolds has observed, "As with so many of the modernists, Hemingway's modernism resided in his style, not in his ideas or value system."[31] As early as 1944, Malcolm Cowley was claiming that the literary lion could be grouped not with those who were attempting to remake reality, but "with Poe and Hawthorne and Melville," writers from the romantic period in American literature.[32]

Although Hemingway implies in all his fictions that romance, chivalry, and knighthood are dead, that does not prevent his characters from trying to think or act in a romantic fashion, or from considering what it takes to be a modern hero. In fact, they seem compelled to do so. Robert Jordan alludes to previous heroes such as the Greeks at Thermopylae, Horatius at the bridge, and the Dutch boy who stuck his finger in the dike (164). Even the drunken revolutionary leader, Pablo, is compared to General Ulysses S. Grant—a grand general but lousy president. In *Across the River and Into the Trees*, Colonel Cantwell describes General George Patton as being "quite rich in money and with a lot of armour" and notes how difficult rank makes it for a man to attain "the Holy Grail" in this day and age.[33]

The Virginian established the Western hero as a knight on horseback who lived by a code as honorable and chivalrous as medieval warriors (74, 208). The Virginian was "deeply proud of his lady," despite the fact that she "had slighted him. He had pulled her out of the water once and he had been her unrewarded knight even to-day" (74). Later, "before a lot of men . . . Trampas spoke disrespectfully of [her], and before them all he made Trampas say he was a liar" (211). Again, one can't help but think of Cohn, the "false knight"[34] who was unable to defend his lady's honor, and, in fact, violated the code even more by talking about his affair with her to Jake (100–1). Or one recalls Maria's "rescue" from the fascists, where one of the men who helped her later confesses that he was "glad thou wert hanging over my back when the shots were coming from behind us" and grateful to "hold onto thy legs." Hearing this, Maria holds her composure and simply says, "My heroes. . . . My saviors" (133).

However outdated or reductive the notion of a Hemingway code hero might now be considered, the fact remains that the code by which Hemingway's heroes live too closely resembles the code of the Western hero to be considered anything but an embracing of Western myth—even down to the ironic endings. Though Wister romanticized the West, Haycox and genre writers to follow would have their heroes lose for winning— solving the problems of the community, but riding off alone and feeling empty. Despite readings of *For Whom the Bell Tolls* as a subversion of the Western myth, then, the Inglés can be read as another Virginian, but with a later genre-style ending, since he experiences a letdown after blowing the bridge (447) and cannot ride off into the sunset with his beloved Maria. Even so, it may still be too much to claim that the Hemingway code hero is derived strictly from the Western hero, since Wister himself wrote that the cowboy hero was himself a reincarnation of "the medieval man. It was no new type, no product of the frontier."[35]

Nevertheless, the shadow cast by the Western hero upon American culture has been significant. And if the mountains of the American West loom as large as Fiedler and others have observed in Hemingway's fictional world, they seem to have cast a technical as well as thematic shadow. In *The Virginian,* Wister used the mountains as a sundial of sorts, returning to them in his fictional descriptions as a way of heightening pre-showdown tension. As the shadow creeps closer to town, where the Virginian and Trampas must "slap leather" on Main Street, the reader experiences what it must feel like for the participants, sensing the magnitude of the moment drawing closer. Perhaps not so coincidentally, repetition of select descriptive elements is a technique Hemingway has employed often in his fiction. In *For Whom the Bell Tolls,* Hemingway uses the movement of sunlight across a landscape as Wister did, in order to create suspense and set up the two-part tragic ending: Jordan's injury, and Jordan's impending death. Readers are told that Robert Jordan "lay on his belly behind the pine trunk, the gun across his left forearm and watched the point of light below him. . . . Robert Jordan lay there and waited for daylight" (410–11). Hemingway returns to descriptions of Jordan, the pines, and shifting sunlight again and again,[36] until finally the novel ends with Hemingway's version of the showdown:

> Robert Jordan [lying] behind the tree, holding onto himself very carefully and delicately to keep his hands steady. He was waiting until the officer reached the sunlit place where the first trees of the pine forest joined the green slope of the meadow. He could feel his heart beating against the pine needle floor of the forest. (462)

For Jordan and other Hemingway code heroes, as with the Virginian and every Western hero before them, and after, it often comes down to this simple maxim: in life and in the face of death, a man's gotta do what a man's gotta do.

NOTES

1. Michael Reynolds, *Hemingway: The 1930s* (New York: Norton, 1997), 4.

2. Leslie Fiedler, "Men Without Women," in *Hemingway: A Collection of Critical Essays*, ed. Robert P. Weeks (Englewood Cliffs, N.J.: Prentice-Hall, 1962), 90, 92.

3. John J. Teunissen, *"For Whom the Bell Tolls* as Mythic Narrative," in *Ernest Hemingway: Six Decades of Criticism*, ed. Linda W. Wagner (East Lansing: Michigan State University Press, 1987), 221–37. See also Ben Merchant Vorpahl's "Ernest Hemingway and Owen Wister: Finding the Lost Generation," *Library Chronicle* 36 (Spring 1970): 126–37; Frank Scafella's *"The Sun Also Rises*: Owen Wister's 'Garbage Pail,' Hemingway's 'Passage of the Human Soul'," in *The Hemingway Review* 6 (Fall 1986): 104; and Alan Price's "'I'm Not an Old Fogey and You're not a Young Ass': Owen Wister and Ernest Hemingway," in *The Hemingway Review* 9.1 (Fall 1989): 82–90.

4. Dean Rehberger, "'I Don't Know Buffalo Bill'; or, Hemingway and the Rhetoric of the Western," in *Blowing the Bridge: Essays on Hemingway and "For Whom the Bell Tolls,"* ed. Rena Sanderson (New York: Greenwood Press, 1992), 161, 163.

5. Michael S. Reynolds, *Hemingway's Reading: 1910–1940, An Inventory* (Princeton, N.J.: Princeton University Press, 1981), 42–43.

6. Charles A. Fenton, *The Apprenticeship of Ernest Hemingway* (New York: New American Library, 1961), 16.

7. Scafella, "Wister's 'Garbage Pail,'" 104.

8. Reynolds, *Hemingway's Reading*, 202.

9. Rehberger, "Buffalo Bill," 160.

10. Will Wright, *Sixguns and Society: A Structural Study of the Western* (Riverside: University of California Press, 1975).

11. Jane Tompkins, *West of Everything: The Inner Life of Westerns* (New York: Oxford University Press, 1992), 45, 48.

12. Cynthia S. Hamilton, *Western and Hard-Boiled Detective Fiction in America: From High Noon to Midnight* (London: Macmillan, 1987), 10.

13. Tompkins, *West of Everything*, 31.

14. Owen Wister, *The Virginian* (New York: New American Library, 1970), 270. Subsequent references are from this edition and will be given as page numbers in the text.

15. Owen Wister, *Owen Wister's West: Selected Articles*, ed. Robert Murray Davis (Albuquerque: University of New Mexico Press, 1987), 38.

16. Owen Wister, *Owen Wister Out West: His Journals and Letters*, ed. Fanny Kemble Wister (Chicago: University of Chicago Press, 1987), 246.

17. Wister, *Owen Wister's West*, 42–43, 50.

18. Ernest Hemingway, *The Sun Also Rises* (New York: Scribner's, 1954), 10. Subsequent references are from this edition and will be given as page numbers in the text.

19. Robert Penn Warren, "Ernest Hemingway," in *Ernest Hemingway: Five Decades of Criticism*, ed. Linda Welshimer Wagner (East Lansing: Michigan State University Press, 1974), 79.

20. Matthew J. Bruccoli, *Conversations with Ernest Hemingway* (Jackson: University Press of Mississippi, 1986), 63.

21. Ernest Hemingway, "The Short Happy Life of Francis Macomber," in *The Short Stories of Ernest Hemingway* (New York: Scribner's, 1987), 4. Subsequent references are from this edition and will be given as page numbers in the text.

22. Ernest Hemingway, *The Old Man and the Sea* (New York: Scribner's, 1980), 32. Subsequent references are from this edition and will be given as page numbers in the text.

23. Ernest Hemingway, *For Whom the Bell Tolls* (New York: Scribner's, 1987), 4. Subsequent references are from this edition and will be given as page numbers in the text.

24. There are numerous instances of such behavior in *For Whom the Bell Tolls*, most strikingly on pages 43, 52, 62–3, 136–37, and 470–71.

25. Ernest Hemingway, *A Farewell to Arms* (New York: Scribner's, 1969), 104. Subsequent references are from this edition and will be given as page numbers in the text.

26. Philip Young, *Ernest Hemingway* (Minneapolis: University of Minnesota Press, 1964), 11.

27. Ibid., 10–11.

28. Jackson J. Benson, *Hemingway . . . The Writer's Art of Self-Defense* (Minneapolis: University of Minnesota Press, 1969), 102.

29. Rehberger, "Buffalo Bill," 162.

30. Gertrude Stein, *The Selected Writings of Gertrude Stein*, ed. Carl Van Vechten (New York: Modern Library, 1962), 204.

31. Michael S. Reynolds "The *Sun* in Its Time: Recovering the Historical Context," in *New Essays on "The Sun Also Rises*," ed. Linda Wagner-Martin (Cambridge: Cambridge University Press, 1987), 43–64.

32. Malcolm Cowley, in *The Portable Hemingway*, ed. Malcolm Cowley (New York: Viking, 1944), vii.

33. Ernest Hemingway, *Across the River and Into the Trees* (New York: Scribner's, 1950), 144–45.

34. Mark Spilka, "The Death of Love in *The Sun Also Rises*," in *Hemingway: A Collection of Critical Essays*, ed. Robert P. Weeks (Englewood Cliffs, N.J.: Prentice-Hall, 1962), 127.

35. Wister, *Owen Wister's West*, 43.

36. See especially pp. 431, 433–34, 450, 458, and 461–62.

Hemingway's Constructed Africa: *Green Hills of Africa* and the Conventions of Colonial Sporting Books

LAWRENCE H. MARTIN

In Part III of *Green Hills of Africa,* Hemingway, P.O.M., and Pop are sitting by the campfire one evening after a day's hunt, relaxing, drinking, and discussing politics, revolutions, writing, and, especially, writing about Africa. With a characteristic slant, Hemingway at one point insists on the writer's fidelity to personal observation: "It's very hard to get anything true on anything you haven't seen yourself," he says.[1] He goes on, "But if I ever write anything about this [his 1933–34 African trip] it will just be landscape painting until I know something about it" (193). To Hemingway's plan to write about the African hunting trip, the wise and experienced Jackson Phillips—"Pop"—retorts, "Most of the damned Safari books are most awful bloody bores" (193). Hemingway agrees, "They're terrible" (194).

In what ways are safari books boring and terrible? Pop explains: "They all have this damned Nairobi fast life or else bloody rot about shooting beasts with horns half an inch longer than someone else shot. Or muck about danger" (194).[2] Pop has just identified three conventional themes in colonial African sporting literature: the safari as recreation for the rich and socially prominent, competition for trophies, and thrilling accounts of dangerous game and narrow escapes. Disparaging this "muck" and "bloody rot," Pop tells the visiting American writer-sportsman, "I've never read anything, though, that could make you feel about the country the way we feel about it" (194). After this inviting lead, Hemingway responds, "I'd like to try to write something about the country and the animals and what it's like to someone who knows nothing about it" (194).

In the well-known Foreword to *Green Hills*—probably added, like all prefaces, after the book was finished—Hemingway states his literary principle: "to write an absolutely true book to see whether the shape of a country and the pattern of a month's action can, if truly presented, compete

[87]

with a work of the imagination" (vii). This idea, together with the writer's remarks to his safari guide, comprise the announced rhetorical intention of the book: to tell the truth about Africa and the hunt while avoiding the mistakes and melodrama of other books of the type, and thus to be the best, the most original, the most truthful of the genre, communicating personal experience in such a way to make the armchair sportsman feel the country and the chase.

Hemingway's 1935 *Green Hills of Africa* was by no means the first book of its kind, or the last. It belongs to a long, long tradition of accounts by British writers (and, later, Americans) of adventure, exploration, and big-game hunting in Africa. When Pop speaks of "Safari books," he has in mind a clearly established genre of writing, whose golden age was the half-century or so from about 1880 until the Second World War. Hemingway's book comes near the end of the era of safaris and safari stories in the old, grand style.

There is a canon of safari literature, with its leading authors, and with certain themes and conventions, as well as social, political, and economic origins and implications. Hemingway evidently knew this literature well, and he owned books by the best-known safari writers of the nineteenth and twentieth centuries.[3] Although he claims that safari books by others are worthless and that his yet unwritten book will outdo them all in honesty and verisimilitude, *Green Hills of Africa* owes a great deal to the writing of hunters and adventurers who preceded him. The sporting writers whose books were in Hemingway's library, and from whom he appears to have learned, include the leading English safari writers Frederick Courteney Selous and Chauncey Hugh Stigand, the American president-naturalist-explorer Theodore Roosevelt, and, perhaps most interesting of all, the Kenyan game ranger Blayney Percival, brother of Philip Percival, Hemingway's "white hunter" and the model for Mr. Jackson Phillips—the "Pop" of *Green Hills*. It is possible that Hemingway had read Blayney Percival's African adventure books before ever meeting Philip Percival, who then figures so importantly in both the actual 1934 safari and in Hemingway's book about it. The outlooks and experiences of these writers almost certainly influenced Hemingway's attitudes toward the African land, its people, and the hunt, and they taught him how to compose a safari book employing most of the traditions of the genre while he also "improved" the narrative in his own ways.

Safari books of the late Victorian and early modern era have some distinctive themes and conventions. One must remember, first of all, that this period coincides with the apex of the British Empire and with the era of European colonialism in general. The African country most suitable for big-game shooting—Kenya, Tanganyika—was (or became) British territory, and the sporting and exploration literature emanating from them had a decidedly British colonial cast. The English hunters and explorers were an adventurous lot, eager to see the new—to them—land and to live lives different from those in their homeland. They were physically strong, good hunters and skilled marksmen, and curious about African life. Some were educated and well-read; Latin terminology abounds, as does reference to classical authors. Some were soldiers, looking for exciting adventure beyond the battlefield. Above all, they were observant naturalists, filling their books with elaborate descriptions and frequently with artistic sketches of fauna and flora.[4] Some writers appear to be expert zoologists and botanists, whether by schooling or self-taught. The best of them were gentlemen-naturalists, recalling for the modern reader those amazing Victorians who, it seems, knew science, literature, history, languages, and geography, and who wrote about what they knew for an audience presumably interested in far-off lands, striking adventures, and exotic customs. Indeed, the very act of writing is part of the character, for these gentlemen-adventurers wrote long, very long, books in the slightly stiff prose of our great-grandparents.

As for the accounts of shooting, there were also fixed, if unwritten, standards. The hunter had to know his quarry's habits, and he had to respect the animal. Indiscriminate, careless shooting was outside the rules, as was greedy trophy-taking. Sportsmen followed their rules of fair play, and market-hunters—ivory-hunters—followed their rules of practicality. In the course of hunting, whether for sport or profit, the colonial writers paid attention to the land, the rivers, the mountains, the veldt, and the savannah, and, of course, to the Africans, who were, on the one hand, obviously (to British eyes) an uncivilized servant race but, on the other, superior in their ancient knowledge of land and animals.

This survey is hardly an exhaustive index of the themes of the classic safari books, but it may serve to give an idea of the conventions influencing *Green Hills of Africa,* while suggesting also what happens when an original artist works in, and beyond, a fixed tradition, in an effort "to write something about the country and the animals and what it's like."[5] A look at some of the safari books Hemingway owned will further illustrate the close resemblance and show how *Green Hills* derives many of its attitudes about the African land and people.

If English-language safari narrative has an originator, he is Frederick Courteney Selous, born in 1851, the year of the Crystal Palace Exposition, and killed in action (at age 66!) as an infantry officer in 1917. Selous lived most of his life in Africa as an explorer, ivory hunter, and (among other employment) an agent for Cecil Rhodes in Mashonaland. The Selous book in Hemingway's library was *A Hunter's Wanderings in*

Africa, an 1881 account of Selous' epic nine-year (1871–80) "wander-ings." In an 1880 letter with striking foreshadowing of a later writer, Selous explains his plan to write "a true book" about his adventure.[6]

His true book, which sold quite well, set the standard for later works. The Rugby-educated Selous wrote about personal privation and physical danger, and in a matter-of-fact way about his own daring. He practiced the profession of naturalist, writing a long disquisition on "varieties of the Bushbuck," and devoting a long passage to the "koodoo," including some fine engraving plates to illustrate zoological points. About the kudu he dwells on the animal's admirable grace, and he emphasizes its rarity and the difficulty of hunting "the handsomest antelope in the world" (116). He was interested in "native" hunting skills and African culture in gen-eral, especially language and dress, and he had an African native servant with a nickname—"Cigar"—whose wisdom and skill he respected. The attentive modern reader of "Macomber" as well as *Green Hills* will be sure to notice Selous' drawing of a hunter shooting point-blank at a charging lion (opposite 244), another of a hunter about to be trampled by a buffalo (opposite 280), and yet another of a hunter, rifle at the ready, pursuing a wounded buffalo in thick bush (opposite 320). Although Selous is typically a factual, quick-paced writer with a sense of ongoing action, perhaps his most effective passage is a nostalgic (in 1881) reflec-tion on the "splendid hunting grounds which still exist" (443), for even by his day the game was endangered, and Africa—the Africa of colonial English experience—was threatened too. Hemingway, of course, ends *Green Hills* on a similar sentiment: gratitude for having seen a wonderful land before it vanishes.

Other African books in Hemingway's collection, ones whose author rivals Selous in importance in the genre, are two by Chauncey Hugh Stigand, born in 1877 and killed in action (recall Selous) in the Sudan, where he was Bey, or governor, in 1919. Stigand opens his 1913 book *Hunting the Elephant in Africa,* a volume whose preface was contributed by Theodore Roosevelt, with the sad observation that he lived "fifty years too late"[7] for the great years of safaris in the East African Highlands. Despite the title, which refers to only five of twenty-three chapters, this book is a discontinuous collection of how-to hints and African curiosities, including the habits of lions, African sayings and ideas, and a chapter on "The Happy Bantu." The book's significant contribution to science and African entomology in particular, according to Stigand's friend Roosevelt, is a section on insect mimicry and protective coloration—the naturalist superseding the sportsman, in effect.

An earlier publication by Stigand, also in Hemingway's possession, was *The Game of British East Africa* (1909). This piece is interesting because it focuses on the ethics of sport shooting, the author's distaste for trophies ("heads"), and especially the influence of European presence in British East Africa. Although Stigand claims that he has put trophy hunting behind him, he simultaneously says that the game field has been overrun by "town-bred sportsmen" and consequently ninety-nine percent of the heads are "worthless."[8] His implication is that novice or unprincipled sportsmen have devalued the experience of the hunt. Stigand's central theme is the difference, as he says in a chapter title, between "Hunting versus Shooting." The question of sportsmanlike ethics and fair play should recall Hemingway's June 1934 *Esquire* article "Shootism versus Sport," originating in his African hunt, in which Hemingway decries the use of motorcars, favoring instead a sporting, though dangerous, approach on foot. In a parallel passage, Stigand demands "shooting [a lion] in the sporting way; that is, by tracking him up or hunting him unaided on foot" (6). Hemingway's attitude toward sportsman and lion, his regard for bravery and dignity, and indeed his phraseology, are almost identical to Stigand's. Overall, Stigand focuses on the land and the animals, keeping hunting exploits to a minimum. He has favorable opinions of the Masai and Wandorobo, and he remarks on the scarcity and wariness of the greater kudu. Some of his chapters are titled "The Plains," "The Bush," and "The Forest," confirming not only his practical knowledge of the territory but, significantly, his recognition that geography precedes human use.

Hemingway's ownership of Theodore Roosevelt's 1910 *African Game Trails* should come as no surprise, given the widespread appeal of the Rough Rider to a generation of young men. This particular book is an account of Roosevelt's 1909 expedition with his son Kermit on an elaborate safari—F. C. Selous made the plans—to collect specimens for The Smithsonian Institution. On the title page Roosevelt styles himself "an American Hunter-Naturalist," but the manner of collecting usually involves high-power rifles and long-range shots. The image of the hunter as dashing hero overwhelms the picture of the naturalist expanding scientific knowledge. Interspersed with information about lions, rhinos, and buffaloes are opinions about Balzac, Dumas, and Shakespeare. Indeed, one appendix to the 468-page book lists the 512 animal specimens collected, and another appendix ("Appendix F") gives the titles of the Great Books the expedition carried—reminding one of the "book bag" of Russian and British novels carried by the Hemingway-Percival safari. *African Game Trails* describes the geography and reports on the game, but essentially it features one person—TR, hero, sportsman, naturalist, marksman, *litterateur.*

It is worth noting, by the way, that Roosevelt the sportsman had both admirers and detractors, as Hemingway did. Foremost among the admirers, and the man who inspired TR to go to Africa, was Carl E. Akeley, whose 1923 memoir *In Brightest Africa,* dedicated to the memory of Akeley's hero the late President—"the truest sportsman of them all"⁹— was in Hemingway's collection. Akeley was an American original, an adventurer-artist, a science-minded young man who trained as a taxidermist and then raised that "trade to an art" (175), eventually creating the African Hall of the Museum of Natural History in New York, doing everything from designing the building to personally collecting the animals for display in natural settings, which he also devised. He was an African explorer and hunter, a zoologist, a student of evolution who shot animals to study them but feared for their extinction, the inventor of technically advanced motion picture cameras for wildlife photography, the inventor of industrial equipment, a sculptor whose works were sought by important collectors, and a tough, self-reliant man of heroic constitution who survived crushing by an elephant and once strangled to death a leopard that attacked him. Akeley's book covers several African safaris made to collect specimens for the Field Museum in Chicago and the Museum of Natural History, as well as private trips. Though Akeley was a naturalist on a scientific expedition, much of his activity resembled the adventures of Selous, Stigand, and many others. Collecting specimens meant shooting them, and, to make the museum displays impressively realistic, it meant shooting baby elephants and grayback gorillas as well as prime trophies. Nonetheless, Akeley frequently asserts his scientific and artistic aims earnestly and without irony.

These tales of adventure, danger, and straight shooting, all in the name of science and art, show why Roosevelt admired Akeley, invited him to the White House in 1906, and befriended him, and why Akeley later dedicated his African book to the memory of his ideal sportsman, Roosevelt. But romanticizing the strenuous life may be a superficial and sentimental response. The genuine article, the British-born African hunter, sometimes found Roosevelt's dash and heartiness (and egocentricity) a bit too much. Hemingway owned a copy of Denis D. Lyell's 1935 *African Adventures: Letters from Famous Big-Game Hunters,* an anthology of correspondence to Lyell, a famous big-game hunter in his own right, from his friends F. C. Selous, C. H. Stigand, W. D. M. "Karamojo" Bell, R. J. Cuninghame (Roosevelt's safari leader), Sir Alfred Pease, Blayney Percival, and many more, interspersed with commentary by Lyell. Much of the book is taken up by professional opinions of various rifles and calibers, the effectiveness of certain bullet types, techniques for tracking, and other campfire chat. But throughout the letters runs a strong theme of proper conduct in the hunting field, tempered by nostalgia such as Leslie J. Tarlton's in 1927: "The sad thing of it all is, that there is a regular leavening of genuine good sportsmen, who long for the real thing, but who find that modern methods have driven the game so far afield, that the old-time methods are no longer possible."[10] Lyell sustains Tarlton's opinion by explaining that safaris traveling by car are evidence of the decline of sporting ethics, resulting in "a disgraceful proceeding . . . this nefarious kind of butchery" (73). Readers of Hemingway's *Green Hills of Africa* and his other African stories will recall that the 1934 Hemingway-Percival safari moved by car much of the time, and that pursuing game by car is an important (and historically realistic) plot element in "The Short Happy Life of Francis Macomber."

Yet it is not the specifically illegal acts that offend Lyell and his friends as much as the attitudes of the new sportsmen, "the modern game-slaughterer," as Tarlton called them in a 1926 letter (69). Writing nearly ten years after Roosevelt's safari—in *African Game Trails* TR calls it a "scientific expedition"[11]—to collect specimens for The Smithsonian Institution, John G. Millais confesses that "the only thing I have against Roosevelt, who is a delightful man and a personal friend, is that he has an abominable habit of being photographed with every zebra and Kongoni he shoots for the pot as if it were some feat" (103). Millais goes on to criticize the practice in general: "I loathe these wretched amateur photographs, and of the successful hunter posing in front of mangled corpses. It is of no earthly use or scientifically instructive and gives no correct representation of the animal, whilst it displays a cheap conceit which future generations will only laugh at" (103). Lyell himself recollects Colonel Roosevelt's "shooting exploits . . . and his liking to be photographed standing over his harmless victims" (108). Lyell quotes Sir Frederick Jackson, who in his *Early Days in East Africa* publicly expressed "great regret" to learn that Roosevelt had "so unduly exceeded reasonable limits . . . particularly the White Rhinoceros" (109). To Jackson's claim that TR was "so utterly reckless in the expenditure of ammunition" (109), Lyell adds a personal note that "in 1911 I happened to follow the trail taken by an American party, and the empty cartridge-cases lying about the veld reminded me of places I had seen in South Africa during the progress of the Boer War after an engagement had taken place, for they were often as thick as peas. This is hardly playing the game as it ought to be played" (109). Playing the game: In this phrase inseparably connected to British notions of fair play and personal uprightness, as well as to the infinite rituals of sport, Denis Lyell touches the central issue of African sporting literature. It's not the number of heads, the size of the horns, or the rarity of the kudu that counts, but the approach, the attitude, in effect the style of pursuit and capture that matter most.

Perhaps the most provocative coincidence among the African books in Hemingway's collection is a pair of volumes by A. Blayney Percival, "late of the Kenya Colony Game Department." Blayney Percival was the brother of Philip Percival, Hemingway's 1934 guide and "white hunter."[12] Philip, from Somersetshire, in England, had come to Kenya in 1905 to join Blayney, already established there. In 1934, Hemingway was directed to Philip Percival, then Director of the Kenya Guides, Ltd., by Bror von Blixen, a noted big-game hunter and the former husband of Isak Dinesen.[13] In his first book, *A Game Ranger's Note Book* (1924), Blayney sets forth in serviceable, literate prose a comprehensive how-to about stalking, game habitat, and details about individual species such as kudu and lion. His explanations of stalking game at salt-licks, the cowardice of setting grass on fire to drive out wounded lions, and shooting hyenas without compunction should sound familiar to readers of Hemingway's African writing. He is particularly keen on the greater kudu, "the greatest prize of the sportsman,"[14] difficult to hunt, perfectly camouflaged, "almost invisible" (309). As a professional game ranger, Blayney Percival says that he has "always liked the man . . . who has no lust of slaughter," and he laments that certain districts are "shot out" (334), suggesting the postwar impact of the European sportsman on game populations. In his second book, *A Game Ranger on Safari* (1928), Blayney again regrets changing times: "A great change has come over the colony during the last quarter of a century," especially the deleterious effect of "motor cars."[15] To a large extent he repeats or merely expands the practical advice of the earlier book, but this one differs by a pronounced wistfulness for the passing of an earlier, less settled, more "natural" Africa.

What do all of these old books have to do with Hemingway's writing, especially *Green Hills* but also the African stories and even the journalism? What do they have to do with his understanding of the African natural world?

The books cited here (and many more) illustrate the tradition in which Hemingway was working. Furthermore, the books that Hemingway actually owned (and presumably read) suggest the specific ways in which his knowledge, attitudes, and beliefs were formed and conditioned. The genre of safari book is by definition an expression of colonial values. Selous, Stigand, Denis Lyell, Blayney Percival and their type were Englishmen, and they brought to Africa their notions of society and sport. The same is true of the United States president Theodore Roosevelt and the American naturalist Carl Akeley, whose books Hemingway owned, for whom Africa was a distant land in which to collect specimens of nature for exhibit in museums at home.

The overseas foreigners, from Selous to Roosevelt to Hemingway, went to Africa to use the land in one way or another. Selous went to make a living in ivory and also to collect African experiences for a profitable book. Roosevelt, representing a prestigious museum, went on a shooting expedition in the name of science and also produced an adventure book. Hemingway, coming late in the tradition, indeed in its last days, traveled to Africa to hunt exotic animals and take trophies in the world's greatest game fields, and to have an exhilarating adventure, while also gathering information for literary use. For the safari hunter, the land was there to supply lions and rhinos and kudu. The foreigners, regardless of their claims of being naturalists, explorers, or ethnologists, were essentially consumers who had come to Africa for a brief visit—for Hemingway, a couple of months—eager to reap as great an experience, as Hemingway says in *Green Hills,* as could be had in a fixed time. The visitors consume not only the game animals, but even the landscape, which is recorded because it is picturesque or grand, and the native way of life, which is to foreign eyes curious or strange.

While the narrative and descriptive body of *Green Hills* and other of Hemingway's African stories is about the quintessential colonial enterprise, the shooting safari, occasionally another Africa breaks through the surface of these tales. The attentive reader might remember that Kandisky, in *Green Hills,* is a labor recruiter working for a rich Indian who runs a sisal plantation. In this tiny aside is a volume of Kenyan and Tanganyikan history. Kandisky, an Austrian (Tanganyika is the prewar German East Africa), is engaged in the business of finding African field hands to work in the agricultural industry created when Europeans expropriated and redistributed native lands, usually to immigrants from the colonial homeland but also to East Indians, who had a reputation as profit makers.[16] This interesting aspect of African life goes undeveloped for it has no place in a sporting tale. Early in *Green Hills* Hemingway recounts meeting Africans traveling westward, "away from the famine" (34–35)—apparently a reference, left as a fragmentary fact, to the starvation that resulted from epidemics of disease in livestock. While all of this real life is going on, evidently elsewhere, Hemingway the hunter is obsessed by the idea of shooting a kudu with record-breaking horns. Even so, Hemingway fatalistically reflects that bad weather and disease are everyone's enemy, and he even admits that while "[t]he natives live in harmony with [a place]. . . . the foreigner destroys [it] . . . we are the intruders" (284).

Green Hills, Hemingway's safari book in the tradition of Selous and Stigand, ends with a rambling and sentimental passage on the rightness of living "where a man feels at home" (284). "I knew a good country when I saw one," Hemingway says. "Here there was game, plenty of birds, and I liked the natives" (285). The passage is meant, it seems, as praise for Africa as "a good country," but it is actually an I-centered reference to the use he could make of the place. For Hemingway, as for the hunter-writers of the past, the African land was a pleasant and productive commodity, and he, like them, was a consumer.

NOTES

1. Ernest Hemingway, *Green Hills of Africa* (New York: Charles Scribner's Sons, 1935), 193. Subsequent references will be from this edition and given as page numbers in the text.

2. For a contradiction of the "Nairobi fast life" idea, which had some truth to it, see Alyse Simpson, *The Land That Never Was* (1937; reprint, Lincoln and London: University of Nebraska Press, 1985).

3. See James D. Brasch and Joseph Sigman, *Hemingway's Library: A Composite Record* (New York and London: Garland Publishing, Inc., 1981). Hemingway's library, as represented in this index, contained approximately 250 volumes on hunting, shooting, and game animals. More than thirty of these books were about African hunting, including many of the classic texts of the genre.

4. Books of this type are often illustrated with drawings, photographs, or engravings. The "decorations" by Edward Shenton in *Green Hills of Africa* recall this practice.

5. Hemingway, *Green Hills*, 194.

6. Frederick Courtney Selous, *A Hunter's Wanderings in Africa* (1881; reprint, Bulawayo: Books of Zimbabwe, 1981, African Hunting Reprint Series, Volume 5.) Subsequent references will be given as page numbers in the text.

7. Captain C[hauncy] H[ugh] Stigand, *Hunting the Elephant in Africa*, with a foreword by Theodore Roosevelt (1913; reprint, New York: St. Martin's Press, 1986).

8. Captain C[hauncy] H[ugh] Stigand, *The Game of British East Africa,* 2nd edition (London: Horace Cox, 1913), 2. Subsequent references will be given as page numbers in the text.

9. Carl E. Akeley, *In Brightest Africa* (New York: Garden City Publishing Company, 1923), 158. Subsequent references will be given as page numbers in the text.

10. Denis D. Lyell, *African Adventures: Letters from Famous Big-Game Hunters* (1935; reprint, New York: St. Martin's Press, 1988), 72. Subsequent references will be given as page numbers in the text.

11. Theodore Roosevelt, *African Game Trails* (New York: Charles Scribner's Sons, 1910), 3.

12. On the Percival brothers, see Carlos Baker, *Ernest Hemingway: A Life Story* (New York: Charles Scribner's Sons, 1969), 609 n. I am also indebted to

journalists expert in colonial Africa, Sam Fadala and Cameron Hopkins, for information about the Percivals.

13. von Blixen is himself the author of a safari book. See Bror von Blixen-Finecke, *African Hunter*, trans. F. H. Lyon (1938; reprint, New York: St. Martin's Press, 1986).

14. A. Blayney Percival, *A Game Ranger's Note Book* (New York: George H. Doran Co., 1924), 307. Subsequent references will be given as page numbers in the text.

15. A. Blayney Percival, *A Game Ranger on Safari* (London: Nisbet & Co., Ltd., 1928), 244–45.

16. See Rudolf von Albertini, with Albert Wirz, *European Colonial Rule, 1880–1940: The Impact of the West on India, Southeast Asia, and Africa*, trans. John G. Williamson (Westport and London: Greenwood Press, 1982). See also Hemingway, *Green Hills of Africa*, 29.

Memory, Grief, and the Terrain of Desire: Hemingway's *Green Hills of Africa*

ANN PUTNAM

"The grass was green and smooth. . . . I could not believe we had suddenly come to any such wonderful country. It was a country to wake from, happy to have had the dream."
    "'I'll bust the son of a bitch.' . . . I heard the whonk of the bullet, and. . . . [then] we heard a deep, moaning sort of groan. . . . ending this time like a blood-choked sigh. . . ."[1]

Green Hills of Africa is a book about the loss of the pastoral, visionary landscape and the ultimately tragic search for redemption. It chronicles the narrator's attempt to fix an image, to bring home both trophy and text, against the remorseless rush of time found on every page. It is a book to break your heart. But what is the nature of that loss and the nature of the dividedness out of which it comes?

The natural world in Hemingway's fiction is compellingly beautiful, at once mysterious and sacred, and watched over by protagonists who see images and shadows of the self reflected there, and who find in its presence wholeness and balance. But equally compelling are those same characters who will one day pit themselves against the very nature they most love, will forge the boundaries of personality against this most beautiful and yielding world. And so standing on the pastoral shore, they will turn, finally, toward the shadowy regions of the swamp, the deep forest, the uncharted depths.

The heart in Hemingway's fiction is always divided against itself. The pastoral impulse to merge with nature is always working against the "tragic" impulse to master it.[2] Actions that honor and respect the natural world compete with actions that would destroy it, actions which create either the pastoral experience or the tragic adventure. It is this dividedness that is at the heart of the conflict of *Green Hills of Africa*. One side beholds nature in reverence and love while the other side seeks only to master it. It is a conflict which shows itself through the narrator's urge to create a pastoral dream on the one hand, and the urge to unflinchingly record its loss on the other. It is a conflict played out in the very structure of the book, in the rhythmic alternation of lyric and narrative, stillness and movement. This sense of dividedness develops in ever-widening circles of memory and action, beholding and mastery, reverence and destruction. The book is built upon a linear narrative driven by the certainty of the coming rains that will put an end to the hunting. It is a time-driven chronicle out of which emerges a pastoral, lyric evocation of memory and desire. But the two urges—one to enter into the very relentlessness of time itself and the other to merge into the timelessness of the pastoral compete in strange and unsettling ways.

Nature in the Hemingway world is always experienced as feminine, but whether it is experienced as pastoral or tragic depends upon whether it is perceived as bountiful mother, as mirror of the self, or as seductive Other who must be mastered. Annette Kolodny explores this distinction in her discussion of gender and landscape in *The Lay of the Land: Metaphor as Experience and History in American Life and Letters*—concepts which provide a useful way of talking about the sense of dividedness at the heart of *Green Hills of Africa.*[3] Either way, the narrative is played out across a paradisaic landscape which holds images of both unspeakable beauty and appalling destruction, images which depict the divided heart of the narrator himself and his two, equally held and opposing attitudes toward nature—a reverential sense of nature where beholding is sufficient, and the sense of nature as an Other to be possessed at all cost. What is most loved must finally be slain, for in the end the pastoral impulse to merge with nature is silenced by the tragic impulse to destroy it.

The green hills of Africa over which the narrative unfolds is Nick Adams' "last good country," a landscape recognizable from the earliest Hemingway fiction. It is the "good place," at once familiar and new, homelike and exotic, the place Hemingway would seek out his whole life—the forested islands and sunstruck rivers of Michigan, the blue waters of the Gulf, the green hills of Africa. It is the place forever lost and forever found, past and present, earth and sky, land and sea, all good places all at once: "[T]he trees were as big, as spreading, and as green, the stream as clear and fast flowing, and the camp as fine as when we had first been there"(123).

It is the place you have always known and the place you have never been. It is a dream country, a "country to wake from, happy to have had the dream. . . ." (218). It is landscape given in descriptions of such beauty they shimmer with the power of the dream—locusts filling the sky, pink and "flickering," "like an old cinema"; at twilight, trees filled with white storks; a lake full of flamingoes who rise and descend as a wondrous, pink cloud then float back onto the lake (184, 287, 133). It is country that creates such longing, the narrator lies on his cot listening to the night sounds of Africa, and misses it already. In the landscape of the dream, one can repeat the sequence of action across familiar terrain, and get "all the old feeling,"[4] but also know that ahead, somewhere beyond the next rise, a new, "virgin country" will be waiting once more.

The pastoral landscape is washed over with a radiant immediacy, which the sojourner traverses with quiet, deliberate movement, stillness of soul, and an eye which holds the "first chastity" of sight.[5] It is a setting accessible only to the sojourner who sees nature as both a reflection of the self and as sacred Other in perfect and controlling balance. Perception, in the Hemingway world, has always held a moral value. Learning "what it was all about" for Jake Barnes means learning how to see it.[6] And it is what Nick Adams meant in the fragment "On Writing" when he said that a writer must learn to "live right with his eyes."[7] Seeing with this "first chastity" of vision means seeing innocently, disinterestedly, for the beauty of the thing itself, divested of all self-interest or gain. Beauty is the one quality that must be loved in order to be seen; yet in the Hemingway world, what is most loved must finally be slain. Thus the eye of the narrator as sojourner and the eye which looks through the sights of the gun emblematize the conflict which drives this book from the first page to the last, placing as it does its competing desires edge on edge.

The pastoral landscape is the true "home" for the Hemingway protagonist, for like Thoreau, it is not wildness—not the swamp, or the deep impenetrable forests, or the uncharted depths of the sea—but the island of pine forests, the golden beaches of Africa where young lions play, the green hills which become "the good place," now and forever "home." As Pop says, "'It's damned strange how you can love a country'" (151). And as the narrator himself says, "where a man feels at home . . . is where he's meant to go" (284).

In this pastoral landscape there is no knowledge of hunter or gun—a landscape where "Kudu came out into the open and. . . . they were so unsophisticated that it was really a shame to topple them over" (143). It is a landscape where you spotted the boar twenty-yards away and raised the rifle, while he just "watched and did not . . . [show] any fright" at all (218). But it is what happens in the deep forest, what happens in the swamp, in the ocean depths, that ultimately expels the Hemingway protagonist from the paradisaic home.

For the Edenic, visionary landscape is also the home of the spirit animal whose encounter with the narrator eventually thrusts him out of the pastoral and toward the "tragic adventure." In Green Hills of Africa it is the hunt for the kudu—an animal glimpsed in bits and snatches, in the sunspots between shadows, an animal which comes to attain totemistic, almost mythic proportions. "[H]e gave a loud bark . . .and was gone, making no noise at first, then crashing in the brush . . . and we never saw him" (10). It is a miracle of nature, appearing as a vision or dream. It can't be true, protagonists say again and again at the first glimpse of it. This transcendent image moving across a paradisaic landscape is the visionary experience granted to the sojourner who has stepped lightly on the forest floor, who has rested in the shade of the spreading trees, who has reverently carried the weight of the pack until he comes to the green hills at last, who when it finally appears, apprehends the spirit animal in wonder and love.

The spirit animal is perceived androgynously by the sojourner as an image of wholeness and integration—at once male and female, familiar and strange, earth-bound and ethereal, holding both life and death.[8] Like the mysterious two-tusked elephant with the light side and the dark side, the elusive kudu of the African safari is also a mythic, two-sided, spirit animal. Pursued for three days through forests and plains, it appears and disappears, showing in flashes its tender eyes, the elegant curve of the neck, its feminine rounded body and the masculine thrust of its "great, curling, sweeping horns"(231)—its earth-bound body and "heart-shaped . . . tracks" (5) made by hooves so "long [and] narrow, and springy . . . he seemed to walk on tip-toe"(234). But the slaying of this animal sets off a series of hurried and unthinking actions that result in the loss of the paradisaic vision, and finally, expulsion from the paradisaic terrain.

And so the landscape darkens, for the sojourner cannot resist the pressures to act out of the male principle alone, untempered by any "softening feminine influence,"[9] as Hemingway himself worded it, writing of *Men Without Women*. The impulse to merge "passively with the maternal landscape,"[10] in Kolodny's words, is overcome by the growing need to "master and act upon that same femininity."[11] In the end, the sense of timelessness cannot be sustained, for the pressure is always to rush things, to hold what cannot be held.

No longer the sojourner, the narrator as hunter plunges into the very heart of nature and penetrates the sacred terrain in search of the secret hidden there. Now the lush green hills, the sunlit river, the shifting colors of the Gulf give way to creepers and vines, dark primal forests, and deep, impenetrable waters where nature keeps hidden its greatest secret—the presence of the spirit animal. Like Nick in "The Last Good Country" it is an encounter with the spirit animal that ultimately thrusts the protagonist out of the pastoral setting. It is a deer shot out of season, slain against Nick's willing almost, that banishes him from the paradisaic landscape. He can never again enter the forest without looking over his shoulder, without "[having] to think about things."[12] Gone is the "first chastity" of sight, for the wondering, wandering eye must always be looking back as well as ahead, conscious now and forever of the stream of time.

It is a familiar narrative, one which serves as the heart of many Hemingway works—"Big Two-Hearted River," "The Last Good Country," the elephant hunt of *The Garden of Eden*, *The Old Man and the Sea*. It is a narrative of pursuit that weaves together the complexities of love, grief, and the pastoral terrain first seen in "Big Two-Hearted River," culminating in the story of a single pursuit of a single, spirit animal in *The Old Man and the Sea*. This seemingly simple story brings together such equal and opposing desires it becomes a distillation of the complexities played out over *Green Hills'* sprawling narrative.[13]

Green Hills of Africa begins as a pastoral evocation of Africa, given in shimmering images apprehended in reverence and wonder. But the images are shadowed by the malign presence of the hunter, and soon turn darkly ambivalent—for the flamingoes which rise from the lake in a wondrous pink cloud do so in panic at the sound of the gun. Two sets of images recur throughout the book that illustrate this tension—one full of sensuousness and beauty, depicting a wondrous landscape of unspeakable beauty. But another set of images bespeaks a different attitude toward nature—violent, jarring images, none more telling than the picture of the convoy of safari Jeeps that grinds its way over the terrain, carving out rutty scars across the virgin landscape. Accruing to it are other dark images—frenzied slashing of underbrush to make way for the safari cars, the wheels cutting through the grass, spinning in the "slick greasiness" (223). It is a painful contrast from the simplicity of Nick's camp in "Big Two-Hearted River" and shows the difficulty of sustaining the pastoral vision in a world of such competing urgencies.

The land itself becomes defiled by the increasing presence of the machine in the garden which permits a deeper penetration into the "virgin country." "This was the kind of hunting that I liked," the narrator says. "No riding in cars" (55). But riding in cars is the only way they can keep up with the rush of time and the coming rains. The description of the race between the beautiful Masai runners who race alongside the safari Jeep, the "cruel pacemaker" (221) which inevitably defeats them, foreshadows darkly the inevitable consequences of the machine's growing presence. Yet perhaps it is the image of the man with the rifle slung over a shoulder, plunging into the heart of the pastoral terrain that most keenly represents the hunter's stance, as does the homage paid to the Springfield rifle with its "sweet clean pull . . . [and] the smooth, unhesitant release at the end" (101), as well as a whole litany of images of animals shot in the neck, shoulder, leg, lung.

Africa, as well as the river and the sea, is experienced first as bountiful Mother, but increasingly as "virgin country" to be assaulted—a feminine landscape which both embraces and resists the male presence. "I loved the country so that I was happy as you are after you have been with a woman that you really love. . .and you want more and more. . . to possess now again for always. . . ." (72). Thus the maternal green hills of Africa become the rounded contours of the lover-mistress who waits to be taken. The landscape as Mother, as reflection of the self, is transformed before our eyes into the landscape as mistress, as an Other who must be possessed at all cost. Though the narrator is able to "hold steady" against the competing urge to master on the one hand and to behold on the other, it is only for the moment.

In the pastoral moment, time seems to stand "so very still that afterwards you wait to hear it move, and it is slow in starting" (72). But stillness and hurry compete in wrenching ways in this book, and reveal the narrator's inability to hold in balance the timelessness of the pastoral moment and the time-driven urgencies of the hunt. Thus the narrator of *Green Hills* is doomed to forever seek, forever lose "that long, sudden-ended always" (72), forever doomed to experience loss in the midst of plenitude, joy forever tinged with sorrow. "All I wanted to do now was get back to Africa," the narrator says (72). Though he has not yet left Africa, the narrator lies awake at night missing it already. Though the pastoral dream of the African plain is held temporarily, it is finally lost. Though the narrator desires to "have time to be in it and to move *slowly*," he admits he was also "hungry for more of it," (73, my emphasis). Soon that hunger propels the narrative out of the timelessness of the pastoral moment and toward the frenetic, unthinking actions that culminate in the crisis of the book. The consequences of this shift become completely clear in the record of everything that follows.

Green Hills of Africa begins on the tenth evening of the kudu hunt, with the fading of the light and the shadow of the coming rains. Soon the moments of stillness and quietude are made precious by the sense of hurry which increasingly fires the narrative. The balance between beholding and mastery, feminine and masculine, cannot be sustained, and the hurried gesture born of desperation propels the protagonist out of the pastoral landscape and toward the tragic adventure. "[I]t is not pleasant to have a time limit by which you must get your kudu or perhaps never get it" (11), the narrator explains at the beginning of the book. Then when time has all but run out, he wonders whether he will even see a kudu before the rains come and he must leave Africa. Phantom kudu tracks appear and disappear and no kudu are anywhere in sight, becoming finally an emblem for the passing of the irretrievable moment: "How the hell do I know we can ever get back here again? . . . I've only got tonight" (206).

Pop tells the narrator to take his time, and so the narrator resists the urge to shoot before he can get off a clear shot. But finally the kudu, object of the spirit quest, is killed cleanly and honorably, according to the rules Hemingway in 1934 had set for himself. The sojourner has loved what the hunter must slay precisely because it is so loved. And so the death of the kudu takes on a transcendent, spiritualized quality as hunter and hunted, sojourner and hunter become one: "I looked at him, big, long-legged, a smooth gray with the white stripes and the great curling, sweeping horns . . . the great, lovely heavy-maned neck, the white chevron between his eyes and the white of his muzzle and I stooped over and *touched him* to try to believe it. . . . there was not a mark on him and he smelled sweet and lovely like the breath of cattle and the odor of thyme after rain" (231, my emphasis).

But it is a dangerous moment. For the act of slaying what had been loved, is loved still, is always unbalancing and fraught with potential sorrow. All too quickly the urge to master overtakes the narrator. He can no longer "hold steady," and soon his adoration turns to competitiveness, envy, and pride which begin to taint the memory of the cleanly-killed kudu. Hemingway wrote that more than anything else, he had wanted a single good kudu, but as it turns out he wants a good kudu *bigger* than all the rest. "Suddenly poisoned with envy, I did not want to see [my kudu] again, never, never" (291). And as Pop explains: "It's impossible not to be competitive. Spoils everything, though" (293).

What happens next always comes to pass in dark, tangled places where creepers and vines make it impossible to see, where there is no "first chastity" of sight—not in the green hills or the pastoral shores. The narrator's pursuit of a sable bull the next day becomes a brutal, pride-driven assault on nature itself. Here is no nature as bountiful mother or passive, waiting virgin; this is a nature to be ravaged: "My eyes, my mind, and all inside of me were full of the blackness of that sable bull and the sweep of those horns. . . . But it was excited shooting . . . [and] now I had wounded him . . . [and] the hyenas would eat him, or, worse, they would get him before he died. . . . But I felt rotten sick over this sable bull. . . . I wanted him more than I would admit. *Why did I have to make a one night stand?* Was that any way to hunt?" (259, 271–2, 282, my emphasis). Rushing in and crouched low like that, the narrator could only get off a "gut shot," shooting it the only way he *"fucking well could"*[14]—by aiming "at the whole animal," instead of the sure and fatal spot (259).

It is a posture and a scene repeated in the elephant tale of *The Garden of Eden* and reminds us instantly of Nick's description of what fishing the swamp would be like: Here the branches grow so low "you would have to keep almost level with the ground to move at all."[15] "They looked as though they had a dirty secret," Davey says of his father and Juma, as they stalk the miracle elephant. Rifles in hand, they plunge into the "thick [forest] cover" as "[Davey] watched their backs and their asses go in and out of sight."[16] Now the protagonist as hunter abandons the upright stance of the sojourner, and crouching low to the ground, moves "quietly as snakes" (254). Pop, the safari guide, explains how to do it: "You want to get in fast and do the dirty and get out fast" (212-3). Hide in the blind by the salt lick, duck low, and pull the trigger. It is an ambush, a stalking, and as Santiago says, a "trick" and a "treachery" every time. Here again is the essential contrast between clean and dirty and the moral complexities of those competing values.

What happens to the sojourner who becomes the hunter? The narrator explains what happens just before the kill: "I was watching, freezing myself deliberately inside, stopping the excitement as you close a valve, going into that impersonal state you shoot from" (76). The eyes narrow, the spirit hardens, the heart becomes a closed fist. For ultimately the hunter must forge his identity against a resisting sense of nature and not a passive one, imposing his desire and his will upon the creatures of the earth. But the cost of such mastery results, finally, in an "emotional and psychological separation" from nature,[17] a fact the narrator makes clear in the sorrow that fills every page to come. For now they are in purgatory. They follow the sable bull through rocky, brutal terrain, no water, shade, or yielding path. Nothing but the merciless sun with its punishing heat and the vanishing trail of blood. Later, after they have given up hope of ever finding the wounded bull, they come to the path leading back through the "broken sunlight and shadow" of the woods. Here the forest floor is "smooth and springy" and it is almost as though the narrator has found his way back to the green hills once more. He comes upon a herd of sable looking back at him through the trees. He raises the rifle and seeks out the biggest set of horns. But they scatter and run and the narrator drops his rifle. "All cows," he says to M'Cola as they watch them "running in a panic through the sun-splashed timber" (273). It is as haunting an image of an Eden defiled, a paradise lost, as anywhere in the book.

This is a book filled with terrible images, and with a longing for an innocence that is terrible in its own way, too. For on the ride back to camp, the kudu horns resting in the back of the car, the narrator attempts to return to the innocence of the pastoral dream. He would return to nature as bountiful, all-giving mother; he would live out this vision which is the heart of the book. He would return to Africa, he thinks, but this time he would "lie in the fallen leaves and watch the kudu feed out and never fire a shot. . . . I'd lie behind a rock and watch them on the hillside *and see them long enough so they belonged to me forever*" (282, my emphasis). Memory would be all he would need, and time enough, and "first chastity" of sight. For in the dream there is always "virgin country" to be found. Now the narrator longs for quietude, for the stillness that follows frantic movement, longs for the return to a beholding complete unto itself. There is no need to master now.

But the vision, like the pastoral experience itself, cannot be held. Nor can the moment of memory. For the hunter-protagonist has entered the fatal stream of time, a fallen world where there is envy, pride, and the "virgin country" all worn out. The timeless presence of the pastoral vision is replaced by images of relentless time—drought, disease, and the country all shot out. "A continent ages quickly once we come," the narrator admits, recognizing for a moment the effects of such mastery. "The natives live in harmony with it" (284). But the foreigner destroys it everywhere he goes. The pastoral exists now only as longing—but a longing that fires the desire of the narrator to fix through art what could not be held in life. Yet the artist depends as much upon the *loss* of the pastoral landscape as upon the landscape itself, depends upon grief as much as joy.

From the first it is clear that *Green Hills of Africa* is a book about writing as well as hunting. In the first chapter, the narrator positions his discussion of the pursuit of the kudu in the context of a discussion of literature and the pleasures and sorrows of the writer's life. To the Austrian, Kandisky, who cannot believe anyone would dedicate himself to the pursuit of a single animal, he explains that hunting the kudu is as genuine an aesthetic experience as a visit to the Prado, and as "necessary" (25). As the narrative unfolds, it is clear that the quest of both the artist and hunter holds the potential for tragedy, because both quests are forged against the passing of time. The narrator explains that the greatest difficulty facing the writer is to "survive and get his work done" (27). Just as "[t]he way to hunt is for as long as you live against as long as there is such and such an animal; . . . [the writer must] write as long as [he] can live and there is pencil and paper or ink" (12). Both hunter and artist are forever "caught by time" (12). Like the hunter in search of the elusive, spirit kudu, the writer attempts to catch and hold something not meant to be held, something luminous and unearthly and trembling with life, and freeze it for all time. As the narrator explains, the writer strives for "a prose that has never been written"—strives to capture the "fourth and fifth dimension"(26–7).

But what will stay the image? How finally to capture the kudu? Photograph it? Try to remember it? Mount it on the wall? And at what cost? After the killing of the kudu, the guides race frantically up the hill against the failing light to get the photograph before the kudu is skinned out. Again the sense of hurry, again the sense of the race against time to capture the image before the light is gone, finally dragging the kudu out of the growing shadows and into the fading light. And what of the other-worldly leap of the kudu, its airy footsteps suspended between earth and sky? M'Cola makes the first incision and the narrator turns away. He would not look at it. He would remember it as it had been, as he had first seen it, though he later changes his mind and decides it would be safe to watch. His memory would fix the image. But at the close of the book the narrator brings up the problem of memory again. P.O.M. says, "'I can't remember Mr. J. P.'s face. . . . In a little while I won't be able to remember him at all'" (295). Neither memory nor the camera will stay the rush of time. And what about the trophy mounted to the wall?

In the end, the shaded, sardonic denouement, given in wasteland images and subdued, chastened tones, shows the dream already fading. They sit beneath the thin sunlight, orphans all, looking out over the "stagnant," "dreary" waters of the Sea of Galilee, no water to walk on here. What will there be to stay the remorseless rush of time now? He would write a book better than any trophy on the wall.[18]

NOTES

1. Ernest Hemingway, *Green Hills of Africa* (New York: Charles Scribner's Sons, 1935), 217–8, 76–8. Subsequent references to this work are from this edition and will be given as page numbers in the text.

2. For his discussion of the relationship of the pastoral to the tragic, and its application to Hemingway's works in general and *The Old Man and the Sea* in particular, I am indebted to Glen Love's "Hemingway's Indian Virtues: An Ecological Reconsideration," *Western American Literature*, 22.3 (November 1987): 201–3.

3. I am particularly grateful for Annette Kolodny's exploration of gender and landscape in *The Lay of the Land: Metaphor as Experience and History in American Life and Letters* (Chapel Hill: University of North Carolina Press, 1975). Especially helpful was her study of Charles Audobon and the conflicts arising from his roles as both naturalist and hunter. I should also note that Mark Spilka's *Hemingway's Quarrel with Androgyny* (Lincoln & London: University of Nebraska Press, 1990) provided intriguing background for my thinking on *Green Hills*.

4. Ernest Hemingway, "Big Two-Hearted River," *The Complete Short Stories of Ernest Hemingway* (New York: Charles Scribner's Sons, 1987), 164.

5. Ernest Hemingway, *For Whom the Bell Tolls* (New York: Charles Scribner's Sons, 1940), 239, cited in Tony Tanner, "Ernest Hemingway's Unhurried

Sensations," *The Reign of Wonder: Naivety and Reality in American Literature* (Cambridge: Cambridge University Press, 1965), 242. See Tanner's fine essay for a discussion of the role of perception and memory in the Hemingway canon.

6. Ernest Hemingway, *The Sun Also Rises* (New York: Charles Scribner's Sons, 1954), 167.

7. Ernest Hemingway, "On Writing," *The Nick Adams Stories* (New York: Charles Scribner's Sons, 1972), 218.

8. For further discussion of the symbolic qualities of the animals pursued in *Green Hills of Africa* see Carl Bredahl's "The Body as Matrix: Narrative Pattern in *Green Hills of Africa*," *Midwest Quarterly: A Journal of Contemporary Thought* 28.4 (Summer 1987): 455–72 and Gerry Brenner's discussion of *Green Hills of Africa* in *Concealments in Hemingway's Works* (Columbus: Ohio State University Press, 1983). Especially interesting was Brenner's discussion of the concept of "trophy hunting." For a discussion of this concept as it relates to the masking and unmasking of the masculine persona, see Thomas Strychaez's "Trophy-Hunting as Trope of Manhood in *Green Hills of Africa*," *The Hemingway Review* 13.1 (Fall 1993): 36–47.

In addition, I should note what the bullfight tells us about the nature of the spirit animal. Because of its scripted, ritualized nature, the bullfight clarifies the function of the spirit animal in a particularly striking way. Hemingway found in the bullfight a rich metaphor for the artist's relationship to the natural world. To be sure, the bull becomes a version of the spirit animal—and source of great mythic, totemistic power—whose death is necessitated by the art itself. Bred and nurtured for a single afternoon in the sun, the bull realizes its destiny in a solitary transcendent and fatal moment. There is no apparent androgyny here, for the bull seems all vengeance and muscle and horns. Yet the choreography of the bullfight itself is a complex blend of masculine and feminine gestures— seductive, balletic pirouettes and dips, and a shocking passivity as the feet of the matador stand firm against the onrush of the bull. It is a *pas de deux* of death, a seduction of color and movement and mysterious, tiny gestures until suddenly the sword is driven up over the top of the massive head and neck and into the one feminine place—the tiny soft place between the shoulder blades that receives the sword up to the hilt. It is the final consummation, a reversal in which the matador becomes all-penetrating male, the bull all-receiving female. "[A]nd the bull charged and Villalta charged and just for a moment they became one. Villalta became one with the bull and then it was over." ("Chapter XII" of *In Our Time*.) I am grateful to Allen Josephs for his mention of two fine sources on the bullfight: the first, his own study of Andalusian culture, *The White Wall of Spain: The Mysteries of Andalusian Culture* (Ames: Iowa State University Press 1983), 133–60; and secondly for Richard Wright's *Pagan Spain* (New York: Harper & Brothers 1957), 68–136.

9. Carlos Baker, *Ernest Hemingway: Selected Letters, 1917–1961* (New York: Charles Scribner's Sons, 1981), 245. This is in reference to Hemingway's second story collection, *Men Without Women*.

10. Kolodny, *Lay of the Land*, 28.

11. Ibid., 4.

12. Ernest Hemingway, "The Last Good Country," *The Complete Short Stories of Ernest Hemingway* (New York: Charles Scribner's Sons, 1987), 541.

13. See Ann Putnam, "Across the River and Into the Stream: Journey of the Divided Heart," *North Dakota Quarterly*, 63 (Summer 1996): 90–98 for a discussion of this theme as it is played out in *The Old Man and the Sea*.

14. Ernest Hemingway, *The Garden of Eden* (New York: Charles Scribner's Sons, 1986), 198, my emphasis.

15. Hemingway, "Big Two-Hearted River," 179.

16. Hemingway, *The Garden of Eden*, 180, 198.

17. Kolodny, *Lay of the Land*, 28.

18. An intriguing concept which addresses the nature of the dividedness I am talking about in this essay is Bickford Sylvester's "compassionate violence." He sees this as a contradiction ultimately resolved into a truly cosmic sense of "harmonious opposition," whereas I see this paradox as a wrenching dividedness that is never resolved—a conflictedness which makes so many of Hemingway's characters forever divided and, as David Bourne describes it, absolutely "riven." See Sylvester's "Hemingway's Extended Vision: *The Old Man and the Sea*," *PMLA* 81 (1966): 130–38.

"The African Book": Hemingway Major and Late in the Natural World

ROBERT W. LEWIS

Among his other works Ernest Hemingway's largely unpublished "African Book" as it has been labeled (Hemingway himself seems not to have entitled it) is most like *Green Hills of Africa*, the 1935 narrative based on Hemingway's 1933–1934 safari, but the similarities are mainly, I think, less interesting than the differences.[1] In both narratives, a famous American writer and his wife go on an extended trip to East Africa. (On each safari a male friend was included, but during the second, Mayito Mencocal has returned to Cuba before the time of its narrative.) Both writings concern hunting, the natives and their culture, the landscape, the author's reflections on the art of writing, and recollections of his past. Settings, characterizations, and narrative lines show many parallels. Themes and styles are somewhat more different than those prior three elements, but they clearly connect to the protean genius and his remarkable oeuvre. If the manuscript had been lost and discovered without any internal hint as to its author, any literary detective familiar with his writing would rightly attribute it to Hemingway based on extensive parallels. Well, the Inspector Clouseaus among us could wonder, and, as a matter of fact, I will here stress some differences, but I do so mindful of Hemingway's own recognition that some of his readers expected strict continuity among his books à la some writers of formula novels. His rhetorical riposte was "Does Yogi Berra have a grooved swing?" What Hemingway meant were tributes to the unorthodox but outstanding baseball player and to the writer who constantly challenged himself to try something different, not being content with a groove (in spite of what William Faulkner said about Hemingway in ranking John Dos Passos and fellow Southerners Erskine Caldwell and Thomas Wolfe ahead of Hemingway because they took more risks as writers).

I don't mean to suggest that "The African Book" is going out too far, as Santiago thought he had, or that it is as different (and surprising) as *The Garden of Eden*, but like all of Hemingway's late works it is innovative, unendingly interesting, and unexpected if one thought he had a grooved swing.

Hemingway himself knew that his second African sojourn was "material." To his lawyer Alfred Rice he wrote, "This time I have really wonderful stuff to write. . . . This was a very rough year even before we smashed up in the air-craft. But I have a diamond mine if people will let me alone and let me dig the stones out of the blue mud and then cut and polish them."² Four months later when he was well into writing the African book, he wrote to Buck Lanham: "I'm in a bell époque writing if they [various intruders and distracters] leave me alone."³ Hemingway seemed to be happy writing the book and confident of its merit. He worked steadily on it for a year and a half beginning soon after returning to Cuba and ending in February 1956. Marginalia dates in the last chapter range from February 2 to February 27. In his *Hemingway Chronology*, Michael Reynolds dates the finishing of the African book in April 1956.⁴ Hemingway may well have continued working on the manuscript through March. It contains numerous typed and holographic changes. Other circumstances indicate Hemingway felt some sense of closure to his work on the book. In April 1956 he securely wrapped the 800-plus pages and on May 22, after he and Mary had returned from Peru where he had fished for marlin and film footage for *The Old Man and the Sea*, he deposited the manuscript in his safe-deposit box in Miami.⁵

Yet another letter is interesting in its *omission* of reference to the work-in-progress. That is, if Hemingway felt he had finished the book in April 1956, it is curious that in a seven-paragraph letter of 25 May 1956 to Philip Percival, the Pop of both *Green Hills of Africa* and its sequel, he writes not a word about the African book.⁶ Such an omission is of course no evidence one way or the other as to Hemingway's intentions regarding the state of completion of the book. But his marginalia such as the early "Put in Pop's leaving EH"⁷ and his very last words that end mid-sentence indicate that although the typescript-manuscript was literally in a vault it was not in the metaphoric vault Hemingway sometimes referred to as the storage place of completed work to be published in good order, the judicious spacing out of the work from the atelier of a craftsman who lived by his art.

Without question, it is unfinished. In a number of places, Hemingway left blanks to be filled in and questions and directions to himself. I've cited "Put in Pop's leaving" from chapter 1. He opens chapter 2 with a reference to "mystical countries . . . of one's childhood" that "are as lovely at night as they were when we were children."⁸ He then parenthetically wrote "Put in why," a note that *Sports Illustrated* editor Ray Cave faithfully includes as a note in this published section of the book and wisely does not try to do himself.[9] On this same typescript page, Hemingway wrote on the left margin alongside a passage on good and bad childishness, "Throw out or re-write all this EH."[10] Since Ray Cave was not going to rewrite Hemingway, he chose instead to follow Hemingway's other option and deleted it. But Hemingway's note to himself at this point well illustrates an editor's headache if not nightmare. Hemingway's marginal comment is to himself, for he was still writing and rewriting. But this imperative direction, unlike "Put in why" is initialed by him (as the first note, "Put in Pop's leaving EH" also was) and that difference could be interpreted as an authorization for someone else to make a decision to delete or even rewrite. But to what did Hemingway refer? His holograph comment vertically spans eight sentences, but his writing about childishness (good and bad) goes on for another fourteen sentences that Cave also omitted. He was careful to convey that omission with ellipses, but those fourteen sentences are to me, and perhaps many others, of much interest. Furthermore, I'd rather know *both* Hemingway's complete text *and* his editorial notes to himself or others. In fact, such a combination would produce a postmodern text to bug the eyes of a deconstructionist. And what a delight it would be to lovers of Hemingway's craft to peek over his shoulder, as it were, to witness a small part of his writing process. One of the most interesting and even exciting aspects of reading the unpublished book in the 832-page combined typescript-manuscript version in the Kennedy Library lies in the sense one may have of witnessing his writing process.

Furthermore, this passage deleted from the *Sports Illustrated* version is a fine example of the thematic unity of the narrative. On first reading one might well agree with Cave's decision to take up Hemingway's offer to "throw out" what could be judged a digression on childishness versus the virtues of mature humans keeping, in Hemingway's words, "a child's heart, a child's honesty, and a child's freshness and nobility."[11] Those words are gone from the *Sports Illustrated* version, and indeed if Cave judged that they are digressive there, in the narrative as a whole they introduce a repeated motif of the holy fool. In many places in the narrative Mary admonishes Ernest on his adolescent or immature (to her) behavior. And Ernest humorously apologizes or fends her off, knowing that he is seeking not childishness but that "heart," "honesty," "freshness," and "nobility" of the innocent, the very characteristics he finds in those Africans he admires and would emulate. They know little of the spirit-wasting life of industrial capitalism which Hemingway despised, and their life now offered him an alternative. Put up or shut up. And among other divergent behavior he took up hunting barefoot with a spear at night. Childlike? Perhaps. Grooved swing? No.

Also in these twenty-five lines that Cave deleted is another theme central to the narrative, the relationship of human to nonhuman, animal life, and Hemingway as a student of ethology and anthropopathy. Easily moving on from the imagined dialogue on the difference between humans as either childish or childlike, Hemingway extends his thoughts to animals and to young gazelles in particular that are "well balanced and well adjusted at the age of four weeks."[12] This four-sentence aside that brings animals into the discussion is dispensable in the excerpted story focusing on "Miss Mary's Lion," but it is an interesting piece in the mosaic that emerges of Hemingway's journeyman ethology throughout the narrative.

One might also note another kind of deletion that does not come from a permissive marginalium nor is covered by Ray Cave's introductory statement that he followed "stringent editing rules" and thus marked all omissions with ellipses. In the first paragraph of the *Sports Illustrated* version, Cave (or someone else) omitted a phrase unmarked by ellipses and only discoverable by a collation of texts. It is not profanity which Cave notes he did change to dashes, but it clearly refutes Cave's statement "No other changes have been made."[13] Yet in a sense the omission is more explosive than profanity. In *Sports Illustrated* the narrator says of Pop, "I respected him and he trusted me which was more than I deserved."[14] In the original, the first phrase of the sentence reads, "I respected him as I had never respected my father."[15] Emendations, deletions, and additions on the much revised manuscript pages indicate the comment on his father was an addition and thus a reconsideration, not the kind of first-draft idea that is often later changed or discarded.

Thus no matter how well the three-part *Sports Illustrated* excerpts read they are only about 55,000 of the approximately 200,000 word total, and the third part, "Imperiled Flanks," is especially heavily edited.[16] From examples such as these, may we not conclude that whatever the degree of incompletion, the manuscript is of immense importance? Familiarity with it will likely enhance Hemingway's reputation as readers see familiar safari "material" freshly through Hemingway's more mature eyes, particularly in an age of enhanced concern for the natural environment. And even though the narrative ends on the last page with a sentence in mid-flight, itself incomplete, perhaps that would be a fitting ending for a narrative in which process is more important than ends. The day-by-day living as fully as one can is more important than illusional "accomplishments." (There are, however, a few loose pages, one of which might be very apt as a conclusion.) And we know from the firsthand sources such as his letters and his "The Christmas Gift" and Mary's *How It Was* that the safari extended long beyond the 1953 year-ending of the manuscript. Although it foreshadows the postponed Christmas-present

flight over Murchison Falls that Mary had allegedly begged from a reluctant Ernest, it ends before that misadventure—a plane crash and an
attempted but aborted "rescue" takeoff in a second airplane. This really is
another story he had already told ("The Christmas Gift" in *Look* magazine of 20 April and 4 May 1954).

One might endlessly speculate as to why Hemingway did not finish the
long book so well begun. Perhaps it was virtually finished. Perhaps he
wanted it to end on the Kenya plains with Kilimanjaro overlooking every
day so rich in joy. Mary wrote that Ernest seemed as happy there as on
the *Pilar* on the Gulf Stream, and nowhere else so happy.[17] The ensuing
disasters could not complete the pastorale that the manuscript is. In contrast to another of his posthumous books titled *The Garden of Eden* and
alluding to a moral "fall," if this late book were to encompass the conclusion of the safari, it would end in a literal fall. Furthermore, the ele-
phant-hunt episode of *The Garden of Eden* connects closely to this
supposedly nonfiction book in which Hemingway abjures elephant hunting, even of marauding elephants he is empowered (as an acting game
warden) to kill. The plot and the complex sensitivities of Hemingway's
writing always thicken, and regardless of the obvious (but minor) omissions where Hemingway noted to himself the need to look up or check
this or that detail, the manuscript is in an important way complete. Linda
Miller, a former Hemingway Foundation board member who has also
read the restricted manuscript, wrote me, "I thought it read straight
through all-of-a-piece. Slow-moving, nuanced, wonderful."

But Carlos Baker gives the manuscript short shrift, describing it as
begun in the late summer of 1954 (about a year after the safari had
begun), and summarizing it in one paragraph. Baker presumably read all
of "The African Book" (sometimes also referred to as "The African
Journal" because of the title of the *Sports Illustrated* excerpts). In his
biography he described it as the first writing (apart from letters) that
Hemingway undertook after the African trip ended in March 1954, about
six weeks after the back-to-back airplane crashes of January 23 and 24.
About a year, then, after the beginning of the safari in September, 1953,
Hemingway (in Baker's words)

> began a series of stories based on his recent experiences in Africa.
> One of them expanded so steadily under his hand that he thought it
> might become a novel. In fact it was more like a slightly fictionized
> day-to-day diary of the safari, almost completely formless, filled
> with scenes that ranged from the fairly effective to the banal. He and
> Mary and Denis Zaphiro [nicknamed G. C. for "Gin Crazed" by
> Hemingway] were in the foreground, and the safari servants and other

Africans moved in and out as the occasion required. He made much of N'gui and Charo, whom he called by their actual names, while the Wakamba girl Debba appeared several times—short-haired, hard-handed, and impudent. . . ."[18]

In a letter to Adriana Ivancich of 15 August 1954, about two months after Ernest and Mary had returned to Cuba from their safari and the following two-and-a-half month sojourn in Europe, Ernest wrote that he had begun writing about their African experiences (that is, about five months after their departure from Africa).[19] In letters to other friends like Archibald MacLeish he seemed to be warming up to his new project as when he compared his Wakamba "fiancée" (as both Mary and Ernest waggishly wrote of her) to Prudy Boulton of his Michigan youth and also as "a dark version of Marilyn Monroe."[20] In the aforementioned letter to Buck Lanham of 10 November 1954, about three months after beginning the book, Ernest apologized for not having time to visit Buck. The reason was that he was "back into the country and I live in it every day and some of the stuff I think you'll like. . . . [But] mustn't put my mouth on it."[21]

A letter to Bernard Berenson of 18 September 1955 also helps us to gauge the progress of the book. Hemingway tells Berenson that he is handwriting the letter because page 594 of the African book is in the typewriter, "and it is unlucky to take the pages out."[22] By 24 January 1956, he wrote again to Alfred Rice that in spite of his illness he had continued writing and was up to page 810, only forty pages shy of the last page misnumbered 850.[23] But given the evidence of marginalia, including dates and word counts that Hemingway often used to assess his progress, it is possible that he composed much if not all of the book in longhand and then revised it as he typed it.

Besides Carlos Baker and Linda Miller, other readers who have commented on "The African Book" or the published parts of it include Philip Young and Charles Mann, John Howell, Ray Cave, Rose Marie Burwell, and Gerry Brenner and Earl Rovit; their comments may introduce a few of my own observations.

Young and Mann provided for most of us the first description of and name for "The African Book." But their brief description is in some details inaccurate because they assumed pages were missing when in fact Hemingway simply occasionally misnumbered pages. They also wrote: "Autobiographical account of duties as volunteer ranger at the Masai game preserve at foot of Mt. Kilimanjaro in late 1953. . . . Unfinished."[24] I cannot recall what my thoughts were on reading that first brief description in 1969, but mild curiosity might have been a strong reaction to what in retrospect, after reading the lively narrative, seems an insipid description. Following the 1971–72 publications of excerpts in *Sports Illustrated*, Mann extended his views of the manuscript. He recalled discussing "the enormous fragment . . . with Mary Hemingway" and his and Young's enthusiasm for the potential publication of it, in spite of its length. Mann saw the *Sports Illustrated* publications as "a compromise" but still "judicious." Furthermore, Mann wrote,

> This is not unfamiliar material where Ernest Hemingway is concerned; but there is, however, a wonderful difference, for the selections record the sensitive response of an aging man suddenly given a job to do—a real one, that of a game warden in a vast African park. It was work for which he was nobly suited, crammed with the minute need for attention to detail which he loved, and his handling of it left him with no shame. This time was also, despite its terrible finale of two separate plane crashes, arguably the happiest period of his life. The anecdotes are rather mystical; a touch of religion presumably in keeping with the Christmas season in which the events occur seems pervasive. Also in his characteristic way, Ernest Hemingway has stylized his material. As in *A Moveable Feast* it is a kind of fiction about true happenings. . . . Let us hope that the remainder of the "African Journal" may appear in hard cover. It would find a ready audience among those who read Hemingway for his own sake, and who are unconcerned with critical reactions and speculations.[25]

With Mann's conclusion I think most of us would agree, even though the preceding favorable description of the book is somewhat misleading, it is not wrong but incomplete. An annoying habit of mine is to see many Hemingway critiques as illustrations of the fable of the blind men and the elephant. But because real elephants do figure in "The African Book," may I not use the analogy again to consider several other responses?

John Howell has done good work on Hemingway, especially his African-set writings, and his review of the *Sports Illustrated* excerpts must be qualified by his limitation to them. He had not read the entire narrative when he rather harshly judged the published sections: "Though the edited narrative is always interesting and at times compelling, it seldom, if ever, lives up to the standard Hemingway establishes in the earlier work. . . . [O]ne looks in vain for the lovingly detailed pictures of animals and landscape that are the poetry of *Green Hills*."[26]

His is, I believe, a remediable assessment if he could consider those published fragments in context. And perhaps Howell's valuing of *Green Hills of Africa* illustrates the "grooved swing" school of Hemingway criticism. If one book or story on a similar topic is good, how does the sequel correspond? It may not, as I don't think "The African Book" does. It is a related but very different book.

Earl Rovit and Gerry Brenner had a similar reaction to the published parts of "The African Journal," describing it in terms of their useful tyro-tutor pattern, Mary being the tyro and Ernest the tutor. But they conclude that the excerpts in *Sports Illustrated* are "contrived" and a "failure."[27] As with Howell's negative reaction, Brenner and Rovit's may be at least partly attributable to the special sports-magazine context of the excerpts.

In introducing the *Sports Illustrated* three-part publication of "African Book" excerpts (20 Dec. 1971; 3 Jan. 1972; 10 Jan. 1972), Ray Cave usefully named "five primary plot lines or themes." The first was "nature, hunting and the hunter, subjects," Cave wrote, upon which Hemingway had no "peer in the English language."[28] (Had Cave or Hemingway read Ortega y Gasset's *Meditations on Hunting*? Neither Baker's *Life* nor *Letters* indexes the great Spanish writer, but Hemingway did own copies of two other Ortega y Gasset books, *The Revolt of the Masses* and *Invertebrate Spain*.) Cave also admits that, given the assumed readership of *Sports Illustrated*, his excerpts emphasized the subject of the hunt. Indeed, the manuscript as a whole does center around two main hunts, Mary's for a predatory black-maned lion and Ernest's for a leopard who had been raiding African *shambas* of their domestic livestock. But these hunts are so heavily interlarded with other matters that it would be reductivist (as, say, with Faulkner's "The Bear" or Melville's *Moby Dick*) to consider the "African Book" as merely a hunting story.

But to his credit Cave goes on to name four other themes in the manuscript less present in his edited selections. The second of the five themes is "the Africanization of Hemingway," which includes his steeping himself in the languages, mores, and religions of East Africa, including his paternalistic "engagement" to a nubile Wakamba woman, Debba.[29] This theme is important to my reading of the narrative because much more so than in *Green Hills of Africa* Hemingway writes himself into the tradition of Melville, Gauguin, Robert Louis Stevenson, Pierre Loti, Lafcadio Hearn, and others who, jaded by their own culture, discover a more holistic way of life in a far different one.

For instance, a passage about drinking, the Nobel Prize, writing (or not writing), and Swahili is wonderfully sardonic in Hemingway's inimitable style. Hemingway, Mary, G. C. the game warden, and Harry Steele the policeman eat lunch together and Mary notes that a heavy drinker like Hemingway "needs to eat. This was not only a very old truth but had been the basis of an article in the *Reader's Digest* that we had all read.

That number of the *Digest* was down in the latrine tent now." Yet
Winston Churchill, who reportedly drank more than Hemingway, had
just been awarded the Nobel Prize for literature. Hemingway remarks, "I
was just trying to step up my drinking to a reasonable amount when I
might win the prize myself; who knows?" Both G. C. and Harry think
Ernest has a good chance to win the Nobel for his bragging, which would
match Churchill's oratory (G. C. says) or "for my [Hemingway's] work in
the religious field and for my [his] care of the natives" (Harry suggests).
Mary avers that "if I would try to write something, I might win it for writing. This moved me very deeply . . ." and he vows to write to please her.
Will it be "something about how mysterious Africa was and . . . in
Swahili?" Harry teases. But Ernest can neither write nor speak Swahili
correctly, Mary states. "I don't know how anyone can speak a language as
badly as you do."

Mary's cutting remarks lead Ernest at this point to break off the mocking talk and to reflect elegiacally about his love of Africa. His use of
Swahili had begun on his first safari, and he could have learned "to speak
it quite well. But . . . I had been a fool not to have stayed on in Africa and
instead gone back to America where I had killed my homesickness for
Africa in different ways." Then he had become involved in the Spanish
Civil War and World War II. He muses, "It had not been easy to get back
nor to break the chains of responsibility that are built up, seemingly as
lightly as spider webs but that hold like steel cables."[30]

New ties, African ones, he often expressed in his descriptions of and
feelings for the land, and repeatedly for the virtually sacred mountain,
Kilimanjaro, that loomed over the plains and that he had so well used in
the 1936 story "The Snows of Kilimanjaro." For instance, there is nothing
self-deprecatory in his beau gesture to the long-hunted and now dead
lion that Mary, G. C., and Ernest have slain. Pictures will be taken, and
Mary will be celebrated by the natives as a great lion killer (she having hit
the lion first, if not fatally). But Ernest, whose fabulous shot brought
down the fabulous beast, "lay down by the lion and talked to him very
softly in Spanish and begged his pardon for having killed him and while
[he] lay beside him [he] felt for the wounds." The prior account of the
hunt prepares us for his next simple sentence: "There were four," but it
also takes us beyond the literal slaying of a marauding lion to connections
with other worlds, including the one of the God-man Christ who dies
with four wounds. Yet the dead lion and Hemingway share their sacramental world with mundane flies: "I was stroking him and talking to him
in Spanish but many of the flat hard camel flies were shifting from him to
me so I drew a fish in front of him with my fore [and four]-finger in the
dirt and then rubbed it out with the palm of my hand."[31] After this

unique rite (that nonetheless relates to worldwide hunter-hunted rites), Hemingway remembers like Santiago and other great hunters the greatness of his prey, which could run a hundred yards in three seconds, weighed "over *four* hundred pounds and . . . was strong enough to have leaped over a high thorn *boma* carrying a cow . . . and he was very intelligent" (my emphasis). If the hunt had not gone perfectly, at least before its climax Hemingway experienced a holistic vision of the great lion in his great home: "I was happy that before he died he had lain on the high rounded mound with his tail down and his great paws comfortable before him and looked off across his country to the blue forest and the high white snows of the big mountain."[32]

On his third theme, "a commentary on the graces of age and the pleasures of power," Cave does not elaborate.[33] Although I understand his idea, it is for me a distortion contradicted by Hemingway's praise of innocence and his own attempts at reinvigoration. Cave, remember, deleted the passage praising the virtues of the adult who can be childlike; and Hemingway at fifty-four was hardly aged. To Cave's "pleasures of power" should be added "responsibility," the concomitant of that authority or power. Indeed Hemingway acted responsibly in his duties as an acting game ranger and for the most part acted with pleasure even when dealing with a Uriah Heep of a Masai, whom Hemingway named "The Informer," a character neither of life nor death but a spirit-denying functionary like Malvolio of Shakespeare's *Twelfth Night*.

Cave's fourth theme dealt with matters that were "bloody and topical, involving the Mau Mau" whose rebellion was in full flood in the 1950s against "the British colonial rule in Kenya."[34] I would prefer to name this subject a background issue and a minor part of the setting. True, Hemingway seems to introduce a red herring by writing about the Mau Mau in the first paragraph of the narrative, violating, perhaps, Chekhov's admonition that a pistol on the mantle in the first act must be discharged before the final curtain. But the Mau Mau are always somewhere else, never with Hemingway, Mary, and their friends and safari servants. The rebellion is at most a frisson, similar to the stalking of the lion, which seems more functional, not as a topic with interest and development (for I see none), but as another contextual detail that highlights the themes of *carpe diem* and eschatology. That is, if angry, panga-wielding Mau Mau threaten, all the more reason to live each moment as if it were your last and to consider "death, judgment, heaven, and hell," as Hemingway does with his naive but fascinated African friends.

Cave points in that direction in naming his fifth and final theme of religion. Cave notes that "It came up repeatedly, often in a humorous connotation, but at heart it was no laughing matter."[35] Cave may have saved that theme for dessert, and to me it is the sweetest course in his five-theme presentation. Yet he admits he allowed "only small portions of these last four aspects of the manuscript" into his edited version. "Religion" may not be the best term to name this theme, for there is nothing organized, official, or instrumental about the motif in the narrative. (See, for instance, the improvised rite of propitiation of the dead lion.) Rather, it seems to me, Hemingway is playing, in a serious way, with philosophical problems as only an artist can, released as one is from conventions and restraints of Aristotelian or Cartesian logic. Cave aptly cites the humor of the treatment of this theme, but it is the humor and play of Johan Huizinga (*Homo Ludens*) and Bergson and Freud, not Robert Benchley or Dorothy Parker (as the quoted passage on the Nobel prize illlustrates). More contemporaneously, it is *The Comedy of Survival*, to borrow the title of Joseph W. Meeker's book with its equally apt subtitle *Literary Ecology and a Play Ethic* (third edition).[36]

And although Rose Marie Burwell (in her recent book *Hemingway: The Postwar Years and the Posthumous Novels*) is more interested in the connections among Hemingway's posthumously published books and the partly published "African Book" than she is in a separate study of it, she too repeatedly describes it as a comic narrative, revealing "Hemingway at his most human, writing of himself with sustained comic irony we have never been allowed to see."[37] I agree with this description of "The African Book," but his humor and keen sense of the comic, especially the sardonic rather than ironic, flashes forth throughout his writing. From juvenilia in imitation of Ring Lardner to the homage to Henry Fielding in *Torrents of Spring* to the wonderfully sardonic *The Sun Also Rises* and *A Farewell to Arms* and numerous short stories, Hemingway became one of our best comic writers. Because he was most praised for other qualities, and because he thought "The bastards [critics] don't want you to joke because it disturbs their categories," perhaps his humor has yet to be fully appreciated.[38] Still, he may have anticipated a time when we would awaken to this marvelous dimension of his writing. As early as 1933 he wrote, "By jeesus [*sic*] will write my own memoirs sometime when I can't write anything else. And they will be funny."[39] Along with *A Moveable Feast*, "The African Book" certainly is funny. An example is this interchange (real or imagined) between Mary and Ernest after she has killed her lion, with more help from Ernest than she liked:

> Mary: "What have you been thinking of all morning when you've been so uncommonly silent?"
> Ernest: "About birds and places and how nice you are."
> Mary: "That was nice of you."

Ernest: "I didn't do it as a spiritual exercise."

Mary: "I'll be all right. People don't just jump in and out of bottomless pits."

Ernest: "They're going to make it an Olympic event."

Mary: "You'll probably win it."

Ernest: "I have my backers."

Mary: "Your backers are all dead like my lion. You probably shot all your backers one day when you were feeling especially wonderful."

Ernest: "Look, there's another field of storks."

Mary: "Yes," she said. "Look, there's another field of storks."[40]

The passage epitomizes much of the best of the narrative in its good humor and its subjects (in order of appearance here): introspection, wildlife, the importance of places, human relationships, spirituality and its absence, death and last matters, and, once again, with emphasis, wildlife. This Hemingway, this mellowed, thoughtful, sardonic naturalist, is a man worth knowing. His extraordinary capacity for both childlike joy and elegiac sorrow is nowhere more well present than in his "African Book."

* This essay was presented in Sun Valley, Idaho, in 1996 and so predates the essays of Joan Didion, Tom Jenks, and others that have preceded it into print.

NOTES

1. The typescript-manuscript (hereafter identified as "The African Book") is in the Hemingway collection in the John F. Kennedy Library in Boston and is copyrighted by The Ernest Hemingway Foundation, 1988. At least one other version exists; see note 37.

2. Ernest Hemingway, *Ernest Hemingway: Selected Letters, 1917–1961*, ed. Carlos Baker (New York: Scribner, 1981), 832f.

3. Ibid., 839.

4. Michael Reynolds, *Hemingway: An Annotated Chronology* (Detroit: Omnigraphics, Inc., 1991), 129.

5. Ibid., 129.

6. Hemingway, *Letters*, 860f.

7. Hemingway, "The African Book," 13.

8. Ibid., 30.

9. Ernest Hemingway, "An African Journal," *Sports Illustrated*, 20 December 1971: 47.

10. Hemingway, "The African Book," 30.

11. Ibid., 31.

12. Ibid., 30.

13. Ray Cave, introduction to "An African Journal," by Ernest Hemingway, 41.

14. Hemingway, "An African Journal," 44.

15. Hemingway, "The African Book," 2.

16. Hemingway, *Letters*, 841. In note 1, Carlos Baker estimates that less than thirty percent of the manuscript was published in *Sports Illustrated*. Rose Marie Burwell's estimate that approximately "half of the African Book appeared in magazines" is based on her assumption that "Safari" (*Look*, 26 Jan. 1954) and "The Christmas Gift" (*Look*, 20 Apr. and 4 May 1954) were parts of "The African Book." Rose Marie Burwell, *Hemingway: The Postwar Years and the Posthumous Novels* (Cambridge: Cambridge University Press, 1996), 220.

17. Mary Hemingway, *How It Was* (New York: Alfred A. Knopf, 1976), 371.

18. Carlos Baker, *Ernest Hemingway: A Life Story* (New York: Scribner, 1969), 626.

19. Baker, *Life*, 660.

20. Ibid., 526 and 660.

21. Hemingway, *Letters*, p. 839f.

22. Ibid., 847.

23. Ibid., 850.

24. Philip Young and Charles Mann, *The Hemingway Manuscripts* (University Park: Pennsylvania State University Press, 1969), 6.

25. Charles Mann, review of "An African Journal" by Ernest Hemingway, *Fitzgerald/Hemingway Annual 1972* (Dayton: NCR Microcard Editions, 1973), 395ff.

26. John Howell, review of "An African Journal" by Ernest Hemingway, *Hemingway Notes* 2 (Spring 1972): 21–22.

27. Earl Rovit and Gerry Brenner, *Ernest Hemingway*, rev. ed. (Boston: G. K. Hall, 1986), 165f.

28. Cave, Introduction, 40.

29. Ibid., 4.

30. Ernest Hemingway, "An African Journal," *Sports Illustrated*, 3 January 1972: 39.

31. Ibid., 43.

32. Ibid., 43.

33. Cave, Introduction, 40.

34. Ibid., 40f.

35. Ibid., 41.

36. Joseph W. Meeker, *The Comedy of Survival: Literary Ecology and a Play Ethic* (Tucson: University of Arizona Press, 1997).

37. Burwell, *Postwar Years*, 135. Burwell worked with the Princeton University Library copy of "The African Book," obtained from Charles Scribner's Sons. Although she claims that "Safari," and "The Christmas Gift" were, like the *Sports Illustrated* publications, parts of "The African Book," they do not appear in the copyrighted version and were written before Hemingway began work on "The African Book." Burwell's dates are wrong for "Safari" (26 January not 25 January), for the second part of "The Christmas Gift" (4 May not 27 April) and for the second and third parts of "The African Journal" (3 January 1972, not 27 December 1971, and 10 January not 2 January 1972).

38. Hemingway, *Letters,* 385.

39. Ibid., 388.

40. Ernest Hemingway, "An African Journal," *Sports Illustrated,* 10 January 1972, 24.

Dead Rabbits, Bad Milk, and Lost Eggs: Women, Nature, and Myth in *For Whom the Bell Tolls*

LISA TYLER

In a fascinating article entitled "Pilar's Tale: The Myth and the Message," Robert E. Gajdusek dissects the mythic dimensions of the atrocity tale that Pilar tells Robert Jordan and Maria in Ernest Hemingway's *For Whom the Bell Tolls*.[1] Gajdusek contends that Hemingway contrasts the Apollonian qualities of the fascist order with the Dionysian qualities of the Republican revolutionaries.

While I agree that Hemingway was working with myth in this novel,[2] I want to suggest that he was perhaps invoking an older myth than that suggested by Gajdusek—that Hemingway was in fact evoking the Eleusinian mysteries of Demeter and Persephone.[3] This proposal is not inconsistent with Gajdusek's interpretation, for the two myths are related; in *Greek Folk Religion*, Martin Nilsson observes "that from the late fifth and early fourth centuries B.C., there was a certain mixing up of the Mysteries of Eleusis and the cult of Dionysus."[4] In fact, according to Helene Foley, Dionysus is sometimes presented as Persephone's child.[5] However, "Dionysus, young male god of the grapevine, wine, intoxication, revelry, frenzy and destruction, as well as of resurrection, was added rather late to the rites of Demeter."[6] Certainly the themes of the older myth, described by Mara Lynn Keller in "The Eleusinian Mysteries of Demeter and Persephone," closely parallel the themes of *For Whom the Bell Tolls*:

> The rites of Demeter and Persephone speak to the experiences of life that remain through all times the most mysterious—birth, sexuality, death—and also to the greatest mystery of all, enduring love. In these ceremonies, women and men expressed joy in the beauty and abundance of nature, especially the bountiful harvest; in personal love, sexuality and procreation; and in the rebirth of the human spirit, even through suffering and death.[7]

[125]

I suggest that it is the matricentric myth of Demeter and Persephone which Hemingway contrasts to the patriarchal myth he associates with the Nationalist order, and that he explores this contrast throughout the novel, not simply in Pilar's tale. Hemingway evokes the myth to mourn what he sees as Spain reenacting the myth's shift "from relatively egalitarian and peaceful clan communities to urbanized, warfaring, male-dominant, and slave based class societies"[8]—a startlingly apt description of twentieth-century fascism.

In the myth, which is developed at length in *The Homeric Hymn to Demeter*,[9] a young maiden, Persephone, is abducted and raped by Hades, god of the underworld. Her grief-stricken mother Demeter searches for her daughter and begs Zeus to order Hades to return Persephone, but he refuses until Demeter, goddess of the grain, causes a famine to starve the mortals of the earth. Persephone is finally restored to her mother, but because Persephone has eaten pomegranate seeds given to her by Hades, she must remain in the underworld a part of each year. The mother-daughter reunion is such a joyful one that when Persephone returns to her mother, spring returns to the earth. The myth thus explains the seasons and establishes a cult whose initiates receive the secret of immortality.

The mother and maiden of the myth are doubles for each other, as Jane Ellen Harrison points out in her *Prolegomena to the Study of Greek Religion*: "It is important to note that primarily the two forms of the Earth or Corn-goddess are not Mother and *Daughter*, but Mother and Maiden, Demeter and Kore. They are, in fact, merely the older and younger form of the same person; hence their easy confusion."[10] Pilar and Maria are similarly doubles for each other, as Hemingway signals in his choice of names for these two women. Jordan insists that Maria's name is signifi-cant: "Sweetheart, *cherie*, *prenda*, and *schatz* [sic]. He would trade them all for Maria. There was a name."[11] Later, when she insists on its common-ness, he disagrees (263–64). It is "not common" both because it belongs to his love and because it invokes the Virgin Mary. But so, of course, does the name Pilar, as Hemingway makes clear when he later refers to the "Blessed Virgin of Pilar" (303). According to Catholic tradition, the Virgin Mary miraculously appeared to Saint James in Zaragoza in 40 A.D., and the stone pillar on which she stood became first a venerated shrine and later the site of a cathedral established in her name. Her appearance is celebrated during the Pilar Festivals with parades and bullfights.[12] Ironically (especially, perhaps, given Hemingway's noted predilection for madonna/whore characters), both Maria and Pilar are also referred to as whores (53, 150, 311, 388).

Again and again, Hemingway suggests the similarities between the two women. Immediately after Pilar tells Robert and Maria, "I was born ugly" (97), Maria insists that she, too, is ugly (98). At one point, waking abruptly from his sleep, Robert momentarily mistakes Pilar for Maria (360). When they see that Robert is wounded, both women react the same way. Robert thinks, looking at Maria, "her face was twisted as a child's contorts before it cries," and later, "He looked up at Pilar. Her face had the same expression as Maria's" (462). The two women are in some ways identical. Theodore Bardacke notes of Hemingway's characters, "Maria is symbolically the daughter of Pilar, who had rescued the girl and nursed her back to health. Maria is, however, also Pilar's vicarious youth, almost as if Pilar, who has become desexed with age, had recreated her sexual youth by identification with this young girl."[13]

In *Of Woman Born: Motherhood as Experience and Institution*, Adrienne Rich contends that the myth of Demeter and Persephone celebrates "mother-daughter passion and rapture."[14] Certainly the two women in Hemingway's novel are unusually close, and one scene, in which Pilar caresses Maria and confesses her jealousy, suggests that the relationship has a homoerotic component (154–55). Joseph Waldmeir suggests that Pilar was based on Gertrude Stein and notes, "though Gertrude [Stein] was an avowed [l]esbian, Pilar was, in her sexual attraction to Maria, at least a homosexual *manqu*[é]."[15] In an earlier draft of the novel, Hemingway hinted even more strongly that the two women had once shared a sexual bond.[16]

Several festivals were associated with the Demeter cult, and most of them were for women only. Keller explains: "Probably through these celebrations, elder women shared with girls and young women what they would need to know about menstruation, sexuality, marriage, pregnancy, childbirth, and childrearing."[17] Similarly, Pilar teaches Maria about life in lessons that Maria compares to "religious instruction" when she explains them to Robert: "'It is something like that.' She blushed again. 'But different'" (324; see also 349).

Like Demeter, the Grain-Mother,[18] Maria is associated with agriculture.[19] As Robert Jordan notices in their first encounter, "Her hair was the golden brown of a grain field that has been burned dark in the sun" (22). He later notices it is "tawny as wheat" (158) and compares it to "a wheatfield in the wind" (345; see also 23 and 346). Like Persephone, Maria is also associated with images of fertility, among them animals and flowers. Her hair is "little longer than the fur on a beaver pelt" (22), and "[s]he stroked under his hand like a kitten" (68). Maria sits in the heather to hear Pilar's story (96), and later she and Robert Jordan make love in a meadow of heather (159), in a plot development which echoes what Froma I. Zeitlin terms the Eleusinian Mysteries' "sacralization of sexuality . . . by the widespread pattern of a human couple performing sexual intercourse in a field."[20] John J. Teunissen uses the phrase "hierogamy, the sacred marriage" to describe their union, which he sees as a reenactment of ancient fertility rituals.[21] Elsewhere in the novel Robert explicitly compares Maria to the life force: "He held her feeling she was all of life there was and it was true" (264).

Maria is also, of course, given the problematic nickname of "little rabbit."[22] As Edward F. Stanton notes:

> The reader with a knowledge of Spanish who is aware, for example, that *"conejo"* or rabbit can be used to refer to the female organ finds it difficult to read without smiling those passages in which Jordan uses the assumed Spanish word as an endearing nickname for Maria ("little rabbit"). Either Hemingway himself was unaware of the figurative meaning of the word, or he used it as a kind of private joke, unconcerned about the reaction of the few readers who might understand the sexual connotations.[23]

I want to argue that Hemingway both knew the meaning of the word and *intended* to invoke its sexual connotations. After all, it has sexual connotations in English as well, albeit not such explicit ones. (Consider the expressions "breeding like rabbits" and "Playboy bunny.") Moreover, classicists speculate that a display of the female genitals (or a representation of the female genitals) may have played an important role in the celebration of the Eleusinian mysteries.[24] It seems to me that Hemingway's use of the word "rabbit" in this context is therefore meant to suggest fertility, not smuttiness. It is Hemingway's taste, not his intelligence, which is in question here.

Maria, then, is a fertility figure, but fertility is endangered in the no-longer-peaceful agrarian world of Hemingway's novel. It is not coincidental that the first rabbit to appear in the novel is eaten (22; see also 300) and other specimens are shot (42 and 274). Nor is it an accident that later in the novel Maria's hair is compared to the fur of a marten in a trap (378). Like Persephone, Maria is brutally raped. It is clear that she was a virgin at the time. She does not even know how to kiss (70). She tells Robert Jordan she has "never" loved others, "But things were done to me" (71); her experiences are so terrible that Robert perceives her "going dead in his arms" when she first tries to tell him about them (71). When she finally tells Robert the details of her story, she clearly indicates that she was gang-raped (350–53).

It was her "mother," the maternal figure of Pilar, who rescued her from that underworld of male brutality. Rafael explains:

> We would have left her after the train. Certainly it was not worth being delayed by something so sad and ugly and apparently worthless.

But the old woman tied a rope to her and when the girl thought she could not go further, the old woman beat her with the end of a rope to make her go. Then when she could not really go further, the old woman carried her over her shoulder. When the old woman could not carry her, I carried her. . . . And when I could no longer carry her, Pablo carried her. But what the old woman had to say to make us do it! (28)

Ever since, Agustin tells Robert, "you cannot imagine with what fierceness [Pilar] has guarded her" (290). As Adrienne Rich writes, "Each daughter, even in the millennia before Christ, must have longed for a mother whose love for her and whose power were so great as to undo rape and bring her back from death. And every mother must have longed for the power of Demeter, the efficacy of her anger, the reconciliation with her lost self."[25] It is precisely this that happens in Hemingway's novel: The maternal figure of Pilar undoes Maria's rape and brings her back from near death; Pilar possesses all of the efficacy and anger of Demeter, and in Maria she rediscovers her lost self. But this reunion, unlike the reunion of mother and daughter in the myth, takes place in a hostile world of war and violence. Pilar has even coached Maria on how to cut her own throat to kill herself most efficiently should she be captured. As a horrified Robert thinks to himself, "So she goes around with that all the time, . . . as a definitely accepted and properly organized possibility" (171).

Maria's case is not an isolated one, as Hemingway makes clear. Mothers and children are endangered in the war-torn world of the novel. Even the usually submissive Maria recognizes this danger. When Robert hesitates to let her try whiskey, saying "it is not good for a woman," Maria rather dryly replies, "And I have only had things that were good for a woman" (343). Pablo refers to one of the fascists to his face as "You who would shoot your own mother" (101). The gypsy exclaims to Robert Jordan, "we have just seen the sky full of airplanes of a quantity to kill us back to our grandfathers and forward to all unborn grandsons" and complains of the "[a]irplanes making a noise to curdle the milk in your mother's breasts" (79). Many pages later, a fighter in El Sordo's band tells a comrade, "Wipe the pap of your mother's breasts off thy lips and give me a handful of that dirt" (309). In place of mother's milk, the Spanish people have dirt. Defeated by the masculine violence of the fascists, the maternal breast can no longer nourish. No wonder El Sordo mentally (and ungrammatically) compares the hill on which his band makes its last stand to "the breast of a young girl with no nipple" (309).

Similarly, Pilar speaks of the "smell of death" in a remarkable passage in which various traditional images of fertility are reversed: Chrysanthemums are dead, the women are old and clearly past menopause, the blood they drink is from *slaughtered* bulls, the whores mate against cold iron railings, and the flower beds are rotting (254–56). War, she suggests, perverts human fertility by replacing life with death.

One of the most cryptic references to fertility in the novel occurs when Robert, Anselmo, and Fernando return to Pablo's cave:

> "*El Palacio del Miedo*," Anselmo said. "The Palace of Fear."
>
> "*La cueva de los huevos perdidos*," Robert Jordan capped the other happily. "The cave of the lost eggs."
>
> "What eggs?" Fernando asked.
>
> "A joke," Robert Jordan said. "Just a joke. Not eggs, you know. The others."
>
> "But why are they lost?" Fernando asked.
>
> "I don't know," said Robert Jordan. "Take a book to tell you. Ask Pilar[.]" (199)

Gajdusek contends, "On the simplest of levels, the reference to the lost eggs is, of course, to lost testicular power or male potency."[26] Similarly, Stanton asserts, "The repeated allusions to milk in the novel refer to semen."[27] These interpretations, which rely on slang meanings of the Spanish words at the expense of the literal meanings of the English words Hemingway actually uses, are more than a little strained; surely these images are as feminine as they are masculine. On the *simplest* level, images of milk and eggs suggest maternity and offspring; bad milk and lost eggs suggest blighted maternity and destroyed fertility. According to Maria, Pilar has speculated that Maria may have literally lost her fertility to the fascists (354). It is Maria herself who suggests the importance of this possible loss when she asks Robert: "And how can the world be made better if there are no children of us who fight against the fascists?" (354).

Maria's losses are representative of those her nation has suffered: "Her parents have been murdered, her village sacked, she has been violated as Spain herself has been pillaged and raped by foreign and native soldiers for centuries."[28] Another image of lost eggs further emphasizes the loss of procreativity that the Spanish people—both men and women—have sustained in this civil war: Andres, on his trip to notify Golz that the fascists know of the coming offensive, inadvertently startles a partridge and thinks to himself that the bird's nest must be nearby. He wishes he could mark the nest with a handkerchief, return for the eggs, and watch the birds hatch and grow in his own courtyard: "I would like such small and regular things" (367). Andres would like to return to his agrarian pre-war Spain; he would, perhaps, like to have children, the children that the egg imagery suggests.

But instead of eggs, this world has explosives, which Robert Jordan had "packed as carefully as he had packed his collection of wild bird eggs when he was a boy" (48). The only babies left in this world are "baby" tanks, and they, too, are to be destroyed, as Agustin acknowledges when he boasts of the baby tank, "If I had a baby bottle full of gasoline I would climb up and set fire to him" (453).

In using these startling images, Hemingway emphasizes the fundamental contradiction between mothering and war that Sara Ruddick describes in her book *Maternal Thinking: Toward a Politics of Peace*: "All of women's work—sheltering, nursing, feeding, kin work, teaching of the very young, tending the frail elderly—is threatened by violence. . . . Mothering begins in birth and promises life; military thinking justifies organized, deliberate deaths."[29] Ruddick suggests that the image of the *mater dolorosa*—whose name Maria and Pilar share—is often invoked to emphasize this contradiction.[30] Of course, mothers can often become violent themselves,[31] but Hemingway, while drawing on the idealized images of myth, is no essentialist. He acknowledges that many mothers participate in war: Pilar, who is so maternal toward Maria, ultimately advocates killing the untrustworthy Pablo for the good of the cause (217), and La Pasionaria urges young men to fight while allegedly sending her own son to Russia (309).

Interestingly, the fascists have no problems with fertility; they have abundant supplies of hay and grain (363), and the mistresses of the fascists are all pregnant (399). They are, after all, winning the battle—and when Hemingway wrote the book, he knew they had already won the war. Allen Guttmann suggests that, "for Hemingway the Spanish Civil War was dramatized as, among other things, a struggle waged by men close to the earth and to the values of a primitive society against men who had turned away from the earth, men who had turned to the machine and to the values of an aggressive and destructive mechanical order."[32] The alternatives are "on the one hand, fertility and spontaneity, and on the other, sterility and repression."[33] What was happening in Spain must have seemed to Hemingway a reenactment of the archetypal conflict inscribed in the myth: "The Mysteries of Demeter and Persephone embodied the values of the relatively peaceful farming and trading mother-clan societies of the Goddess-preeminent Neolithic, before the sacrifice of sons in war became common practice as patriarchal warrior clans forced their way to power."[34] Similarly, Martin Nilsson contrasts the "warring Homeric knights" with the "ideal of peace and justice created by agriculture" and writes, "I venture to speak of an Eleusinian piety founded on this idea that agriculture created a civilized and peaceful life worthy of human beings."[35] Early in the novel Robert recognizes of Pilar, "She is a damned sight more civilized than you are"

(168). It is the loss of the civilized and peaceful life Pilar represents that Hemingway mourns in this novel.

The Eleusinian Mysteries, the rituals linked to the myth of Demeter and Persephone, were open to both men and women.[36] Helene Foley observes, "If the Mysteries in some sense permit universal access to (and imitation of) a secret or private world of the female, and to the mysteries of death, fertility, magic, and even anger connected with her, one can perhaps understand some of its appeal . . . for the male initiate" (140).[37] It is intriguing to see Robert Jordan as an initiate to these sacred rites. It is possible to interpret the "dark passage which led to nowhere" as a descent into Hades (159). Interestingly, Herman Nibbelink writes of Robert at the novel's conclusion, "In his final moments of life, he achieves union with nature. . . . All the traditional religious imagery of the novel is resolved now as Jordan accepts a nature religion."[38] At least one feminist theorist, Sara Ruddick, has suggested a possible link between maternal thinking and a mystical attitude toward nature.[39] Anselmo's anguished insistence that a public atonement ceremony will be necessary after the war to cleanse the souls of those who have killed (196) recalls the ancient Greek belief that those guilty of unatoned murder could not participate in the rites of Demeter.[40] It is also interesting to note that Gerry Brenner "read[s] Jordan's reminiscences of [his] father as a psychological 'descent to the underworld,' for such journeys traditionally feature conversations with the dead."[41] Given this reading, then, Jordan reenacts Persephone's descent into the underworld, much as initiates of the Demeter cult might have done.

Like Demeter and Persephone, Pilar and Maria introduce Robert to what he thinks of as "mysteries" associated with the earth-moving sexual experience he and Maria share: "Nobody knows what tribes we came from nor what our tribal inheritance is nor what the mysteries were in the woods where the people lived that we came from. All we know is that we do not know" (175). He thinks uneasily, "I am no mystic" (380) and says, "I do not believe . . . in supernatural things" (250). He later tells Pilar, "Don't be so mysterious" and adds, "These mysteries tire me very much"; he finally asks her to "leave the mysteries" (176).

Uncomfortable with these matricentric mysteries as he seems, however, Robert Jordan may have gained from them a kind of immortality. He insists to Maria that he will live through her: "As long as there is one of us there is both of us" (463). There is also the suggestion of a more literal kind of immortality in that there is at least a possibility that Maria may be pregnant. When Robert, worrying about the future, tells Pilar, "I can't take a woman where I go," she responds, "You may take two where you go" (84). Pilar seems unperturbed by the prospect of Maria's pregnancy.[42] Rafael, the gypsy, is less sanguine; disgusted that Jordan slept with Maria and did not kill Pablo, he rather comically exclaims, "You were supposed to kill one, not make one!" (79). Appropriately, the Demeter cult gave its initiates "a hope of immortality and a belief in the eternity of life, not for the individual but for the generations which spring from one another."[43] Regardless of whether he has fathered a child, however, Robert has learned the mysteries: "in losing his isolate self in Maria, Jordan gains eternal life beyond his insignificant mortality."[44]

The novel ends just as June is presumably beginning. Nilsson and Zeitlin point out that in Eleusis, grain is sown in October or November, reaped in May, and threshed in June, before the blazing heat of summer scorches the earth. The seed "corn" (what Americans would call grain) was then stored underground until the fall, when it became necessary to obtain seed from the old crop to plant for the next year's harvest. Thus June is the month that Nilsson felt, given the growing season for grain in Greece, was most likely the time for Persephone, the Corn Maiden, to descend to the underworld.[45]

Hemingway knew, when he wrote the novel, that the Republican forces had lost the war—that Spain, like Persephone, had descended unwillingly into an underworld of violence and death.[46] But he ended the novel with Jordan's sacrifice, which transcends that loss and gives hope to the novel's readers. Although Hemingway mourned for the rape and abduction of Spain in his novel, he remained hopeful nevertheless. Hemingway described his vision for the Spanish people in an article titled "On the American Dead in Spain" which was published in the 14 February 1939 issue of the *New Masses*. In it, as in the novel, he again evokes the ancient Greek myth—and the immortality it promised: "[O]ur dead are a part of the earth of Spain now and the earth of Spain can never die. Each winter it will seem to die and each spring it will come alive again."[47]

NOTES

1. Robert E. Gajdusek, "Pilar's Tale: The Myth and the Message," *The Hemingway Review* 10.2 (Fall 1990): 19–33, reprinted in *Blowing the Bridge: Essays on Hemingway and "For Whom the Bell Tolls,"* ed. Rena Sanderson (New York: Greenwood Press, 1992), 113–30.

2. Other critics who have explored the mythic dimensions of the novel include Robert W. Lewis, Jr., *Hemingway On Love* (Austin: University of Texas Press, 1965), 141–78; J. B. Michael, "The Unspanish War in *For Whom the Bell Tolls*," *Contemporary Literature* 13 (Spring 1972): 204–12; Edward F. Stanton, *Hemingway and Spain: A Pursuit* (Seattle: University of Washington Press, 1989); Robert O. Stephens, "Language Magic and Reality in *For Whom the Bell Tolls*," *Criticism* 14 (Spring 1972): 151–64, reprinted in *Ernest Hemingway: Five*

Decades of Criticism, ed. Linda Welshimer Wagner (East Lansing: Michigan State University Press, 1974), 266–79; John J. Teunissen, *"For Whom the Bell Tolls* as Mythic Narrative," *Dalhousie Review* 56 (1976): 52–69, reprinted in *Ernest Hemingway: Six Decades of Criticism*, ed. Linda Welshimer Wagner (Ann Arbor: Michigan State University Press, 1987), 221–37; and Delbert E. Wylder, *Hemingway's Heroes* (Albuquerque: University of New Mexico Press, 1969), 127–64.

In a related vein, Carlos Baker identified the novel's parallels to Homeric epic in *Hemingway: The Writer as Artist* (Princeton, N.J.: Princeton University Press, 1963), 248–50. Gerry Brenner later developed those parallels at much greater length in "Epic Machinery in Hemingway's *For Whom the Bell Tolls," Modern Fiction Studies* 16 (Winter 1970–71): 491–504; this essay was revised and reprinted in *Concealments in Hemingway's Works* (Columbus: Ohio State University Press, 1983), 124–36.

For explorations of the novel's references to Christianity, which Hemingway often conflates with Greek myth, see Patrick Cheney, "Hemingway and Christian Epic: The Bible in *For Whom the Bell Tolls," Papers on Language and Literature* 21 (Spring 1985): 170–91; Robert D. Crozier, S. J., "For Thine is the Power and the Glory: Love in *For Whom the Bell Tolls," Papers on Language and Literature* 10 (1974): 76–97; and H. R. Stoneback, "'The Priest Did Not Answer': Hemingway, the Church, the Party, and *For Whom the Bell Tolls," Blowing the Bridge: Essays on Hemingway and "For Whom the Bell Tolls,"* ed. Rena Sanderson (New York: Greenwood Press, 1992), 99–112.

3. Mimi Reisel Gladstein, in *The Indestructible Woman in Faulkner, Hemingway, and Steinbeck* (Ann Arbor, Mich.: UMI Research Press, 1986), 67, notes the novel's parallel to the Demeter/Persephone myth but devotes only a paragraph to developing the comparison.

4. Martin Nilsson, *Greek Folk Religion* (New York: Harper, 1961), 48.

5. Helene Foley, ed., *The Homeric "Hymn to Demeter"* (Princeton, N.J.: Princeton University Press, 1994), 110.

6. Mara Lynn Keller, "The Eleusinian Mysteries of Demeter and Persephone," *Journal of Feminist Studies in Religion*, 4.1 (Spring 1988): 49.

7. Ibid., 27.

8. Ibid., 37.

9. Foley, *The Homeric "Hymn to Demeter,"* 1–27. Some readers may be more familiar with the Roman version of the myth, in which Pluto is the god of the underworld, Proserpine is the daughter, and Ceres is the mother.

10. Jane Harrison, *Prolegomena to the Study of Greek Religion* (New York: Meridian, 1957), 274. See also Froma I. Zeitlin, "Cultic Models of the Female: Rites of Dionysus and Demeter," *Arethusa* 15 (1982): 149, and Nilsson, *Greek Folk Religion*, 48.

11. Ernest Hemingway, *For Whom the Bell Tolls* (New York: Scribner's, 1940), 167. Subsequent references to this text will be given as page numbers in the text.

12. Stoneback, "The Priest Did Not Answer," 103–4, and Allen Josephs, *"For Whom the Bell Tolls": Hemingway's Undiscovered Country* (New York: Twayne, 1994), 74–75.

13. Theodore Bardacke, "Hemingway's Women," *Ernest Hemingway: The Man and His Work*, ed. John M. McCaffery (New York: Cooper Square Publishers, 1969), 51.

14. Adrienne Rich, *Of Woman Born: Motherhood as Experience and Institution* (New York: Norton, 1986), 237.

15. Joseph Waldmeir, "Chapter Numbering and Meaning in *For Whom the Bell Tolls*," *The Hemingway Review* 8 (Spring 1989): 44.

16. Thomas E. Gould, "'A Tiny Operation with Great Effect': Authorial Revision and Editorial Emasculation in the Manuscript of Hemingway's *"For Whom the Bell Tolls*," *Blowing the Bridge: Essays on Hemingway and "For Whom the Bell Tolls*," ed. Rena Sanderson (New York: Greenwood Press, 1992), 73–75. See also Nancy R. Comley and Robert Scholes, *Hemingway's Genders* (New Haven, Conn.: Yale University Press, 1994), 47–48.

17. Keller, "The Eleusinian Mysteries," 38.

18. Harrison, *Prolegomena*, 272.

19. See Lewis, *Hemingway on Love*, 174; Wylder, *Hemingway's Heroes*, 152; and Josephs, *Hemingway's Undiscovered Country*, 138, for discussions of Maria as an archetypal goddess figure.

20. Zeitlin, "Cultic Models of the Female," 148.

21. Teunissen, *"For Whom the Bell Tolls"* as Mythic Narrative," 233.

22. On the inappropriateness of Maria's nickname, see Arturo Barea, "Not Spain but Hemingway," *Horizon* 3 (May 1941): 350–61, reprinted in *The Merrill Studies in "For Whom the Bell Tolls*," ed. Sheldon Norman Grebstein (Columbus: Merrill, 1971), 88; F. Allen Josephs, "Hemingway's Poor Spanish: Chauvinism and Loss of Credibility in *For Whom the Bell Tolls*," in *Hemingway: A Revaluation*, ed. Donald R. Noble (Troy, N. Y.: Whitston, 1983), 205–23; and Wolfgang E. H. Rudat, "Hemingway's Rabbit: Slips of the Tongue and Other Linguistic Games in *For Whom the Bell Tolls*," *The Hemingway Review* 10 (Fall 1990): 34–51. Josephs later presented a more sympathetic view in his discussion of the novel's language in his book, *"For Whom the Bell Tolls": Ernest Hemingway's Undiscovered Country*, 155–60.

On the other hand, Mimi Reisel Gladstein notes that the comparison to a rabbit has "connotations of fertility" (68).

23. Stanton, *Hemingway and Spain*, 159.

24. Foley, *The Homeric "Hymn to Demeter*," 46; Zeitlin, "Cultic Models of the Female," 144; Marilyn Arthur, "Politics and Pomegranates: An Interpretation of the Homeric *Hymn to Demeter*," *Arethusa*, 10 (1977): 7–47, reprinted in *The Homeric "Hymn to Demeter*," ed. Helene Foley (Princeton, N.J.: Princeton University Press, 1994), 228–29.

25. Rich, *Of Woman Born*, 240.

26. Gajdusek, "Pilar's Tale," 126.

27. Stanton, *Hemingway and Spain*, 155.

28. Ibid., 175.

29. Sara Ruddick, *Maternal Thinking: Toward a Politics of Peace* (Boston: Beacon Press, 1989), 148.

30. Ibid., 149.

31. Ibid., 154–56.

32. Allen Guttmann, "Mechanized Doom: Ernest Hemingway and the Spanish Civil War," *Massachusetts Review* 1 (May 1960): 541–47, reprinted in *The Merrill Studies in "For Whom the Bell Tolls*," ed. Sheldon Norman Grebstein (Columbus: Merrill, 1971), 76.

33. Ibid., 77.

34. Keller, "The Eleusinian Mysteries," 28.

35. Nilsson, *Greek Folk Religion*, 57. See also Teunissen, *"For Whom the Bell Tolls* as Mythic Narrative," where he puts it more prosaically: "The Republicans are peasants, primitive man, while the Loyalists are petty bourgeoisie, modern man" (233).

36. Foley, *The Homeric "Hymn to Demeter*," 66.

37. Ibid., 140.

38. Herman Nibbelink, "The Meaning of Nature in *For Whom the Bell Tolls*," *Arizona Quarterly* 33.2 (Summer 1977): 172.

39. Ruddick, *Maternal Thinking*, 76–78.

40. Keller, "The Eleusinian Mysteries," 48.

41. Gerry Brenner, "Epic Machinery in Hemingway's *For Whom the Bell Tolls*," 130.

42. For an odd sidelight, see Rudat, "Hemingway's Rabbit": "Pilar may have arranged the affair not only in her capacity as the girl's 'psychiatrist,' but also as a sociopolitical engineer who, realizing that the struggle for her country's freedom will not be won in her generation, employs a *norteamericano* quite literally for the generation of future Republicans" (49).

43. Nilsson, *Greek Folk Religion*, 63.

44. Earl Rovit, "From *Ernest Hemingway*," in *The Merrill Studies in "For Whom the Bell Tolls*," ed. Sheldon Norman Grebstein (Columbus: Merrill, 1971), 120.

45. Nilsson, *Greek Folk Religion*, 51–52; Zeitlin, "Cultic Models of the Female," 138.

46. In some versions of the myth, Persephone is unwillingly abducted but nonetheless gradually comes to love her abductor. See for example Foley, *The Homeric "Hymn to Demeter,"* 107. Spain's civil war perhaps indicates a similar ambivalence.

47. Quoted in Stanton, *Hemingway and Spain*, 186.

Shifting Orders: Chaos and Order in
For Whom the Bell Tolls

ROD ROMESBURG

In *Nature's Economy*, his book on the development of the science of ecology, Donald Worster writes that his field of study, history, "even very recently, was still compartmentalized into two separate spheres, one for people and one for the rest of the natural world. The first, the human story, had been tumultuous, unpredictable, and destructive; the second had been, with big exceptions on the largest scale of time, orderly, predictable, and conserving."[1] In Western science and art, the privilege, or burden, of being human creates a separation from the natural world. Much of our time and energy goes into showing how we are different from the rest of what goes on around us. Because of this either/or dichotomy (either you are human or you are nature), one of the "two separate spheres" gets labeled superior to the other. Which sphere rests higher shifts from culture to culture and temporally within each culture, but by the 1930s, in a world still reeling from the effects of the First World War and anticipating World War II, a world that had seen much of its economic system collapse and had begun to look to other forms of government for answers, it is not hard to imagine a writer, like Worster's historians, looking to the natural world as a model of order distinguished from human chaos.

Ernest Hemingway's *For Whom the Bell Tolls* reflects this attitude, with the natural landscape providing an antithesis to the chaotic, war-ruled environment of civilization. Beginning and ending with an emphasis on the natural surroundings, Hemingway shows the disconnection between human culture and the environment, questioning the very possibility of order in human affairs. Images of natural order contrast with those of chaotic human societies, and though Robert Jordan reaches an "integration" with the natural environment in the text's final scene, even this attempt at joining the two worlds in a harmonious order is rendered problematic.

Early in his childhood, Hemingway's father introduced him to an appreciation of nature. From his youth he was taught how to camp, hunt, and fish, and Hemingway grew up with a persistent need to be in the wilds. However, with this appreciation came a contradiction common in American society. Carlos Baker says that Clarence Edmonds Hemingway had both a love of nature and a belief that God had provided its trappings for the enjoyment of humanity.[2] This tears the believer in two directions: Nature is to be loved, but man (I use *man* intentionally, and will discuss why later) shows love by possessing or even destroying it.[3] Therefore, nature is a benefit for humans, but also something to be defined against. As Michael Reynolds notes, Hemingway shares the burden of the classic Western hero: He, and his characters, must love and conquer the wilderness.[4]

Comparing Hemingway and Henry David Thoreau, Donald Murray writes, "with regard to nature, both men put a high value on sanitive or 'tonic' wildness."[5] Hemingway often portrays the wilderness as a nurturing parent, knowing what is good for us. Wilderness bears something that is "right," something we are missing. Here, we can find healing. As told throughout Baker's biography, when Hemingway finished a book he immediately escaped to the West or the Florida Keys, where he could recuperate. An obvious example from Hemingway's fiction is his short story "Big Two-Hearted River," when the war-torn Nick Adams finally finds some semblance of mental peace away from all humanity and in the presence of nature.

But Hemingway also recognized that we usually fail to treat nature with the same nurturing it provides us. While writing *A Farewell to Arms*, he and his wife Pauline caught six hundred trout in one month, and after finishing *For Whom the Bell Tolls*, he and his family celebrated by shooting four hundred jackrabbits.[6] In *Green Hills of Africa*, he notes, "a continent ages quickly once we come. The natives live in harmony with it. But the foreigner destroys, cuts down the trees, drains the water, so that the water supply is altered and in a short time the soil, once the sod is turned under, is cropped out and, next, it starts to blow away in every old country, and as I had seen it start to blow in Canada."[7] Glen Love also notes Hemingway's conflict with nature. Love admits that though Hemingway's admiration for wilderness is apparent,

> often [Hemingway] turns against the earth itself in his version of
> primitivism, adopting an isolated and aggressive individualism which
> wars against those natural manifestations he claims to love. . . . His
> unique brand of primitivism characteristically rejects those percep-
> tions—the interconnectedness of all life, the harmonious sense of
> oneness with the world, the ability to understand and use complex
> natural processes without destroying them, the acceptance of death

as part of an inevitable and non-threatening flow of existence—
which enable the actual primitive to exist in the sort of non-destructive relationship with his surroundings which Hemingway
paradoxically admired, and which left the country as he liked it.[8]

Hemingway admires wilderness for its own qualities, but at the same
time needs to make it his own, asserting *his* will. Mimi Gladstein states
that Hemingway, and much of Western culture in general, links nature
with the feminine. The apparent ambivalent character of nature, its willingness to both give life and take it, to be fertile and barren, leads the
male psyche to the solution that nature and women must be conquered.
This is accomplished through a taming of, or a separation from the feminine.[9] Something like a too attentive mother, Hemingway feels nature
can nurture and comfort, but also stifle. Though we may have a need to
go to wilderness for healing, we must also outgrow it, finding our own
character through rebellion and distancing.

In *For Whom the Bell Tolls*, Hemingway removes his protagonist from
the chaos of human society and places him in a natural setting. Baker
notes both the healing possibilities and the inherent separation of this
action, feeling that Hemingway achieves "a kind of idyll in the midst of
war, an island (like that of Nick Adams in his afternoon grove on the way
to the Big Two-Hearted River) surrounded by the sinister . . . an island in
the midst of *nada*."[10] Though there is hope, the distance between the two
worlds of nature and human civilization is present. Images of landscape
throughout the novel reflect the division. Though Robert Jordan is hiding
in the wilderness of the forest with his band of guerrillas, the influence of
humanity prevails. The novel begins with Jordan lying

> flat on the brown, pine-needled floor of the forest, his chin on his
> folded arms, and high overhead the wind blew in the tops of the
> pine trees. The mountainside sloped gently where he lay; but below
> it was steep and he could see the dark of the oiled road winding
> through the pass. There was a stream alongside the road and far
> down the pass he saw a mill beside the stream and the falling water
> of the dam, white in the sunlight.[11]

Of this passage, Brian Way writes that Hemingway has given up his customary use of landscape as indicative of the character's mental state, and
instead Jordan "sees only a bridge, rocks, a mountain torrent, patches of
snow: it is a scene without inner resonance, as empty of meaning as the
mind which observes it."[12] I partially disagree with this assessment. I feel
Hemingway's conscious and careful description may be without inner
resonance, but this is because Jordan himself is empty, and the way he

sees this land mirrors his detachment. What begins as a peaceful interaction with nature—tactile, aural, and visual—is interrupted by the effect of humanity's presence: the oiled road, the mill, the dam. Note particularly how nature is described first, then humanity; the artificial intrudes, and like an ink spot on a blank page, its abrupt and incongruous presence renders it the more distinctive.

A second example of the gulf between Jordan and nature comes early in the novel with his references to weaponry. When Jordan begins thinking about the machines of war—trucks holding infantry, machine guns, and tanks—he tells himself, "he would not think about that. That was not his business. That was Golz's business. He had only one thing to do and that was what he should think about and he must think it out clearly and take everything as it came along, and not worry" (9). The disturbing images of the weapons of human chaos spur him to immediate self-isolation. However, Hemingway promptly follows Jordan's introspection with images of nature, a counterpoising image of order to soothe his disturbance. Jordan looks to a stream, watches it tumbling down, then gathers the watercress he finds there. But even in this scene, as he lowers himself to get a drink, he must reposition his automatic pistol, his own weapon of war, to drink from the fountain of nature's order. Though he finds in nature a nurturance, an order his world lacks, Jordan's disconnection from that world remains ever-present. In both Jordan's thoughts of chaos and his initial view of the landscape surrounding the bridge, Hemingway purposefully removes his protagonist from any sense of correspondence with nature. In both scenes, nature may be first observed, but these passages end with the presence of society.

The disconnection is important, because this ties Jordan to the disconnection of Golz's world. When Jordan begins to grow fond of Anselmo, he forces himself to think,

> and that is not the way to think, he told himself, and there is not you, and there are no people that things must not happen to. Neither you nor this old man is anything. You are instruments to do your duty. There are necessary orders that are no fault of yours and there is a bridge and that bridge can be the point on which the future of the human race can turn. (43)

The important words here are "instruments" and "duty." In the mythology of Golz's society, humans are merely instruments, allowing no compassion. They serve only to do their duty, with connotations not of laws and orders, but of commands from a higher authority, which must be obeyed. Rena Sanderson notes that Golz points out that to blow the bridge is nothing; it must be blown at the right time. Therefore, "individual acts are meaningful only when coordinated with the acts of others."[13] For Golz, no man is an island only in reference to the actions which must be performed, not in any sense of the interconnections existing between people. Jordan accepts this ideology, and it reinforces not only the distance between himself and all of humanity, but between the human race and nature. In order to do the job he feels he must do, he must ignore any calls of bonding between himself and the world around him, human and natural.

Here, ecofeminism can help. Karen Warren posits that the main tenet of ecofeminism is the exploration of the connection between the domination of women and the domination of nature under the system of patriarchy.[14] As Francoise D'eaubonne writes in an essay at the inception of the philosophy of ecofeminism, "at the base of the ecological problem are found the structures *of a certain power*. . . . it is a problem of *men*; not only because it is men who hold world power [but] because . . . power is, at the lower level, allocated in such a way to be exercised by men over women."[15] Control of society has been seized by men, or more generally a system of patriarchal power, and men have used this power not only to differentiate themselves from women and nature, but to build a cultural framework that dominates them both. Ecofeminism contends that because of this, women are associated with nature, and many ecofeminists even embrace this idea and claim that women have a special access to nature that men have lost in their drive to become culture-centered.[16]

In *For Whom the Bell Tolls*, Golz serves as an archetype of patriarchy. Like the foreigner Hemingway speaks of in *Green Hills of Africa* who destroys the harmony of the natural world, the Russian Golz comes to Spain to help the Spanish kill each other. Any order of nature is irrelevant; the abstraction of which type of men will rule becomes the only good. Jordan acknowledges this, distancing himself from the precepts of the Communist ideology even while admiring the discipline—the order—they are trying to bring.[17] The successful man necessarily removes himself from any connections. As Jordan tells Golz when Golz offers to explain the attack Jordan will be assisting, "it is better not to know" (7). Ignorance in this ideology is bliss, because it absolves the sense of responsibility. Better not to know about attacks, the land, or the people you work with. Golz's preference for disconnection stretches to women as well. He advises Jordan to have many girls behind the lines. Jordan first thinks this would be a distraction, but later realizes Golz has "a good system of belief" (169). A whole life is lived in four days, the length of the mission, and then left behind. Again, the disconnection absolves responsibility, which leads to domination. Jordan, however, falls in love with his woman-behind-the-lines, Maria, in a way he knows is more than what Golz advises (169). And the effect of Maria moves the earth that holds his patriarchal foundations.

If Golz epitomizes the chaotic isolation of a patriarchal society, Maria shows Jordan an order of healing present in the natural world. The intentional self-imposed separation is a common trait of the Hemingway hero, but the hero also fights against it and seeks something more. To E. D. Lowry, "the Hemingway hero must learn, then, to detach himself from history and, accepting the normality of death, to surrender the successive personae forced upon him by his world."[18] Murray expands on this idea:

> The Hemingway hero . . . typically does not feel any transcendental blending of his soul with Nature, and his imagination is never such that he could see the fundamental laws of nature operating in the spring thaw at the railroad cut [as Thoreau does]. Yet some of the later Hemingway heroes do have transcendental leanings. Robert Jordan comes close to having spiritual kinship with the pine trees.[19]

To reach his near "spiritual kinship," Jordan has to "detach himself from history," literally to leave behind the dictates of society and adopt a new order. Both critics echo the observation of Sarah Unfried in her study of where Hemingway puts man in the natural order of the universe. For Unfried, Hemingway's works are a search for placement, a search for meaning in life. Not until Robert Jordan does Hemingway create a protagonist who finds space and love in the universe. Unfried connects the tolling of the bell not to the individual human, but to the bond that individual forges with the human race. Success comes, for Jordan, with "an understanding that the human race still survives and is linked to an ever-becoming unreachable something."[20] Jordan's success at reaching this state of transcendence is debatable, but for the progress he does make, Maria becomes his guide.

Like Jordan, Maria is pushed into self-isolation from the chaos of her society. Head shaved and repeatedly raped by soldiers, when Pablo's gang finds her she can barely speak or function. Just as Jordan psychologically removes himself from the people and places that surround him, Maria shuts down mentally as a means of defense, a means of staying alive. Rafael recalls that when the band first picked her up after they derailed the train, "she was very strange. . . . She would not speak and she cried all the time and if any one touched her she would shiver like a wet dog" (28). Maria admits she was "dead in my head with a numbness" (353), paralleling the emptiness Brian Way sees in Jordan. But once in the presence of nature, away from society, she begins to heal, evidenced by the progress of her hair's growth, and, with help from Pilar, learns to trust again. With the reestablished ability to trust, she forms connections with the band,

and especially with Jordan, and passes the desire for connection, healing, and responsibility to Jordan. As he realizes he's falling in love with her, Jordan thinks, "Maria was very hard on his bigotry. So far she had not affected his resolution but he would prefer not to die" (164). Though still beholden to his sense of duty, Jordan loses the sense that he and those around him are instruments. As Maria teaches him to care, he sees for the first time something more than the isolationist "duty" he's lived for. He tells Maria, "I have learned much from thee" (380). Just as Golz reinforces the value of disconnection, Maria awakens the need for connection and responsibility. Just as Golz preaches destruction, Maria promises the possibility of healing.

Again, if Golz represents the extreme archetype of patriarchal human society, men waging war under the shadow of chaos, Maria represents an extreme matriarchal nature, or the benevolent Mother Earth. Mimi Gladstein points out several ways that Hemingway uses imagery to connect Maria to nature: hair like "a grain field in the wind on a hillside" (23), various comparisons to animals like colts and rabbits, and most explicitly when Jordan feels "the long smoothness of her thighs against his and her breasts like two small hills that rise out of the long plain where there is a well, and the far country beyond the hills was the valley of her throat where his lips were" (341).[21] Maria is springtime—all youth, beauty, and fertility. And just as Hemingway's father taught him that the earth was at his disposal, Maria seems to exist only to please Robert Jordan. She tells him, "If thou should ever wish to change I would be glad to change. I would be thee because I love thee so. . . . I will be thee when thou art not there" (263). A. Robert Lee notes that it is not really love between Jordan and Maria, because "the transaction goes all one way, towards fulfilling Jordan's needs, not Maria's, his fantasy, not hers."[22] In opposition to Golz, who asks for Jordan's service under the command of duty and stresses the need for disconnection, Maria serves Robert Jordan and brings him to a reconnection with the people and the land he loves.

In *Hemingway: The Writer as Artist*, Carlos Baker frames *For Whom the Bell Tolls* as a series of concentric circles with the bridge at the center.[23] My reading of the text looks more like a line segment, with Robert Jordan at the center and the extreme masculine and feminine archetypes of Golz and Maria perched on the endpoints. This assumes the ideal Jordan enters the Hemingway-created Spain as a blank slate, or something close to it, and glides back and forth from one endpoint to the other. Between Jordan and the two extremes, however, lie two characters who mediate and confuse the archetypical gender roles. Golz and Maria offer an idealized version of disconnection and reconnection, of masculinity and femininity, that is both impossible and undesirable for Jordan

to attain. But Pilar and Anselmo, the in-between characters, mix traditional qualities of masculinity and femininity and provide Jordan with a
more real-world and honorable way to connect with his surroundings.

Of the two in-between characters, Anselmo is less associated with
nature. He seems to be more important to Jordan as an example of the
forging of some order in the chaos of war. Anselmo loves nature as
Hemingway loves nature: ideally through the sights of a rifle. He is
extremely proud of the hunting trophies he has gathered: the wolf pelts,
the ibyx horns, and, most intriguingly, the stuffed eagle "with his wings
spread, and eyes as yellow and real as the eyes of an eagle alive" (39).
Anselmo wants to possess nature, to have a dead eagle that appears alive,
but as Baker observes, Anselmo's "important function is to serve as a
yardstick of human values."[24] Anselmo remembers with pride killing a
bear, but says with "the killing of a man, who is a man as we are, there is
nothing good that remains" (40). This is the traditionally feminine aspect
of Anselmo's character: Of all the men in *For Whom the Bell Tolls*, he
expresses the only real compassion for the victims of his actions. He tells
Jordan he has killed men in the war, but "if I live later, I will try to live in
such a way, doing no harm to anyone, that it will be forgiven" (41). Since
he denies the existence of God, the reader is left to believe it is Anselmo
who must forgive Anselmo. His compassion is important enough for
Hemingway to have the narrator state directly, "Anselmo was a very good
man and whenever he was alone for long, and he was alone much of the
time, this problem of the killing returned to him" (196), as if to ensure we
will not miss this point. Thus, unlike Golz, Anselmo retains both masculine and feminine qualities, a man who kills other men for the cause, but
weeps into his beard after (435). Anselmo brings a healing order into the
chaotic world of the war and forces Robert Jordan to connect with the
people around him.

On the opposing end of the line segment is Maria. Though she undeniably has an effect on Jordan, placing Maria on the outer edges of the
For Whom the Bell Tolls universe is fitting because, as critic upon critic
has noted, her character is idealized to the point of unreality. Mimi
Gladstein blames the absence of humanity in general in Hemingway's
women characters on the correspondence Hemingway puts between
women and the earth, as has been shown in Maria's case. She writes,
"when woman becomes the symbol for the earth and the body, she loses
her individual humanity."[25] Robert W. Lewis, Jr. compares the love
between Hemingway's men and women to Tristan's quest for Iseult. He
asks, "Does the Tristan ever want a woman, or does he rather not simply
want an object—with a face, with a name, and with a body, of course, but
really, ultimately, without any individuality," a perfect description of

Maria. He concludes that Maria is "not meant to be 'real.' She is an image, a mythic woman much better than any real woman just as Jordan is an oversized hero, an epic lover and fighter."[26] Lewis, of all the critics, is perhaps the most forgiving of the character Maria,[27] but I want to argue here, as Mark Spilka does, that Maria becomes real for Jordan because of Pilar,[28] and that it is the more "realistic" androgynous qualities of Pilar that provide a bridge between Jordan and Maria, as well as between Jordan and nature.

Pilar's androgyny begins with her mixing of traditional male and female roles. After Pablo resentfully abdicates command of the band of guerrillas to Pilar, he sneers, "Now if you are a woman as well as a commander, that we should have something to eat" (59). This comment exemplifies the role-playing Pilar is performing. She does the duty of the traditional woman's job of cooking, which the men of the band expect from her and Maria. But Pablo's sarcastic remark shows that "woman" is not usually associated with "commander," so Pilar is obviously usurping a traditionally male role as well. She does so, too, with the support of the rest of the band. One of the brothers says, "To me the bridge means nothing . . . I am for the *mujer* of Pablo" (53), and he is echoed by the other brother and Rafael. The mission itself comes from an outsider, Robert Jordan, but the insider Pilar has used her authority to convince the men of the band to accept her fully in a masculine role.

Pilar's sexual androgyny has been much written about,[29] centering on Pilar's conversation with Maria after the visit to El Sordo's camp. Maria says, "it was thee explained to me there was nothing like that between us" (154). Pilar replies, "I love thee and he can have thee, I am no *tortillera* but a woman made for men . . . I do not make perversions" (155). As is, the reader senses a temptation that Pilar rejects. She has androgynous attractions to men and women, but chooses to be "a woman made for men." However, as Nancy Comley and Robert Scholes discovered, Hemingway's original draft emphasized Pilar's lesbian attraction even more strongly. For example, in the draft, Pilar's reply to Maria's statement quoted above is "there is always something like that," and then, "There is always something that should not be, and for me to find it now in me." But Hemingway cuts the last nine words and replaces them with, "but with me there is not. Truly there is not" (154–55). Hemingway left enough in the text to allude to Pilar's sexual androgyny, but what he removed shows even more revealingly the strength of the mixing of gender roles he had originally planned.

Pilar's paradoxical androgyny, her tempering of Golz and Maria, make her a more "realistic" earth symbol than Maria herself, because, as noted above, the nature of the earth is paradoxical. Sarah Unfried notes, "Pilar, like the earth, is a paradox of ugliness and beauty, brutality and gentleness, and femininity and masculinity."[30] Robert Gajdusek sees evidence of Pilar's paradoxical ability to link opposites when she equates her boredom with pine trees of the mountain and her love for deciduous trees, in which "each tree differs and there is character and beauty" (*FWBT*, 97). He feels it is Pilar's approach to nature that leads Robert Jordan "to accept the absolute *ever*green needles which, whatever their absoluteness, are nevertheless implicated in cycles and have *fallen* to be the base upon which he lies and on which he will die."[31] Maria may be Jordan's guide to the healing of nature, but the path that makes it accessible, like the path to Maria, goes through Pilar.

Thus, just as Golz and the chaotic society he represents affect the way Jordan views nature at the start of the novel, Maria and Pilar catalyze a shift to an appreciation for the order of nature. Herman Nibbelink points out that "most of the last half of the novel is devoid of extended description" until the last chapter.[32] This fast is broken with another description of the natural setting Jordan finds himself in, emphasizing the more frenetic pace of human affairs the novel has been concentrating on to this point and contrasting with the slower pace of the natural world. As at the start of the novel, in this passage we find both worlds as Hemingway highlights trees and roads, streams and bridges. But the two worlds seem closer to blending, or at least more awareness of the world of nature has become apparent to the narrator. Jordan focuses on the bridge, "straight and rigid across the gap, with the wooden sentry boxes at each end. But as he looked the structure of the bridge was still spidery and fine in the mist that hung over the stream" (431). The man-made effects are beginning to fade and take on less prominence; the bridge dissolves into the dewy character of the stream and looks less like an intrusion and more like a part of the natural landscape. As Jordan completes preparations for his ultimate act of chaos, the destruction of the bridge, the gunshot sounds of men disappear and he hears only the stream below. Wiring grenades, he looks down and sees a trout. Finishing the job, the paragraph ends not with the completion, but with Jordan looking "through the metal of the bridge, [and seeing] the sunlight on the green slope of the mountain. It was brown three days ago, he thought" (428). The chaotic actions of humanity are taking on less importance as he becomes closer to the natural world he has been inhabiting. Cycles of order, the coming of the new growth of grass, are becoming apparent and taking on a higher relevance than his own actions. The two worlds, though still separated, become more closely bound. And, unlike the opening scenes, here nature takes prominence as Hemingway first gives us the images of society, and then reverses Jordan's earlier perceptions and ends with the presence of nature.

But Jordan is still caught up in the chaotic force of history, swept along in the current of humanity. As just noted, in the final chapter Jordan becomes even more cognizant of nature and it begins to overwhelm him, taking on more importance than the job of destroying the bridge. Finally, in the last scene, Jordan reaches a union between the world of humanity and the world of nature:

> Robert Jordan saw them there on the slope, close to him now, and below he saw the road and the bridge and the long lines of vehicles below it. He was completely integrated now and he took a good long look at everything. Then he looked up at the sky. There were big white clouds in it. He touched the palm of his hand against the pine needles where he lay and touched the bark of the pine trunk that he lay behind. . . . Robert Jordan lay behind the tree, holding onto himself very carefully and delicately to keep his hands steady. He was waiting until the officer reached the sunlit place where the first trees of the pine forest joined the green slope of the meadow. He could feel his heart beating against the pine needle floor of the forest. (471)

When he was living in Montana, Jordan "worked summers on engineering projects and in the forest service building roads and in the park" (165). He worked to subdue the land, to make it more accessible and develop it into the world of civilization. Nibbelink feels, "Jordan sees nature from the point of view of the Montana nature lover that he is, yet he realizes that his immediate purpose is not to contemplate but to act, and to act destructively rather than creatively."[33] While I agree that throughout the novel Jordan is aware of nature, his awareness and attitude develop and increase over the course of the text. By the end, as he lies waiting to die, he finally can take the time to contemplate, if only because he is unable to act. But what sort of integration does he reach? There is a sense of nature-inspired peace in the passage, with the stimuli of nature overwhelming his senses to the point that his heartbeat itself becomes a part of the earth. But the integration he's reached comes only with his death. At the point Jordan has learned perhaps his greatest lesson, class is over. In addition, the notion of "duty" remains, as Jordan uses the physical beauty of the natural world as a sighting for one last killing. His last act condemns humanity to a fundamental separation between us and nature. His integration is not himself into the order of nature, but an assimilation of that order into the chaos of human society.

In this essay, I've used the terms chaos and order rather dogmatically. Order is good, chaos is bad. I think *For Whom the Bell Tolls* reflects this attitude, with nature assuming the role of healthy order and human society that of destructive chaos. This hard line stance prejudices against finding a merging point, a place where the two worlds can meet. The modern science of chaos theory tells us that to posit two fields of possibility, chaos and order, is too simplistic. Order can emerge from chaos, just as chaos can from order. Neither can rightly be termed good or bad, simply necessary.[34] Equally, as Victoria Davion points out, to confine ecofeminism to gender generalizations ignores the critique of gender implicit in feminism.[35] Men aren't all one way, women another. Perhaps the characters who most embody our contemporary ideas of shifting orders and genders are the two people Jordan himself seems to admire most in the novel: Anselmo and Pilar. Anselmo: the guide through nature, hunter and lover of animals, willing to kill men, but emotional to the point of sobbing after; Pilar: mystically tied to some natural order but believer in the Republic, leader and cook, willing to teach Maria the ways of women and kill men for the cause. The contradictory qualities of these characters embody the blend of chaos and order that chaos theory shows is present in nature. If Golz and Maria typify chaotic society and natural order, in Anselmo and Pilar Hemingway may get as close as he can to having characters integrated with nature and accepting both chaos and order. However, by forcing disconnection on his main character Hemingway seems to admit he sees no way to truly integrate the two worlds or get beyond the dualism constructed to house them. If he were writing now, maybe chaos theory would give him a way toward integration, but in *For Whom the Bell Tolls*, Hemingway is left to use the tools available and finds no place for chaotic humanity in the ordered world of nature.

NOTES

1. Donald Worster, "Nature and the Disorder of History," in *Reinventing Nature?: Responses to Postmodern Deconstruction*, eds. Michael E. Soulé and Gary Lease (Washington, D.C.: Island Press, 1995), 72.

2. Carlos Baker, *Ernest Hemingway: A Life Story* (New York: Charles Scribner's Sons, 1969), 9.

3. The possible effect of this contradiction may be seen in Hemingway's posthumously published novel, *The Garden of Eden* (New York: Scribner's, 1986). In this book, the narrator tells the story of a boy and his father hunting elephant in Africa and the boy's conflicting emotions at the tracking and killing of the creatures.

4. Michael Reynolds, "Hemingway's West: Another Country of the Heart," in *Blowing the Bridge: Essays on Hemingway and "For Whom The Bell Tolls,"* ed. Rena Sanderson (New York: Greenwood Press, 1992), 33.

5. Donald M. Murray, "Thoreau and Hemingway," *Thoreau Quarterly Journal* 11, no. 3–4 (1979): 15.

6. Baker, *Life Story*, 196 and 352.

7. Ernest Hemingway, *Green Hills of Africa* (New York: Scribner's, 1935), 248.

8. Glen A. Love, "Hemingway's Indian Virtues: An Ecological Reconsideration," *Western American Literature* 22 (November 1987): 203.

9. Mimi Reisel Gladstein, *The Indestructible Woman in Faulkner, Hemingway, and Steinbeck* (Ann Arbor, Mich.: UMI Research Press, 1986), 8.

10. Carlos Baker, *Hemingway: The Writer as Artist* (Princeton: Princeton University Press, 1972), 257.

11. Ernest Hemingway, *For Whom the Bell Tolls* (New York: Scribner's, 1940), 1. Subsequent references will be given as page numbers in the text.

12. Brian Way, "Hemingway the Intellectual: A Version of Modernism," in *Ernest Hemingway: New Critical Essays*, ed. A. Robert Lee (Totowa, N.J.: Barnes & Noble, 1983), 167–68.

13. Rena Sanderson, ed., introduction to *Blowing the Bridge: Essays on Hemingway and "For Whom the Bell Tolls"* (New York: Greenwood Press, 1992), 1.

14. Karen J. Warren, ed., introduction to *Ecological Feminism* (New York: Routledge, 1994), 1.

15. D'eaubonne, Francoise, "The Time for Ecofeminism," trans. Ruth Hottell, *Key Concepts in Critical Theory: Ecology*, ed. Carolyn Merchant, (N.J.: Humanities Press, 1994), 185.

16. Ynestra King, "Feminism and the Revolt of Nature," in *Key Concepts in Critical Theory: Ecology*, ed. Carolyn Merchant (N.J.: Humanities Press, 1994), 202.

17. Stephen Cooper, *The Politics of Ernest Hemingway* (Ann Arbor, Mich.: UMI Research Press, 1987), 106. However, though Jordan admires their efforts to bring order to what Anselmo calls "guerrilla discipline" (*FWBT*, 44), this order, like the utopian society of Marxism, remains a dream.

18. E. D. Lowry, "Chaos and Cosmos in *In Our Time*," *Literature and Psychology* 26 (1976): 109.

19. Murray, "Thoreau and Hemingway," 16.

20. Sarah P. Unfried, *Man's Place in the Natural Order: A Study of Hemingway's Major Works* (New York: Gordon Press, 1976), 1–2.

21. Gladstein, *The Indestructible Woman*, 68.

22. A. Robert Lee, "'Everything Completely Knit Up': Seeing *For Whom the Bell Tolls* Whole," in ed. A. Robert Lee, *Ernest Hemingway: New Critical Essays* (Totowa, N.J.: Barnes & Noble, 1983), 93–94.

23. Baker, *Writer as Artist*, 245–46.

24. Ibid., 244.

25. Gladstein, *The Indestructible Woman*, 8.

26. Robert W. Lewis, Jr., *Hemingway on Love* (Austin, Tex.: University of Texas Press, 1965), 8–9, 178.

27. For example, see Gerry Brenner, "Once a Rabbit, Always? A Feminist Interview with Maria," in *Blowing the Bridge: Essays on Hemingway and "For Whom the Bell Tolls,"* ed. Rena Sanderson (New York: Greenwood Press, 1992), 131–42.

28. Mark Spilka, *Hemingway's Quarrel with Androgyny* (Lincoln, Neb.: University of Nebraska Press, 1990), 250–51.

29. Nancy R. Comley and Robert Scholes, *Hemingway's Genders: Rereading the Hemingway Texts* (New Haven: Yale University Press, 1994), 48.

30. Unfried, *Man's Place*, 84.

31. Robert E. Gajdusek, "Pilar's Tale: The Myth and the Message," in *Blowing the Bridge: Essays on Hemingway and "For Whom the Bell Tolls,"* ed. Rena Sanderson (New York: Greenwood Press, 1992), 116.

32. Herman Nibbelink, "The Meaning of Nature in *For Whom the Bell Tolls,*" *Arizona Quarterly* 33 (1977): 170.

33. Ibid., 166.

34. For explanations of chaos theory accessible to the non-scientist, see John Briggs and F. David Peat, *Turbulent Mirror: An Illustrated Guide to Chaos Theory and the Science of Wholeness* (San Francisco: Harper and Row, 1989) and James Gleick, *Chaos: Making a New Science* (New York: Penguin Books, 1987). For applications of chaos theory to literature, see Harriet Hawkins, *Strange Attractors: Literature, Culture, and Chaos Theory* (New York: Prentice Hall, 1995) and N. Katherine Hayles, *Chaos Bound: Orderly Disorder in Contemporary Literature and Science* (Ithaca: Cornell University Press, 1990).

35. Victoria Davion, "Is Ecofeminism Feminist?" in *Ecological Feminism,* ed. Karen Warren (New York: Routledge, 1994), 17.

Moving Earth: Ecofeminist Sites in Hemingway's *For Whom the Bell Tolls* and Gellhorn's *A Stricken Field*

CECELIA KONCHAR FARR

"Tell me the landscape in which you live, and I will tell you who you are." This quote from Jose Ortega y Gassett prefaces Kathleen Norris's *Dakota*, an intermingling of life-writing, which generally centers on a person in time, with nature writing, centering on a person in space/place. A colleague and I have taken to calling this intermingling "ecobiography."[1]

Ecobiography, or what Norris has called "spiritual geography," is the notion that in "reading" our landscape, we construct selves.[2] Inherent in this concept is a certain relationship with place, a valuing of our interconnectedness with it, and an acknowledgment of the constructedness of both "self" and "nature." As a theorist of autobiographical fiction, I am fascinated by the possibilities of spiritual geography. How much does the exploration of place affect constructions of selfhood? How much does place influence *bios* and its tellings in fiction? These questions took on an added dimension as I drove to Ketchum for the International Hemingway Conference through the mountains and river valleys of Montana and Idaho. As I ran through the adjectives I would use to describe this land (rugged, grand, untamed), it struck me that many have been used to describe Ernest Hemingway. I couldn't help speculating about the nature of Hemingway's relationship to this place. Simply put, do we seek out landscapes that express our personalities, or do we create ourselves in harmony with our landscapes?

Both Hemingway and Martha Gellhorn, I believe, took on these questions in a pair of novels they wrote in 1939. Hemingway's *For Whom the Bell Tolls*, dedicated to Gellhorn, his (soon-to-be) third wife, begins and ends with Robert Jordan pressed against the Spanish earth. Gellhorn's *A Stricken Field*,[3] also about the human cost of military conquests, begins and ends with Mary Douglas viewing the Central-European landscape from above, on a plane. Displaced and expatriated, these two wandering war correspondent authors create suggestively autobiographical characters in these novels, characters whose relationship to place is central to plot development. In exploring Jordan's and Douglas's relationships to the land via the insights of ecofeminist criticism, I will explore ways in which, for these Midwestern writers, constructing foreign landscapes is also constructing character. To a lesser extent I also want to suggest that in constructing these characters, Hemingway and Gellhorn were constructing themselves.

Hemingway sets the stage for his novel in "Landscape with Figures,"[4] a story published in 1987 for the first time, though (most likely) written in 1938.[5] In the story a documentary film team observes the Spanish Civil War from a crumbling, bomb-blasted apartment building that serves "both as an observation post and as an advantage [sic] point to film from" (590). The "Old Homestead" is situated, apparently, on the side of a hill just above the battlefield, so there is a feeling of a panoramic landscape outside it. Because of this, and because the main characters are hidden away in the abandoned half-building filming the war, the story has a sense of detachment and distance, of watching a scene play out on a screen. As the main character, Edwin Henry (who shares Hemingway's initials, E. H.), watches this scene, he also initiates an American woman journalist ("the girl") into the harsh realities of the war playing out below her. "So that's war," she concludes disconsolately, after the battle gets a bit too close. "That's what I've come here to see and write about" (595).

Tellingly, Edwin calls the woman journalist "daughter," just as Hemingway called Martha Gellhorn "daughter" when she first arrived in Spain in 1937.[6] The two main characters seem very much like Hemingway and Gellhorn as they were in Spain early in 1937. The story also parallels Hemingway's work on the documentary film *The Spanish Earth*, a sympathetic view of the loyalists he would portray in *For Whom the Bell Tolls*. Autobiographical connections here are numerous, but are of questionable reliability or significance, as autobiographical connections to fiction tend to be. For the purpose of this study, however, it is clear that Hemingway, as he prepared to write *For Whom the Bell Tolls*, was hard at work on narratives of the Spanish Civil War, that he was making use of landscape in creative ways in these accounts, that he was (as usual) capitalizing on autobiographical details, and that he was working closely with Gellhorn, whom he saw as something of an apprentice. Gellhorn, if we are to believe the biographers, resented this characterization because she perceived their relationship as much more equal—two writers sharing what they knew.[7] Her characterization of their relationship is, not surprisingly, much more like the one Mary Douglas shares with her lover, John, the absent and equally independent fellow journalist in *A Stricken Field*.

By the beginning of *For Whom the Bell Tolls,* Hemingway has removed some of the distance between his main character and the war-torn landscape. Not watching from above like Edwin Henry, this main character, Robert Jordan, "lay flat on the brown, pine-needled floor of the forest . . . studying the country." The country, mountainous and rugged, split by a gorge and inhabited by counter-revolutionaries in rope-soled shoes, is not Hemingway's native landscape. In 1939 Hemingway had been long an expatriate, an expert, if you will, at reconstructing himself in different geographies. In this novel he uses this skill even more effectively than he does in his earlier novels, developing Jordan's character with constant direct reference to the land.

Indeed, nearly every chapter begins with a careful geographic orientation—the forest (Chapter One), "through the heavy timber to the cup-shaped end of the little valley" (Chapter Two), "through the pines of the steep hillside" to the bridge (Chapter Three), "down to the mouth of the cave" (Chapter Four), and so on. Early in the novel Jordan observes the land, as Edwin did in "Landscape with Figures," from behind field glasses. He is looking for airplanes, guards at the bridge, and the best places to detonate his dynamite. With his focus set clearly on his military operation, he sees the surrounding countryside as a challenge to his duty, to "blow the bridge at a stated hour based on the time set for the attack" (5). The first question he asks, as he lies prone on the floor of the forest, is about a constructed and not a natural landmark: "Is that the mill?" (1). This military consciousness (which General Golz emphasizes when he outlines the mission)[8] requires Jordan to detach himself not only from the land, but from the people there as well. They are to be mere figures on the militarized, constructed landscape. And, in the beginning of the novel, Jordan seems to acquiesce to this view. He spreads the military map on the floor of the forest and begins asking questions about the bridge.

By the end of the novel, a dying Robert Jordan has a different relationship to the land. Again lying prone, his elbows on the pine needles, this time he "was completely integrated" (471). When he "took a good long look at everything," everything does not include the bridge, the mill, the dam or even the oncoming enemy vehicles and soldiers. He "looked up at the sky. There were big white clouds in it. He touched the palm of his hand against the pine needles where he lay and he touched the bark of the pine trunk that he lay behind" (471). And when his heart beats, it beats against the floor of the forest, mingling his life with the life of the earth.

Clearly, there is something transcendent in this final scene, but there is also the meticulous development and manifestation of a human character in relationship to the earth. The Jordan we meet at the beginning of the novel, a native of Montana, is experienced in mountaineering, and "he knew from experience how simple it was to move behind the enemy lines in all this country" (4). He was experienced at negotiating this Spanish countryside. What, in the course of this final adventure, changes Robert Jordan's relationship with the earth? I suggest that the land changes when the earth moves—it is Maria who most influences Jordan's changed attitude toward the land.

Certainly the author's attitudes toward the land have been much noted, most helpfully for me in Glen Love's 1987 article on Hemingway's "Indian virtues."[9] In this essay, Love examines Hemingway's opposing modernist orientation and primitivist attitudes. Love notes that Hemingway's "unique brand of primitivism characteristically rejects those perceptions . . . which enable the actual primitive to exist in the sort of non-destructive relationship with his surroundings which Hemingway paradoxically admired and which left the country as he liked to find it."[10] Among the perceptions that he rejects are the interconnectedness of life, the harmonious sense of oneness with the world, and the acceptance of death as part of the flow of existence—all of which Robert Jordan embraces at the end of *For Whom the Bell Tolls*. This later Jordan is, per-haps, the one true primitive in a world of Hemingway sportsmen with notably different values.

Of course, many elements influence this innovative characterization of Jordan, among them the character's camaraderie and identification with the peasants and his self-examination through his philosophical conversa-tion with the dead Kashkin. Nothing, however, is so strong an influence as his relationship with Maria, the "little rabbit."

In their introduction to *Reweaving the World: The Emergence of Ecofeminism*, Irene Diamond and Gloria Feman Orenstein outline some of the basic assumptions of ecofeminism, including the contention that "because of women's unique role in the biological regeneration of the species, our bodies are important markers, the sites upon which local, regional, or even planetary stress is often played out."[11] In *For Whom the Bell Tolls*, Maria's body, bearing as it does the visible and invisible scars of the things done to her in the war, serves as a double for the ravaged land of Spain. In one passage near the end of the novel, Hemingway makes this relationship explicit:

> So now they were in the robe again together and it was late in the last night. Maria lay close against him and he felt the long smooth-ness of her thighs against his and her breasts like two small hills that rise out of the long plain where there is a well, and the far country beyond the hills was the valley of her throat where his lips were. (341)

In coming to understand and love Maria as he confesses he has never loved another woman, Jordan also comes to know himself as part of nature, "completely integrated" (471).

When they make love in the pivotal scene in the mountain meadow, nature and Maria are again coupled: "Then there was the smell of heather crushed and the roughness of the bent stalks under her head and the sun bright on her closed eyes and all his life he would remember the curve of her throat with her head pushed back into the heather roots" (159). When he joins with her in the "dark passage to nowhere, once again to nowhere, always and forever to nowhere," he is again lying prone, "heavy on the elbows in the earth to nowhere." He feels, then, "the earth move out and away from under them" and he is changed. "Then he was lying on his side, *his* head deep in the heather, smelling it and the smell of the roots and the earth and the sun came through it and *it was scratchy on his bare shoulders and along his flanks*" (159) [my emphasis]. Unlike the times before this when Jordan lay against the earth, this time he is part of it. This time he is in the moment, not looking forward to the bridge or backward to his father's suicide. This encounter is with Maria *and with the earth,* which, for him, has "truly never" moved before (160).

The change that comes over Robert Jordan, then, is a change in his orientation both to women and to landscape. He drops the field glasses, drops the futile strategizing, and comes to what ecofeminists would call a "new, more complicated experiential ethic of ecological interconnectedness."[12] Karen Warren, in a definitive essay for ecofeminism, describes this ethic as "conceptualist."[13] It involves, she writes,

> a shift *from* a conception of ethics as primarily a matter of rights, rules, or principles predetermined and applied in specific cases to entities viewed as competitors in the contest of moral standing [as General Golz's military ethics] *to* a conception of ethics as growing out of . . . relationships conceived in some sense as defining who one is.[14]

Relationships in this ethical shift are then based on an attitude of "loving perception" rather than "arrogant perception," she explains, an attitude where difference is acknowledged and valued rather than erased.[15] Jordan's shift from an arrogant to loving perception of nature, then, grows out of his awareness of difference from Maria and his (apparently new) willingness to acknowledge reciprocity in his relationship with her. After all, the earth moves for both of them, and he seems to need Maria's love just as she does his.

This change in Jordan is difficult for him to find language for: "All right. He would write a book when he got through with this. But only about the things he knew, truly, and about what he knew. . . . The things he had come to know in this war were not so simple" (248). I suggest that, rather, the things he had come to know *were* simple, but the complexities of his language and his traditionally masculine experiences up to that point had mediated against his telling them. What he learned was simply a basic tenet of ecofeminism, a concept that many women, allied with exploited Mother Earth in war and in Western philosophical tradition, have been forced to know—that "because human life is dependent on the earth, our fates are intertwined."[16] Joined in a relationship of reciprocity with Maria, Jordan stumbles into a transformational relationship with the earth.

I am unwilling to postulate that Hemingway himself had such a transformational experience with the earth or with Gellhorn and used it as fodder for his novel. But I will posit that the intensity of his newly-developing relationship with Gellhorn, a professional writer who insisted more on their mutual independence and on the reciprocity of their relationship than did his previous wives and lovers, surely contributed to his insights. Because Gellhorn and Hemingway were, as these novels were produced, living and writing together, it is not difficult to locate the influence they had on each other in their texts—from shared language (the unusual use of the word "rare") and phrases ("not politically developed")[17] to shared ideas.

The notions of the interconnectedness of all life and of the complicity of our philosophical and political systems to keep that knowledge from us are key to Martha Gellhorn's *A Stricken Field* as well. Both novels focus on place as a critical locus of character development. And, much as Edwin Henry and Robert Jordan are semi-autobiographical characters, so, too, is Mary Douglas for Martha Gellhorn. Years later Gellhorn acknowledged this, writing in her Afterword to the Virago edition that she "disliked [her]self for taking a fictionalized share" in the tragedy of the story (312). She also confessed in a private correspondence that she felt somewhat "ashamed" of the depiction of herself in *A Stricken Field*.[18]

When Gellhorn met Hemingway in 1936, she was, in her late twenties, already a published fiction writer and journalist. *A Stricken Field* was to be her second novel, a novel that came out of her experience as a European correspondent for *Collier's* from 1937–39, a novel that would express her outrage at the rise of fascism and the incursion of Hitler into central Europe. *A Stricken Field* ends with a less intimate connection to the land than Jordan's at the end of *For Whom the Bell Tolls*, one more reminiscent of "the girl's" view in "Landscape with Figures." Crossing the border from Germany to France, Mary Douglas

> stared down at the neat fields, brown and green, purple brown, yellow. There were the white roads and the white farmhouses and the

pompons of the trees. But the land doesn't look any different, she thought. The land doesn't look different at all. (302)

Because they had entered occupied territory, the narrator explains, they expected "some change in the land to equal the change on the map. There was nothing to see" (3).

Using the same technique as Hemingway does in *For Whom the Bell Tolls*, Gellhorn places her character in the same place for the opening and closing of the novel and repeats the same phrase, "The land doesn't look any different" as Hemingway repeats the phrase about Jordan lying on the "pine-needled floor of the forest." This serves to locate the earth as a constant, highlighting the character's changes. It also serves to link the characters' development directly with the landscape.

The voices of both main characters mirror their authors in passionate political commitment and involvement in the intricacies of pre-World War II Europe. But the green, sun-drenched fields of *For Whom the Bell Tolls* are not to be found in Gellhorn's novel, which is dominated by wet, grey urban landscapes of occupied Prague as in this passage:

> Smeary gray sky rimmed the flat land. There were no trees and the untended fields spread mud-brown, rough and wet around a huge building that might have been a factory or a prison, gray like the sky, with small black windows and rain-streaked walls. Mary could see nothing green or growing, no one moving, and the great, square building rose high and empty from the silent empty land. (73)

Crowds of refugees and lost children wander muddy roads and huddle in warehouses, as apathetic journalists commiserate in smoke-filled hotel lobbies. The city is "cold and shabby" (11), lined with "cement-gray houses" (4) and filled with "gray and empty" people (13). In the midst of this bleak landscape are two women characters, Mary, the American journalist, and Rita, a German refugee.

To the other journalists, Rita is also nondescript, one of "five thousand others" with similar stories. To them, she looks "Like nothing. . . . Like a she-communist" (29). But as Rita leads Mary through Prague, each site removes Mary further from the other journalists, each venue leaves her progressively with less pretense of journalistic objectivity. She becomes increasingly frustrated with her role as detached observer and, by the end of the novel, inspired by her relationship with Rita, she joins in the refugees' struggle. Gellhorn replicates this "conceptualist" ethical involvement in the narrative style of the novel by mingling Mary's voice with Rita's, and sometimes shifting point-of-view from the two women to the children, to Peter, another refugee and Rita's partner, and even to a German soldier. Though Mary's story remains central, this unconventional shifting from her perspective reinforces the theme of interconnectedness and the sense of "loving perception" of others and of the land.

But while Jordan's changing character is tied directly to the land as we have viewed it (rather narrowly) in ecocriticism, Mary's transformational connection to place comes by way of a revealing twist in the plot of Gellhorn's novel. Gellhorn moves away from wilderness—from rivers and pine-needled forests, from broad views and rural landscape—into a tiny, urban, domestic space.

Because the main characters of the novel are displaced and wandering, they are, as Gellhorn carefully repeats, homeless. From the reporters who, like Gellhorn and Hemingway, move from hotel to hotel as they follow tragedy across Europe, to the refugees, forced from their farms, deprived of their land, these characters are a study in loss. One scene, made even more moving by historical perspective, has a group of young refugees (some who had never been away from home before the previous week when soldiers drove them out) scanning "a geography book, a school text, dog-eared, and with soiled pages, open at a map of the world," looking for a safe country to go to, a new homeland (58). Most of their real-life counterparts, we know now, died in their own homeland in concentration camps.

Gellhorn's narrative seems to redirect, slightly but significantly, the emphasis on place that is central to both novels. Given the human connection to landscape and the interconnectedness of life, Gellhorn seems to ask, how does the lack or loss of place affect character development? In this novel, politics change, borders shift, people starve, are separated from their families, die. But the rural landscape is unchanged. Instead of the nurturing motherland of Hemingway's novel, this landscape takes on the characteristics of the "lucky" countries such as Britain, France, and the U.S., which were, Mary Douglas discovers, bent on ignoring what was happening in central Europe in 1938. This Czechoslovakian land, now German, won't acknowledge border changes or political wind shifts. It won't change because the people who once lived on it are gone.

The novel follows Mary as she watches Rita respond to this disruption. Mary's transformational relationship, the one that the plot turns on and that parallels Jordan's with Maria in the Spanish country, is with Rita in the intimate space of the shabby apartment Rita shares with Peter. Rita is perpetually a refugee from her native Germany, an early prison camp survivor, robbed by politics of her family (her father, also a refugee, lives penniless in Greece, and her mother and brother are dead). Rita has no homeland in this novel, and she has no freedom. Timid, she looks over her shoulder constantly. Gellhorn portrays her hiding, running, seeking safe spaces for herself and others. Rita's task, then, is to create a concept of place for the displaced, to make a space in this wretched urban landscape for herself.

Rita's apartment becomes that place, and represents a broadening of the concept of "landscape." Furnished with bookcases made from packing boxes, chairs on loan from the Socialist Club, and a bedspread made from discarded parade banners, it is the single location in the novel where hope enters. Rita fills it with connotation the first time she utters the word "home" to Mary early in the novel, "bringing it out as if it were a rare word, and one that she wanted Mary to hear" (17). Mary catches the undercurrent:

> They shook hands and Mary waited a moment, watching Rita weave through the crowds in her hurry to get home. Home, Mary repeated to herself, hearing Rita's voice again. Then she walked up the street towards the fish restaurant, to dinner, to meet again her odd portable world, but she no longer noticed the muted people around her. She thought: Rita's not a refugee anymore. It's finished. She's lost that floating, empty-hearted look they have. She's happy. That's the same thing as having a country, anyhow. (17–18)

Gellhorn here makes the connection that allows Rita's domestic space to function as the equivalent of Jordan's Spanish landscape. Though in the end this home, too, proves temporary, torn apart by the presence of German soldiers who torture Peter to death, the idea of "home" has a hold on both Mary and Rita.

Indeed, being in Rita's apartment changes both Rita and Mary. There Rita becomes more confident, smiling, with an air of privilege. Mary becomes dreamy, connecting the idea of home tentatively to marriage and to John: "We aren't like that, we'll never be settled," she thinks. But adds, "Maybe marriage was also for absence: if she were married she could now say, 'My husband John thinks . . .'" She looked at Rita and Peter, and practiced saying it silently, with delight" (87). In this space, with Peter and Rita, Mary's voice becomes plural: "They're just like us, Mary thought. They love each other the same way" (88).

"Home" here, however, is not conceptually similar to the carpeted suburban retreat of our family-values rhetoric. "Rather, it is the place," in Judith Plant's theory of bioregionalism, "where we can learn the values of caring for and nurturing each other and our environments and of paying attention to immediate human needs and feelings."[19] It is, in effect, a training ground for the ethics of caring, of loving perception and of transformational, rather than dominating, relationships. Gellhorn is careful not to give this home any of the trappings of Western consumer society. It becomes, then, a landscape, an ecofeminist location. Plant writes:

> One of the key values of bioregionalism [and of ecofeminism] is the decentralization of power: moving further and further toward self-governing forms of social organization. The further we move in this direction, the closer we get to what has traditionally been thought of as "woman's sphere"—that is, home and its close surroundings.[20]

Peter's behavior toward Rita in the apartment reinforces the notion that home, in this novel, represents not conservatism and tradition but a radical shift in social organization. Here Peter plays a nurturing role, caring for, cooking for and comforting his lover. Visiting the apartment, Mary notices first Peter's "narrow light body" and sees his gentleness, and that he clearly "loved Rita very much" (85). His behavior contrasts sharply with the behavior of the other men in the novel—the gruff, jaded reporters and, especially, the military men who kill him in the novel's most brutal, disturbing passage. Gellhorn uses the military as Hemingway used Golz—as a foil to establish, in opposition, the central values of the novel. In the torture scene the commanding officer corrects his inferior for showing sympathy for Peter: "You make a mistake. We are not dealing with people. This man does not exist. He is a thing, a message in code. He has certain information and we must extract it" (267).

Thus, the invocation of the idea of home undergirds the novel's anti-imperialist values, highlights its sympathy for the oppressed refugees, establishes "loving perception" of others as paramount, and clarifies character development in the same way as For Whom the Bell Tolls—by carefully delineating a concept of place for its main characters. This ecofeminist use of place also invites critics to come down from the mountains and make use of ecocritical concepts indoors, in the urban and domestic spaces most people occupy in everyday life.

I would add one more tentative autobiographical observation—that, clearly, the character of Mary Douglas is inspired by Gellhorn's own experiences, which, on the surface, seem to parallel quite closely Mary's in Spain and Czechoslovakia. Gellhorn, too, had left behind a lover, a fellow reporter, in Spain. She would marry Hemingway two years later, but before she did she established a home for them at Finca Vigía, in Cuba. Soon after she returned to the U.S. from Prague, she left her family to join Hemingway in Cuba. There, according to one biographer, without Hemingway's help and "Using her own money, Gellhorn went ahead, hiring painters, a carpenter, two gardeners, and cook."[21] She made what was, by all accounts, a lovely home in Finca Vigía, but soon left to travel and work again. After she and Hemingway divorced in 1945, Gellhorn continued to live in her "portable world," and, over the years, established homes in Africa, Mexico, Wales, and England. Since she left her family home in St. Louis to attend Bryn Mawr in 1926, she has spent her life traveling, a citizen of the world. She now lives in Wales, and "pictures herself as part of a 'global fellowship' of people fighting for the well-being of the earth and of its most vulnerable citizens."[22]

Thus, like Gellhorn, Mary seems both connected to and detached from the land she observes in her travels. While she does view the landscape from a distance at the beginning and end of the novel, she has also established an intimate bond, similar to Jordan's, with a place and its people. And because of this, she is changed. She has left behind her journalistic ethic, the mandate that "I'm only supposed to write, I'm only supposed to tell what happens, I'm not supposed to do things. Oh, and not for friends, not supposed to take care of friends either" (235).

Foregrounding, as these two novels do, an ethic of interconnectedness and caring located in both natural and domestic spaces, they are a fertile field for ecofeminist analysis. In them, Hemingway and Gellhorn intermingle landscape and life in ecobiographies of compelling, at least semi-autobiographical characters who affirm that by "telling" the landscape in which we live, we, indeed, construct ourselves.

NOTES

1. Phillip A. Snyder, of Brigham Young University, and I first used the term "ecobiography" in "From Walden Pond to the Great Salt Lake: Ecobiography and Engendered Species Acts in *Walden* and *Refuge*," a cowritten essay published in *Essays on Contemporary Mormon Literature*, ed. Eugene England and Lavina Fielding Anderson (Salt Lake City, Utah: Signature Books, 1995).

2. Kathleen Norris, *Dakota: A Spiritual Geography* (Boston: Houghton Mifflin, 1993).

3. Throughout this paper I will be citing from Ernest Hemingway, *For Whom the Bell Tolls* (New York: Scribner's, 1940) and from Martha Gellhorn, *A Stricken Field* (1940; reprint, New York: Penguin/Virago, 1986). For both works subsequent references will be given as page numbers in the text.

4. Hemingway's "Landscape with Figures" was first published in *The Complete Short Stories of Ernest Hemingway*, the Finca Vigía Edition (New York: Scribner's, 1987), 590–96. Subsequent references will be given as page numbers in the text.

5. Publisher's note to "Landscape with Figures," 590.

6. Carlos Baker, *Ernest Hemingway: A Life Story* (New York: Scribner's, 1969), 304.

7. Baker, *Life*, 304f and Carl Rollyson, *Nothing Ever Happens to the Brave: The Story of Martha Gellhorn* (New York: St. Martin's, 1990), 108f.

8. I am indebted to my colleague Rod Romesburg, University of California, Davis, for his observations on how Golz's values counterpoint the influence of Maria in the novel.

9. Glen A. Love, "Hemingway's Indian Virtues: An Ecological Reconsideration" in *Western American Literature*, 22.3 (November 1987): 201–13.

10. Ibid., 203.

11. Irene Diamond and Gloria Feman Orenstein, introduction to *Reweaving the World: The Emergence of Ecofeminism* (San Francisco: Sierra Club, 1990), x.

12. Ibid., xi.

13. Karen Warren, "The Power and Promise of Ecological Feminism," *Environmental Ethics* 12 (Summer 1990): 125–46.

14. Ibid., 141.

15. Ibid., 137.

16. Diamond and Orenstein, *Reweaving the World*, xii.

17. Hemingway, *For Whom the Bell Tolls*, 425; Gellhorn, *A Stricken Field*, 93.

18. Letter to the author from Gellhorn, 10 October 1991.

19. Judith Plant, "Search for Common Ground: Ecofeminism and Bioregionalism" in *Reweaving the World: The Emergence of Ecofeminism*, ed. Irene Diamond and Gloria Feman Orenstein (San Francisco: Sierra Club, 1990), 160.

20. Ibid.

21. Rollyson, *Nothing Ever Happens to the Brave*, 138.

22. Rollyson, 207 facing page.

Hemingway's Gentle Hunters: Contradiction or Duality?

CHARLENE M. MURPHY

From "Big Two-Hearted River" and Nick Adams' care in handling the trout too small to keep to Thomas Hudson's empathy for the creatures he has shot, Hemingway's writing reveals a reverence for nature and a sensitivity that may seem to present a dichotomy when combined with the undeniable part of Hemingway that was the exuberant big-game hunter. This sensitivity concerns not only the living creatures who are prey for the hunter and fisherman but the land itself. The ambivalence of Hemingway's hunters reflects the work of one of Hemingway's favorite painters, Winslow Homer.

From the start of his writing career, Hemingway was keenly aware of man's destruction of the natural environment, and he repeatedly returned to this theme for at least thirty years. In "Game-Shooting in Europe," a 1923 piece for the *Toronto Daily Star*, Hemingway explains "the reason for the continued existence of game in good numbers" in Europe while "game is rapidly being exterminated" in much of the United States. "It is careful protection, rigidly enforced closed seasons, and the fact of government-owned forests, which are really farmed for timber rather than cut over and denuded of trees. Indiana was once a timber country. So was the Lower Peninsula of Michigan. Today there is hardly a patch of virgin timber in the Upper Peninsula of Michigan."[1]

Logging is mentioned (in "iceberg" fashion) in several of the early stories in *In Our Time* ("Indian Camp," "The Doctor and the Doctor's Wife," and "The End of Something"). It is a pervasive activity in young Nick's environment. Likewise, Thomas Hudson in *Islands in the Stream* remembers how, when he was young, he nearly drowned under the logs from the sawmill on the Bear River.[2] Hudson's childhood memories seem related to the experiences of the young Nick Adams, not only in the earliest stories but also in "Fathers and Sons" and especially in the unfinished "The Last Good Country."

In "Fathers and Sons," written in 1932, Nick remembers the logs left "in the woods to rot. . . . It was only the bark they wanted for the tannery

[165]

at Boyne City. . . . and each year there was less forest and more open, hot, shadeless, weed-grown slashing."[3] Hemingway drew the picture in more detail twenty years later as Nick and Littless "go through some bad slashings" in "The Last Good Country."[4] "Damn slashings," Littless says. "I hate them. . . . And the damn weeds are like flowers in a tree cemetery if nobody took care of it" (516). When they get beyond the slashings to the woods that are "all the virgin timber left around here," Nick says "This is the way forests were in the olden days. This is about the last good country there is left" (516). To Nick this "last good country" is like a "cathedral" (517). Nick's feelings in these stories mirror Hemingway's own as he comforted his very ill youngest son Gregory in 1942 by "telling wonderful stories about his life up in Michigan as a boy . . . and how beautiful the virgin forests were before the loggers came."[5]

In *Green Hills of Africa* (1935), Hemingway explains the costs of the exploitation of a natural environment.

> A continent ages quickly once we come. The natives live in harmony with it. But the foreigner destroys, cuts down the trees, drains the water, so that the water supply is altered and in a short time the soil, once the sod is turned under, is cropped out and, next, it starts to blow away as it has blown away in every old country."[6]

Such perceptions were still strong in 1947 when he wrote to William Faulkner about living away from the United States: "My own country gone. Trees cut down. Nothing left but gas stations, sub-divisions where we hunted snipe on the prairie, etc."[7]

From his fiction to nonfiction, and even in his personal correspondence, Hemingway is concerned with the preservation of the natural world.[8] Jack Hemingway, who has labored on behalf of environmental issues himself, describes the "sportsman" and "conservationist" Ted Trueblood as a man "who clearly understood the relationship which allows a man to hunt and fish for a prey he loves, a relationship that eventually leads him to give his best efforts toward preserving intact the natural habitats those species need to survive."[9]

Could we apply this statement, at least in part, to Ernest Hemingway? Analysis of his writing lends credence to such a view. In addition to those passages already cited, there is considerable evidence throughout his work. For instance, in *Islands in the Stream*, Thomas Hudson remembers how his son Tom slept with the first bird he shot, loving that which he had killed—as Davy loves the broadbill and Santiago the marlin. In spite of all those animal trophies on the wall at the Finca, Hemingway's writing and correspondence reveal a man who was thoughtful about the animals he killed, a man who hunted and fished for a prey he loved and respected.

A passage from *For Whom the Bell Tolls* seems especially instructive here. While Robert Jordan says he doesn't like to kill animals, Anselmo catalogs the animals he has hunted and the many hides and horns and so on that adorn his home, which gave him "great pleasure to contemplate."[10] The paw of the bear he killed brought him "pride of remembrance of the encounter with the bear" (40). Hemingway, too, liked to remember the encounter, and he did not kill thoughtlessly. In a 1936 letter to Maxwell Perkins, Hemingway wrote from the Nordquist Ranch in Wyoming that on a recent hunt for "Grizzlies," he got two. "They were beautiful to meet in the timber that way. . . . I could have killed the three I think but they were so damned handsome I was sorry I killed more than one but at the time did not have much time to decide."[11] Mary Hemingway, in an interview with Denis Brian, supports this view that the encounter is more important than killing numerous animals. "A great deal of the hunting was the pleasure of walking through African bush or Idaho sagebrush. . . . It was certainly not killing that engaged him. . . . we passed up a great many animals who were just too sweet to shoot."[12]

In a 1933 letter to Bruce Bliven, Hemingway responded to criticism of his description of the brave bull in *Death in the Afternoon*, fiercely defending the truthfulness of his portrayal.[13] The writer who understood that a Spanish fighting bull could be brave also knew of the native American belief that the bear is man's brother (see *For Whom the Bell Tolls*, 40). There is a respect for animals in Hemingway, an admiration, and a sensitivity toward their suffering. The narrator of *Green Hills of Africa* relates how his own pain from a broken arm caused him to identify with the suffering of a bull elk that might not be shot cleanly (148). In "The Short Happy Life of Francis Macomber," Hemingway even employs the lion's point of view. As a hunter, Macomber is faulted because he doesn't stop to consider what the lion is thinking. Littless, in "The Last Good Country," feels sorry for the birds her brother has just shot because "They were enjoying the morning just like we were" (540). Nick is happy with the kill because he has been concerned with giving his sister enough to eat. He tries, though, to take only what he needs, as was demonstrated earlier in his frustration when he hooked the trout that was large for the skillet and "pretty big for Littless and me." He realizes, however, that he has hurt the trout and will "have to kill him"(530).

In an article published in 1993, I stated that Thomas Hudson's sensitivity toward nature had grown as his mission in the final section of *Islands* drew him closer toward his death. I believe that in spite of Hemingway's well-publicized enthusiasm for the challenge of the hunt, his own sensitivity toward nature was often revealed in his work. I think that Hemingway's complex response to the natural world partly explains the affinity he felt for the work of Winslow Homer[14] and that a comparison of excerpts from Hemingway's writing with a number of Homer's paintings suggests that the writer and painter shared similar concerns in regard to both living creatures and the landscape itself. A recognition of the correspondences may provide a better understanding of apparent contradictions in Hemingway's attitude toward the natural world as well as further insight into how he wrote. This is not to suggest that Hemingway chose to write about certain subjects merely because Homer painted them or that Hemingway hadn't carefully observed similar scenes himself, but that Homer's paintings were probably useful to Hemingway in a variety of ways. For example, as documented in my previous article on Homer's influence on the writing of *Islands in the Stream*, it is clear that personal photographs as well as reproductions of great paintings were visual aids for the writer. There is documentation for thematic correspondences as well. Of course, Emily Stipes Watts, in *Ernest Hemingway and the Visual Arts*, has described the extensive influence of several visual artists on Hemingway's work.[15]

According to American art expert Helen Cooper, Winslow Homer depicted "the callous rape of the land" in numerous paintings.[16] Several of these, such as *Hudson River*, portrayed logging scenes on the river while others depicted hunters in a landscape where trees have been cut, peeled, burned, or otherwise destroyed. A comparison of the first draft of "Fathers and Sons" with the revised version suggests that Hemingway, like Homer, was intent on depicting the "rape of the land." While the first-person narrator of the opening paragraph in the handwritten draft notes "the forest on both sides" and "much more forest than I had thought there would be,"[17] Nick Adams in the published version of the story describes only "the second-growth timber on both sides" (369). Second growth, of course, is that which follows the destruction of virgin forest. Homer's series on "the death of the great woods"[18] seems especially relevant to "Fathers and Sons" and "The Last Good Country." "Hudson River" and the devastatingly powerful *Huntsman and Dogs* are reproduced in Forbes Watson's book on Winslow Homer, a book in Hemingway's collection at the Finca.[19]

Forbes Watson's book on Homer also contains a reproduction of *Right and Left*, an oil painting of two ducks shot in midair at the moment of impact. In my 1993 article, I indicated a correspondence between *Right and Left* and the birds Thomas Hudson sees while chasing Germans and the birds he shot when he hunted as a boy with his father. The older Hudson "could not feel the same about them now and he had no wish to kill them ever"(417). Homer scholar David Tatham explains that the "vantage point" of the painting "is that of the hunted rather than the hunter."[20]

Winslow Homer, *Huntsman and Dogs*
Courtesy of Philadelphia Museum of Art: The William L. Elkins Collection

Winslow Homer, *Right and Left*
Courtesy of National Gallery of Art: Gift of the Avalon Foundation

In *Islands*, when the mortally wounded Hudson says about his injury, "It doesn't hurt any worse than things hurt that you and I have shot together" (462), he seems to share Homer's vantage point,[21] a perspective also shared by the narrator of "The Short Happy Life of Francis Macomber," the author of *Death in the Afternoon* and *Green Hills of Africa*, and Littless and Nick in "The Last Good Country."

In writing about Homer's Adirondacks watercolors of fish and deer hunting themes, Helen Cooper points out that "these share certain concerns, principally Homer's profound admiration for the nervous, shy vitality of the creatures, and the poignancy of their deaths at the hand of man."[22] Such paintings are represented in Watson's book, and Cooper's words may remind us of Nick's responsibility to kill the trout he hurt and his sorrow at having killed the buck which he only intended to crease. "He felt awful about trying to crease it in the first place" (527).

The large trout that Nick catches in "The Last Good Country" is described in much more detail than any of the trout in "Big Two-Hearted River," and the description seems identical to a vivid Homer watercolor:

> and Nick saw how dark his back was and how brilliant his spots were colored and how bright the edges of his fins were. They were white on the edge with a black line behind and then there was the lovely golden sunset color of his belly. (530)

Not surprisingly, revisions in the manuscript for "The Last Good Country" reveal Hemingway's crafting of this watercolor in prose,[23] so close in detail to Homer's *Leaping Trout*.

Undeniably, Hemingway had already observed hundreds of leaping trout himself, but he also spent a great deal of time looking at paintings, and he claimed to learn from them. As he told George Plimpton, "I learn as much from painters about how to write as from writers. . . . They were a part of learning to see, to hear, to think, to feel and not feel, and to write."[24] Learning to see? To see that the edges of the trout's fins were not only bright but specifically white "with a black line behind" when you looked more closely? And perhaps a painting suggested the essential details for conveying the feeling of the way it was. Perhaps Homer's paintings only helped the writer to remember more fully what he had seen for himself—perhaps.

Three of Homer's major subjects—fishing, deer hunting, and the destruction of forests—receive significant treatment in "The Last Good Country." Though "The Last Good Country" was left unfinished, it seems clear that the story continues some of the themes begun in several earlier works, themes strongly connected to the work of Winslow Homer and which have a close identification with the natural world.

Ernest Hemingway was raised by a sportsman who taught him to love hunting and fishing, but he was also lectured "on the needless destruction of harmless animals" when he and a friend killed a porcupine that had tangled (in self-defense) with a neighbor's dog. According to Carlos Baker, "Having shot it . . . they were now obliged" to cook and eat the porcupine.[25] The lesson was obviously internalized as Hemingway later instructed his own young son Jack, "Never waste fish, Schatz, it's criminal to kill anything you aren't going to eat."[26] This respect for the proper use of nature is present in Hemingway's earliest writings. Yet, as he wrote to Bruce Bliven, "My father, my grandfather, and my great-grandfather were all hunters and fishermen and it is impossible for people who do not care to hunt or to fish to realize how those who do feel about it. I have tried to be very honest about those feelings and to make good pictures of those things but people care very little for the truth."[27]

If we look carefully at the pictures made of those things in *A Farewell to Arms* and *For Whom the Bell Tolls*, we see that hunting is associated with gentle, thoughtful people, good people, people who are deeply troubled by the killing of men. The priest, whose "father is a famous hunter," invites Frederic to visit his family in the Abruzzi where "there is good hunting" and "the birds are all good because they fed on grapes" and the peasants warmly welcomed hunters to their homes.[28] Though Frederic is offered this opportunity for a holy communion with nature, he instead spends his leave with women whose names he doesn't know, reality dulled by a nearly constant state of drunkenness. In *For Whom the Bell Tolls*, Anselmo's village may once have been as idyllic as the priest's Capracotta in the Abruzzi. After the war Anselmo encourages Robert Jordan to come to his village, where everyone hunts, but Jordan has no desire to kill animals (39). Anselmo later reflects, "How could the Inglés say that the shooting of a man is like the shooting of an animal? In all hunting I have had an elation and no feeling of wrong" (442). Of course, as indicated earlier, the older Thomas Hudson, in *Islands*, feels differently. Is this because Hudson was created by an older Hemingway and Anselmo by a younger man?

Other scholars have noted a changing attitude toward hunting in the aging Hemingway. Rose Marie Burwell cites both biographical and manuscript evidence to support her view that Hemingway had lost his desire to kill animals by 1953.[29] Glen Love quotes from Hemingway's own hunting article "The Shot" to indicate a change in thinking by 1951.[30] While I agree that the older Hemingway, like the older Thomas Hudson, exhibited a deeper sensitivity in his dealings with living creatures in the natural world, I also believe that sensitivity was long there and became most apparent as the man matured. Examples already cited from the work and the life suggest that even the younger Hemingway questioned the killing and often responded empathetically to the animal's point of view.

Winslow Homer himself conveyed the complexity of the outdoorsman's relationship to the natural world in many paintings. As Nicolai Cikovsky, Jr., points out, while Homer painted "guides, hunters, trappers, woodsmen—often with heroic strength and dignity and in some solemn moments of communion with the land in and from which they lived," he also portrayed the underside, the cruelty and destruction inflicted by man upon the natural environment.[31] Sometimes this duality is apparent in a single painting. "After the Hunt," reproduced in Forbes Watson's book, is a good example of Homer's complex vision in this regard. While the painting is one in a series on the violent hounding of deer, the old hunter is depicted as capable, gentle, and respectful of nature in his handling of the dog completing its part in the process.[32] In the background, however, the lower half of the dead deer is clearly visible.

If we come back to Hemingway's statement that looking at paintings was "a part of learning to see, to hear, to think, to feel and not feel and to write," we might wonder what impact Homer's paintings could have had on Hemingway's evolving depictions of the hunters in his writing and on his own behavior. Did the duality of Homer's vision speak to the writer's sense of himself as a sportsman? It isn't always a pretty picture, but it is the way it was. Did Homer's paintings contribute to an ambivalence that Hemingway was experiencing for himself? Could particular paintings have prompted new perspectives?

Of course there are no definite answers to these questions, but Ernest Hemingway's sensitivity toward nature is apparent in his writing and in his life if one cares for the truth. I am not a sportsman, but his "good pictures of those things" have convinced me that Hemingway hunted and fished for a prey he loved and that he cared deeply for the natural world.

NOTES

1. Ernest Hemingway, "Game-Shooting in Europe," in *Dateline: Toronto*, ed. William White (New York: Scribner's, 1985), 359.

2. Ernest Hemingway, *Islands in the Stream* (New York: Scribner's, 1970), 278. Subsequent references will be given as page numbers in the text.

3. Ernest Hemingway, "Fathers and Sons," in *The Complete Short Stories of Ernest Hemingway* (New York: Scribner's, 1987), 372. Subsequent references will be given as page numbers in the text.

4. Ernest Hemingway, "The Last Good Country," in *The Complete Short Stories of Ernest Hemingway* (New York: Scribner's, 1987), 515. Subsequent references will be given as page numbers in the text.

5. Gregory H. Hemingway, *Papa: A Personal Memoir* (Boston: Houghton Mifflin, 1976), 62.

6. Ernest Hemingway, *Green Hills of Africa* (New York: Scribner's, 1935), 284. Subsequent references will be given as page numbers in the text.

7. Ernest Hemingway, *Ernest Hemingway: Selected Letters*, ed. Carlos Baker (New York: Scribner's, 1981), 624.

8. See Jackson J. Benson, "Hemingway the Hunter and Steinbeck the Farmer," *Michigan Quarterly Review* 24 (Summer 1985): 441–60 and Glen A. Love, "Hemingway's Indian Virtues: An Ecological Reconsideration," *Western American Literature* 22.1 (1987): 201–13 for essays diametrically opposed to my thesis. Though Love admits the beginning of a changing attitude in the aging Hemingway, he essentially sees it as too little too late.

9. Jack Hemingway, *Misadventures of a Fly Fisherman* (New York: McGraw Hill, 1986), 308.

10. Ernest Hemingway, *For Whom the Bell Tolls* (New York: Scribner's, 1940), 39. Subsequent references will be given as page numbers in the text.

11. Ernest Hemingway, *Letters*, 454.

12. Denis Brian, *The True Gen* (New York: Dell Publishing, 1988), 291.

13. Ernest Hemingway to Bruce Bliven, 19 June 1933, Hemingway Collection, John F. Kennedy Library, Boston (hereafter cited as JFK).

14. Charlene M. Murphy, "Hemingway, Winslow Homer, and *Islands in the Stream*: Influence and Tribute," *The Hemingway Review* 13.1 (1993): 76–85 provides a detailed analysis of the influence of Winslow Homer's painting on Hemingway's writing of *Islands in the Stream*. In April 1995, at the John F. Kennedy Library in Boston, when I spoke with Patrick Hemingway about the accuracy of my article, he said that my paper was "right on the button" and that his father "loved Winslow Homer."

15. Emily Stipes Watts, *Ernest Hemingway and the Visual Arts* (Urbana: University of Illinois Press, 1971).

16. Helen A. Cooper, *Winslow Homer Watercolors* (Washington: National Gallery of Art, 1986), 187–88.

17. Item 383, 1, JFK. Cited by permission.

18. Cooper, *Winslow Homer Watercolors*, 188.

19. Forbes Watson, *Winslow Homer* (New York: Crown, 1942). Watson's book contains a number of paintings Hemingway may have "used" in *Islands in the Stream* as well as some paintings relevant to the present discussion. Watson's book is listed in James D. Brasch and Joseph Sigman, *Hemingway's Library: A Composite Record* (New York: Garland, 1981). In addition to the 1942 text by Forbes Watson, Brasch and Sigman indicate that Hemingway also owned a 1958

[173]

text on Homer. See National Gallery of Art, *Winslow Homer: A Retrospective Exhibition* (Washington: National Gallery, 1958) for reproductions of "Huntsman and Dogs," "Deer Drinking," and "Right and Left."

I believe that Hemingway probably viewed additional Homer paintings during his many visits to New York City and that it is quite likely he saw the "Winslow Homer Centenary Exhibition" at the Whitney Museum of American Art in 1936–37. See Carlos Baker, *Ernest Hemingway: A Life Story* (New York: Scribner's, 1969) for dates of Hemingway's visits to the city, including a business trip in January 1937 (299). The catalog *Winslow Homer Centenary Exhibition* (New York: Plantin Press, 1936) includes in its listings "Right and Left," "The Wood Cutter," "Deer Drinking," and "Guide Carrying a Deer" (the watercolor version of the oil, "Huntsman and Dogs"). In *Green Hills of Africa*, when Hemingway listed the few things he "cared about doing," "seeing pictures" was one of the five activities mentioned, though presumably the only one of them difficult to continue in Africa. Then he added, "I could remember all the pictures" (285).

20. David Tatham, "Winslow Homer at the North Woods Club," in *Winslow Homer: A Symposium*, ed. Nicolai Cikovsky, Jr. (Washington: National Gallery of Art, 1990), 128.

21. Nicolai Cikovsky, Jr., "Good Pictures," in *Winslow Homer*, eds. Nicolai Cikovsky, Jr. and Franklin Kelly (Washington: National Gallery of Art, 1995), 374, makes a related comment about "Right and Left": "Its assignment of human feelings to animals is a characteristic posture of Homer."

22. Cooper, *Winslow Homer Watercolors*, 170.

23. Item 542, 68, JFK. Cited by permission.

24. George Plimpton, "The Art of Fiction: Ernest Hemingway," in *Conversations with Ernest Hemingway*, ed. Matthew J. Bruccoli (Jackson: University of Mississippi Press, 1986), 118–19. First published in *The Paris Review* 5 (Spring 1958): 60–89.

25. Carlos Baker, *Life*, 16.

26. Jack Hemingway, *Misadventures*, 18.

27. Ernest Hemingway to Bruce Bliven, 19 June 1933, JFK. Cited by permission.

28. Ernest Hemingway, *A Farewell to Arms* (New York: Scribner's, 1929), 9 and 73.

29. Rose Marie Burwell, *Hemingway: The Postwar Years and the Posthumous Novels* (Cambridge: Cambridge University Press, 1996), 77, 208.

30. Love, "Hemingway's Indian Virtues," 209.

31. Nicolai Cikovsky, Jr., "Something More than Meets the Eye," in *Winslow Homer*, eds. Nicolai Cikovsky, Jr. and Franklin Kelly (Washington: National Gallery of Art, 1995), 251.

32. Cooper, *Winslow Homer Watercolors*, 177–78.

Hemingway's Late Life Relationship with Birds

ROBIN GAJDUSEK

"'I probably could have been a great ornithologist,' Willie said. 'Grandma used to raise chickens.'"

ISLANDS IN THE STREAM[1]

Willie's facetious comment, after he has just observed a Bahamian booby bird on a nearby wreck, presents Ernest Hemingway's apparently mocking but really straight assessment of his *own* interests and abilities. Throughout that novel, the careful and precise observation of birds, their flight and mannerisms and habits, defines and supports action in the book. The studious perception of the flight of birds accompanies the drama. The observation of birds is so intense it resembles that of classical divination to determine the future by reading the patterns of the flight of birds and the entrails of birds.

In 1949, in "The Great Blue River," Hemingway had given an autobiographical basis to his fascination. There, acknowledging that the reason he lives in Cuba is too complicated to explain, he continues, "You do not tell them about the strange and lovely birds that are on the farm the year around, nor about all the migratory birds that come through, nor that quail come in the early mornings to drink at the swimming pool."[2]

In the remark is his recognition of and love for particular birds and their habits. However, he creates a complication as he goes on in the same essay to observe that he lives in Cuba also because "you can raise your own fighting cocks, train them on the place, and fight them anywhere that you can match them and that this is all legal" (403), and he remembers with nostalgia his live-pigeon shooting there.

Elsewhere, in *Death in the Afternoon*, his love for and delight in the birds he eats is patent even as he describes their deaths:

> In front of the barn a woman held a duck whose throat she had cut and stroked him gently while a little girl held up a cup to catch the blood for making gravy. The duck seemed very contented and when they put him down (the blood all in the cup) he waddled twice and found that he was dead. We ate him later, stuffed and roasted.[3]

He deliberately shocks us—with the gentle stroking of "the throat she had cut," the little girl who, like an acolyte, holds up the cup "to catch the blood," the "contented" duck himself who is surprised to discover his own death, and the almost brutal delight of "we ate him later, stuffed and roasted." All that empathy and all that accepted process! Passages like that teach deeply the *un*sentimental meaning of life.

I doubt that there is a more beautiful beginning to any short story than that to "In Another Country," where Hemingway looks carefully and lovingly at the landscape of hunters of animals, birds, and men:

> In the fall the war was always there, but we did not go to it any more. It was cold in the fall in Milan and the dark came very early. Then the electric lights came on, and it was pleasant along the streets looking in the windows. There was much game hanging outside the shops, and the snow powdered in the fur of the foxes and the wind blew their tails. The deer hung stiff and heavy and empty, and small birds blew in the wind and the wind turned their feathers. It was a cold fall and the wind came down from the mountains.[4]

The tenderness and precision and hardness are all there, life seen clearly amidst death that is seen clearly—and all of that in the midst of painfully intense sensation and love. There is the acceptance of process in the midst of an undercurrent and tone of lament—the necessary deaths in life that support the intense delights of life. In a remarkable passage in *Death in the Afternoon* he writes, "Do you know the sin it would be to ruffle the arrangement of the feathers on a hawk's neck if they could never be replaced as they were?" (159). In "The Christmas Gift," he describes "a string of mallard ducks hung out of reach of cats and there were also hung up Hungarian partridges, different varieties of quail and other fine eating birds."[5] Such an observation records pursuit that goes beyond death, just as the memory of taste remains beyond the fact of consumed delight. Such moments of fascinated observation underwrote his ornithological knowledge.

In *Look*, in "A Situation Report," in 1956, he describes:

> The sea birds huddled in the lee of the cliffs, coming out in clouds to dive wildly when a scouting bird would sight schoolfish moving along the shore, and the condors ate dead pelicans on the beaches. The pelicans usually died from bursting their food pouches diving and a condor would walk backwards along the beach lifting a large dead pelican as though it weighed nothing.[6]

This later Hemingway is a writer who not only sees where the driven birds hide but who empathically, feelingly understands their dilemma in the wind and cold, who sees the pattern of their grouped flight, the prey they pursue and how it is pursued. He knows what eats what, what bird can lift what, and how they die and return through their deaths back into the cycle of life. In *Esquire* in May of 1936, he writes:

> So we drifted like that all morning, and in the fall, the small birds that are going south are deadly tired sometimes as they near the coast of Cuba where the hawks come out to meet them, and the birds light on the boat to rest and sometimes we would have as many as twenty on board at a time in the cabin, on the deck, perched on the fishing chairs or resting on the floor of the cockpit. Their great fatigue makes them so tame that you can pick them up and they show no fear at all. There were three warblers and a thrush in the cockpit when Enrique poked his head out to get some air from working in the galley and Lopez Mendez said, "Don't let him see the birds. He would eat them."
>
> "No," said Enrique. "I am a great lover of birds."[7]

Passages like that can only be written by someone who understands the weariness, the desperation, the fear, and the perils of these small creatures, and also places his awareness helplessly in the great enveloping process that includes their coevally dangerous and beautiful lives. He not only participates in their struggle but brings the great undercurrents of nature and time to visibility through them. This sympathetic awareness of their lives and anxieties Hemingway gave fine expression to in *The Old Man and the Sea*, where Santiago binds himself to the creatures of the air as he will later bind himself to the great fish of the sea:

> He was sorry for the birds, especially the small delicate dark terns that were always flying and looking and almost never finding, and he thought, the birds have a harder life than we do except for the robber birds and the heavy strong ones. Why did they make birds so delicate and fine as those sea swallows when the ocean can be so cruel? She is kind and very beautiful. But she can be so cruel and it comes so suddenly and such birds that fly, dipping and hunting, with their small sad voices are made too delicately for the sea.[8]

Such a passage lets the reader close into Hemingway's love. We infer it from the qualities he projects upon his characters—here, as we empathize with Santiago in his feeling perceptions, his reflection upon, and his measurement of man and the birds. He uses the birds as ways to better see more deeply the ironies of beauty and kindness within rapacity and destruction. Letting the birds help him as he labors and suffers, and alive to their suffering, allows him to acknowledge that they participate and share: "The bird is a great help" (38).

The depth at which birds inhabit Hemingway's unconscious life is recognized in the frequent association between the flight of birds in his work and the orgasmic moment of fully completed love, when the soul seems, in the ecstasy of loving, to have been released from and therefore apprehended through the body, so that infinitely heightened life and death become one and the same. It is this love/death, attainment of spirit through flesh, of paradise on earth, that the flight of the bird records—whether for Cantwell with Renata, or with the "rising" and "sailing" and "wheeling" and "soaring" of Robert Jordan and Maria as the two sexually become one, or with Nick Adams and Trudy. Late in Hemingway's life he describes his aged Cantwell's response after his gondola loving with Renata: "She said nothing, and neither did he, and when the great bird had flown far out of the closed window of the gondola, and was lost and gone, neither of them said anything."[9] As Hemingway earlier reached in "Fathers and Sons" for an image of a boy's first introduction to the mystery and wonder of sex, he wrote:

> Could you say she did first what no one has ever done better and mention plump brown legs, flat belly, hard little breasts, well holding arms, quick searching tongue, the flat eyes, the good taste of mouth, then uncomfortably, tightly, sweetly, moistly, lovely, tightly, achingly, fully, finally, unendingly, never-endingly, never-to-endingly, suddenly ended, the great bird flown like an owl in the twilight, only it daylight in the woods and hemlock needles stuck against your belly.[10]

What the passage records is the night bird in the double light as the unending and the suddenly ended are joined: *that* moment. That the relations between love and death not be lost, Hemingway, in "Fathers and Sons," labors the association. Nick's father has given him shells to go hunting black squirrels, only three shells a day because "it wasn't good for a boy to go banging around" (497). The black squirrel hunting is associated with sex and death, and when Nick, at the end of "The Doctor and the Doctor's Wife," offers himself as guide to take his sexually defeated masturbatory father *through the hemlock woods* to where the black squirrels are, the overtones are strong that this is a love/death experience towards which he leads. In "Fathers and Sons," it is the journey through the hemlock woods towards black squirrel hunting and the hemlock tree (where Nick and his Indian girlfriend Trudy make love) that leads towards the orgasmic moment of love. This love/death moment, described as the moment when the "suddenly ended" loving brings Nick to "the great bird flown like an owl in the twilight," leaves him with hemlock needles stuck to his belly (497). In both stories the death journey through sex to renewed life is implied. The experience binds together birth, death, birds, and the feminine:

When you have shot one bird flying you have shot all birds flying. They are all different and they fly in different ways but the sensation is the same and the last one is as good as the first. (498)

My point here is that Hemingway has invested birds, their beauty, their flight, and their role as mediators between the earth and the heavens, with mythological and psychic significance. They are related to the ecstatic love moment of orgasmic transcendence, even as they are related to the polar experiences of heightened life and death. Although he usually distinguishes birds as either male or female, they are metaphorically established as avatars of and the means whereby the male may enter the primal experience of the feminine.[11]

Hemingway's interest in birds has scientific, aesthetic, and religious components. He increasingly gives ritualistic and mythological significance to birds. Late in *Across the River and into the Trees,* he has Cantwell imagine the gift he would most wish to give to his beloved:

> I'd like to give her a vest made of the whole plumage the way the old Mexicans used to ornament their gods, he thought. But I suppose these ducks have to go to the market and no one would know how to skin and cure the skins anyway. It could be beautiful, though, with Mallard [*sic*] drake skins for the back and sprig for the front with two longitudinal stripes of teal. One coming down over each breast. Be a hell of a vest. I'm pretty sure she'd like it. (282)

The vest he describes is really, as he suggests, an investiture for her still-to-be-ritualized adoration/enthronement. Conceived in "the way the old Mexicans used to ornament their gods," the vest he describes barely conceals the way it as costume transforms his beloved into a bird goddess. The sexual and ritual transformations and investments with power that *Across the River* records are further enunciated as this man, who wears a small eagle with wings outstretched on each shoulder (283), finds himself later imagining a real down jacket that he would additionally like to have made for Renata: "I could find out how they are quilted and make one with duck down from here. . . . I'd get a good tailor to cut it and we would make it double-breasted" (289), he continues.

Across the River is filled with the many gifts that Cantwell brings to Renata to lay at her feet: his love, his sense of the past and its meaning, his usually defended prerogatives and command, and, ultimately, his life. It is with an imagery of birds that this level of meaning is enunciated in the novel, which progresses from the first scene and its shooting of the birds, to the last scenes, in which the guns are put away, the killing of birds is abjured. It is a novel studying the ritualized self-overthrow of the male who, in rites of ritual self-castration divests himself of the signs of his authority and power and transfers them to his female consort. It is a studied examination of a shift from the patriarchal to the matriarchal mode, an understanding that the time has come culturally for that shift, and it is told to an extent in "bird language." Lest the reader miss the meaning of his treatise, Hemingway etches the movement to the future iconographically. Following the last words of the preceding chapter, "The shooting's over" (294), the new chapter begins as "the boatman placed the ducks carefully, breasts up, on the bow of the boat and the Colonel handed [up] his guns" (295). As the transference of power ends, Cantwell looks at the injured mallard drake, a "cripple" with a beating heart and "captured hopeless eyes." He asks the boatman to "put him in the sack with the hen" (298). That metaphor is historical and profound.

In "The Last Good Country," an incest story which Hemingway wrote late and never completed for publication, he deals, as he does in so many of his later works, with the sexual inversions and sexual transformations necessary for a transference of power. As Littless says, she is "practicing being a boy,"[12] which echoes Catherine's metamorphoses in *The Garden of Eden*. In "The Last Good Country," as Nick enthrones/invests Littless with power, he brings her gifts of the bird totems that belong to her. Nick and Littless have gone into fresh and virgin territory, where they come on the "last really wild stream there is" (541). There they observe cedar waxwings "calm and gentle and distinguished moving in their lovely elegance with the magic wax touches on their wing coverts and their tails" (540). Littless says, "They're the most beautiful, Nickie. There couldn't be more simply beautiful birds." "They're built like your face," he replies. The birds make her so proud and happy that she cries. Nick then brings to her three grouse that he has shot for her and lays them out on the moss at her feet. She feels them "warm and full-breasted and beautifully feathered." Such ritualized moments in which the male brings the bird costume, the bird beauty, or the bird experience to the woman he loves, should recall to the reader the many moments in Hemingway when the bird is equated with orgasmic transcendence. As he recognizes and fashions bird beauty for his beloved, it is not only adoration but service, self-abnegation in the interest of her empowerment.

Since the dimensions of my subject are large, in the remainder of this essay I will confine myself to and focus primarily on the third book of *Islands in the Stream*, "At Sea," to examine Hemingway's remarkable descriptive passages that define the role of birds in the lives of men. Within a page of its beginning, the discovery of the bodies of the executed villagers causes Ara to remark that "birds haven't worked on them but the land crabs are working on them" (333). Instantly the birds are related to the inescapable voracious food cycle, identified with and related to the lives and deaths of men. But Ara points out that creatures from the sky and from the land both participate in life/death cycles. Shortly after the gruesome discovery of the dead, which sends Hudson and his men into pursuit and ultimately leads some toward their own deaths, Hemingway describes the terns:

> The sand was high like new-made graves and over the island sooty terns were flying in the wind. They nested in the rocks up at the windward end and a few nested in the grass of the lee. They were flying now, falling off with the wind, cutting sharply into it, and dipping down toward the grass and the rocks. They were calling, sadly and desperately. (351)

The birds are invested with the sorrow, the prescience, and the duties of harbingers and heralds. Sooty and calling their lament, they are seen in their customary flight movements and nesting habits. Their beautiful release in the wind leads to an inescapable descent into death: The neutral sand suggests awaiting graves. That chapter concludes as Thomas Hudson informs the lieutenant at the radio shack of what he has seen and what the lieutenant must know. Hudson says, "I saw the birds moving." "'The poor birds,' the Lieutenant said" (354), and the chapter ends. Later, the movement of the birds will reveal the movement of the Germans and foretell Hudson's fate.

As they pursue and search, Thomas Hudson sees

> a tall white heron standing looking down in the shallow water with his head, neck, and beak poised. . . . Then the heron rose and flew further up the beach. Braking widely with his great white wings, and then taking a few awkward steps, he landed. I am sorry I disturbed him, Thomas Hudson thought. (376–7)

Only one who has observed with care could note the triply poised heron, with its braking action and its "awkward" steps; but, more, only one empathically inside the world of birds could feel regret for having disturbed the heron. Later, Hudson notes "One turtle with a sea gull flying around him. I thought he was going to perch on his back. But he didn't" (387). Again, he enters with empathy into the decisions and choices of the bird, wondering about that incidental life. The birds usurp much of his attention. Going behind the lagoon, he had found

> the place where the flamingoes came at high tide and he had seen many wood ibis, the *cocos* that gave the key its name, and a pair of roseate spoon-bills working in the marl of the edge of the lagoon.

> They were beautiful with the sharp rose of their color against the
> gray marl and their delicate, quick, forward-running movements,
> and they had the dreadful, hunger-ridden impersonality of certain
> wading birds. (399)

These observations are ornithological wonders: The recognized "hunger-ridden impersonality" is not only remarkably acute but is used to establish relationship to other birds similarly driven. Like the painter he is, Hudson carefully notes colors and contrasts. The "roseate" and then the "sharp rose" identify his different observations, while the words "delicate" and "quick" establish the birds as he has seen them.[13]

Later, "In the morning light they could see four terns and two gulls working around the shoal. They had found something and were diving. The terns were crying and the gulls were screaming." Willie, sympathizing like Santiago with the birds, notes that "Those poor bastard birds have to get up earlier in the morning than we do to make a living. . . . People don't appreciate the work they put in" (406). Again the appreciation based on empathy and comparison is there, while the crying and screaming dramatically orchestrate the drama. The birds' struggle and pursuit is allied with the mission of Hudson's men as irregular troops, and on the next page it is Willie again who sees the booby bird as "probably come to *reinforce* us" [my emphasis]. Hudson studies the "flocks of shore birds wheeling and settling on the banks to feed" (415), and these predatory cycles echo against their own hungers and pursuit. Throughout this book, the patterns of natural hunger, life, and death are the background to the *un*natural dying and *diving*—this is, after all, a submarine crew they pursue.

Hudson, alone on his *flying* bridge,

> watched the shore birds working on the flats and he remembered
> what they had meant to him when he was a boy. He could not feel
> the same about them now and he had no wish to kill them ever. But
> he remembered the early days with his father in a blind on some
> sand-spit with tin decoys out and how they would come in as the tide
> lowered and bared the flats and how he would whistle the flock in as
> they were circling. It was a sad whistle and he made it now and
> turned one flock. But they veered off from the stranded ship and
> went far out to feed. (417)

Because his memories are thoroughly grounded in his pursuit of birds, Hudson finds his nostalgia, raised by the birds, bringing together both innocence and guilt, and the sense of senseless slaughter together with the strategies of war. The memory of the birds thoroughly structures the drama unfolding between himself and the German submarine crew. Then, quick on the heels of this recognition

> he saw a flight of flamingoes coming from the left. They were flying low over the water, lovely to see in the sunlight. Their long necks were slanted down and their incongruous legs were straight out; immobile while their pink and black wings beat. . . . [Hudson] marveled at their downswept black and white bills and the rose color they made in the sky, which made their strange individual structures unimportant and still each one was an excitement to him. (418)

The flamingoes evoke his artistic self. Their color and form are aesthetically related in his mind. He simultaneously recognizes through them the loss of the individual in the presence of group. Yet even as he understands this, he, as an artist and a significant man, knows that he puts together the universal and the particular, for "each . . . was an excitement to him." The relationship between individual anger as justification for murder and group rage as acceptable in war is debated through Hudson's recognition of flamingo patterns. Hudson accurately portrays the birds' precise neck slant, with "incongruous" legs and "downswept" black and white bills. Their choice for feeding at the mud bank tells Hudson they had been "spooked flying over the key" (419). They have given him an index to the prey he seeks. But the flamingoes are *yet* more important to him. He dismisses his crew because, as he says, "I want to watch the flamingoes for a little while."

> He stood on the flying bridge and watched the flamingoes. It is not just their color, he thought. It's not just the black on that rose pink. It is their size and that they are ugly in detail and yet perversely beautiful. They must be a very old bird from the earliest times. He did not watch them through the glasses because he did not want details now. He wanted the roseate mass on the gray brown flat. Two other flocks had come in now and the banks were colored in a way that he would not have dared to paint. Or I would have dared to paint and would have painted, he thought. It is nice to see flamingoes before you make this trip. (420)

The quasi-prehistoric flamingoes bring to him a reconciliation of opposites, of now and then, of beauty and ugliness, of color against the gray brown flat of things. They establish for him the limits of daring between the real and the fictional, the surreal colors and grotesque forms and the incredible actual beauty. He is fully aware of "the details" that support the abstractions, the way "the roseate mass" and the "flocks" take their origin in each fact that gives him the ability to extrapolate, as artist or hunter of men.

They assure him and enable him to define his aesthetic courage—this, now, for a soldier going into physical battle. The trip looms larger than just an exploration behind the keys: Surely "this trip" will be into death.

As they journey inward toward the center of darkness where their fatal encounter lies, Hudson sees "a night heron rise from the trees in the center and fly away. Then he saw two wood ibis rise and wheel and fly off with quick-flapping, then coasting, then quick-flapping wing beats downwind toward the little key" (432–3). The described flight of the wood ibis is the sort of exact ornithological description Hemingway exhibits in his later years, after he has established his home in Cuba. These birds, exactly described in their manner of flight, pinpoint the movements of Willie and the others, who are scouting for Hudson. But the flight of birds also increasingly establishes the tension. "Occasionally a bird, or a pair of birds would fly up, and they knew these birds had been frightened either by Willie or the others." Ara knows that the birds anger Willie, and Hudson remarks, "He might as well be sending up balloons" (434). Hudson suddenly does "not like any of it now. There were too many birds getting up from the key. . . . it does not look good with so many birds getting up," and just then "Another pair of wood ibis rose not far from the shore" (434). The birds are signals and omens:

> A bittern came out from the mangroves and Thomas Hudson heard it squawk and watched its nervous swooping flight downwind. Then he settled down to trace Willie's progress along the mangroves by the rising and the flight of the birds. When the birds stopped rising he was sure he was headed back. Then after a time they were being put up again and he knew Willie was working out the windward curve of the key. After three-quarters of an hour he saw a great white heron rise in panic and start its slow heavy wing-beats to windward and he said to Ara, "He'll be out now." (435)

How carefully Hemingway distinguishes the "nervous swooping flight" of the bittern from the "slow heavy wing-beats" of the heron, and how intricately he ties the movements of the men to the flight of the birds, so that their danger or safety is read in the skies.

In the later afternoon, the flamingoes are gone from the flat though there is a flock of willets working over it. The willets fly up finally but Hudson notes there are no flamingoes and that the other birds are nearly all the same except for the flocks of golden plover.

> He remembered the seasons when the plover were gray and the others when the black feathers had the golden tinge and he remembered young Tom's pride at the first one he had ever

brought home. . . . He remembered how Tom had stroked the plump white breast and touched the lovely black under markings and how he had found the boy asleep that night in his bed with his arms around the bird. He had taken the bird away very softly hoping he would not wake the boy. . . . As he had taken the golden plover into the back room where the icebox was, he felt he had robbed the boy of it. But he had smoothed its plumage carefully and laid it on one of the grilled shelves of the icebox. The next day he had painted young Tom a picture of the golden plover and the boy had taken it with him when he went off to school that year. In the picture he had tried to get the fast, running quality of the bird and the background was a long beach with coconut palms. (445–46)[14]

This memory triggers another memory for Hudson of when he had painted his sleeping son when he "lay on his back with his arms crossed and he looked like the sculpture of a young knight lying on his tomb" (446). The two memories link the previous death of Hudson's beloved son with the death of the golden plover and with his own approaching death. It also establishes the relations between life, dream, and art, and time and immortality. The attempt to preserve in time that which is devoured by time has been Hudson's dilemma. The boy and the bird are now linked in their fates, the icebox preserves the bird, even as the painting preserves Hudson's beloved son. In the same way memory itself is another variety of preservation of the timelessness of life in time. The delicacy of Hudson's touch and his son's touch of the delicate markings and plumage of the dead bird reveal Hemingway's sense of the delicacy of life in nature in the midst of its deaths. Imagining his son in his Spitfire that he *flew* in combat to his death, Hudson places him *like the bird* in the air out of which he will, like the birds, descend. He remembers his son having said that the only thing he really worried about was the second coming of the ice age— "That and the extinction of the passenger pigeon."[15] With this remark Hemingway again ties together the bird, the suspending qualities that both art and the refrigerator express, and the dead son and his soon-to-be-slain father. We know that it was Hemingway's own father, Dr. Clarence Hemingway, who had lamented the passing of the carrier pigeon. How incredibly memory—implicitly the memory of the artist—unites life and life and life and life despite time.

Islands in the Stream has used the birds throughout as harbingers and prophesiers. Their flight has signaled both safety and danger, but the book ends with Hudson's probably fatal wounding. He suffers it in an ambush that is signaled not by the rising flight of birds but rather by the fact "there were no birds rising from the mangroves" (454): there "were no birds at all and since the tide was high he knew that the birds had to be in the mangroves" (455). The mangroves are already stripped of their birds by the forces of death that wait for Hudson there; he has entered the place where no birds sing, where no birds are, where only silence and darkness wait for him.

NOTES

1. Ernest Hemingway, *Islands in the Stream* (New York: Scribner's, 1970), 407. Subsequent references will be given as page numbers in the text.

2. Ernest Hemingway, "The Great Blue River," in *By-Line: Ernest Hemingway*, ed. William White (New York: Scribner's, 1967), 403. Subsequent references will be given as page numbers in the text.

3. Ernest Hemingway, *Death in the Afternoon* (New York: Scribner's, 1950), 275–76. Subsequent references will be given as page numbers in the text.

4. Ernest Hemingway, "In Another Country," in *The Short Stories of Ernest Hemingway* (New York: Scribner's, 1938), 267. Subsequent references will be given as page numbers in the text.

5. Ernest Hemingway, "The Christmas Gift," in *By-Line: Ernest Hemingway*, ed. William White (New York: Scribner's, 1967), 466.

6. Ernest Hemingway, "A Situation Report," in *By-Line: Ernest Hemingway*, ed. William White (New York: Scribner's, 1967), 473.

7. Ernest Hemingway, "There She Breaches! or Moby Dick Off the Morro," in *By-Line: Ernest Hemingway*, ed. William White (New York: Scribner's, 1967), 247.

8. Ernest Hemingway, *The Old Man and the Sea* (New York: Scribner's, 1952), 29. Subsequent references will be given as page numbers in the text.

9. Ernest Hemingway, *Across the River and into the Trees* (New York: Scribner's, 1950), 154. Subsequent references will be given as page numbers in the text.

10. Ernest Hemingway, "Fathers and Sons," in *The Short Stories of Ernest Hemingway* (New York: Scribner's, 1938), 497.

11. My belief is that this is because Hemingway prejudices either/or and both/and experiences as male and female: The boundaries, oppositions, definitions, and delineations of war or civilization tend to be the terrain of masculine commitment; those of love or joining or reconciling or of unaided nature itself, where the spirit and flesh inextricably cohabit, tend to be the country of the feminine.

The bias is towards heterosexual love, in which the male, unlike Jake Barnes, phallically equipped to enter the "other" undiscovered land, gains in immersion in otherness the compassionate and individuated psyche to enable him to live fully. The flown bird, here and not here, of the earth and then of the sky, in song and flight transcending but not escaping itself, is the emblem of the orgasmic reconciliation.

12. Ernest Hemingway, "The Last Good Country" in *The Complete Short Stories of Ernest Hemingway* (New York: Scribner's, 1987), 533. Subsequent references will be given as page numbers in the text.

13. "As he has seen them" is the point. Hemingway sees as a painter sees: In "The Strange Country," excerpts from an early version of *Islands in the Stream*, he writes:

> That was the year they shot the wild turkey as he crossed the road that early morning coming out of the mist that was just thinning with the first sun, the cypresses showing black in the silver mist and the turkey brown-bronze and lovely as he stepped onto the road, stepping high-headed, then crouching to run, then flopping on the road. (608)

Hemingway not only records the colors and movements of birds and their beauty and its impact but directs others how to observe. He describes an incoming flight of birds:

> They showed white in the cypress hammock . . . the sun shining on them in the dark foliage and as the sun lowered more came flying across the sky, flying white and slow, their long legs stretched behind them.
> "They're coming in for the night. They've been feeding out in the marsh. Watch the way they brake with their wings and the long legs slant forward to land."(611–12)

14. There is a similar scene, where one lovingly cradles a dead bird, in "The Strange Country." In those early version notes for *Islands in the Stream*, Hemingway wrote

> They had put the wild turkey in the back of the seat and he had been so heavy, warm and beautiful with the shining bronze plumage, so different from the blues and blacks of a domestic turkey, and David's mother was so excited she could hardly speak. And then she had said, "No, let me hold him. I want to see him again. We can put him away later." And he had put a newspaper on her lap and she had tucked the bird's bloodied head under his wing, folding the wing carefully over it, and sat there stroking and smoothing his breast feathers while he, Roger, drove. Finally she said, "He's cold now" and had wrapped him in the paper and put him in the back of the seat again and said, "Thank you for letting me keep him when I wanted him so much." (609)

15. The memory of this appears in Hemingway's older sister's reminiscence of her childhood home. She remembers their father reacting to the thought of the extinction of the passenger pigeons: "'And to think they are extinct now,' Daddy said. 'It's wicked!'" Marcelline Hemingway Sanford. *At the Hemingway's: The Years of Innocence* (Boston: Little, Brown and Co., 1962), 11.

Hemingway as a Young Hunter
Courtesy of John F. Kennedy Library, EH 783N

Bird Hunting and Male Bonding in Hemingway's Fiction and Family

JAMES HUGHES MEREDITH

Describing bird hunting in almost mythopoetic terms, sportsman Edward K. Roggenkamp, III, in *American Roughshooting*, muses that

> Autumn days cause a yearning for the hunting fields in the heart of every dedicated outdoorsman, a calling akin to the urges that drive geese south in the fall. This tradition, a rite of season, a ritual that bird-shooting sportsmen have sometimes carried to the level of an art, is marked by fine dogs, high quality guns, elaborate social settings, deep friendships and a rigorous adherence to a code of ethics.[1]

Bird hunting for the Hemingways was also a formative pursuit and an important opportunity for these men to bond together. In *My Brother, Ernest Hemingway*, Leicester Hemingway comments that his father firmly guided Ernest toward nature, fishing, and hunting, "the noncompetitive sports he loved."[2] And as Scott Donaldson notes, Hemingway "avidly mastered those lessons Dr. Hemingway first taught him on the prairie north of Oak Park and in the wilderness of upper Michigan."[3] Because of his father's emphasis on hunting, Ernest would own his first shotgun and become a committed sportsman by the age of twelve. Yet like so many other endeavors Hemingway pursued, this lifelong experience was not without its emotional complexity.

Michael S. Reynolds observes in "Hemingway's Home: Depression and Suicide" that although Hemingway's father "still loved the woods and the lake," after 1912, when Hemingway would have been about thirteen years old, the father increasingly "loved them alone," and began "shutting out his son."[4] Ernest acquired his first shotgun—thus ending his hunting novitiate—about the same time he reached puberty and about the time his father began to hunt alone. By shutting out his son, Hemingway's father ended hunting as a nurturing, father-and-son experience, and Ernest could not help but link the shotgun with his father's withdrawal, an experience which must have created immense emotional confusion within the young boy.

[189]

Commenting on this link between hunting and the absent father, Jackson L. Benson, in *The Writer's Art of Self-Defense*, observes that "[h]unting becomes for Ernest-Nick the male direction."5 Moreover, hunting becomes "not only a means of escape and masculine identification for the Hemingway protagonist," but "a release from the anxiety . . . that is often produced from the continual effort of trying to be a man . . . when there is only a weak pattern to follow."6 Thus, Hemingway and some of his fictional characters, in such short stories as "Fathers and Sons," "The Doctor and the Doctor's Wife," "Now I Lay Me," "A Day's Wait," and "I Guess Everything Reminds You of Something," not only pursue this blood sport to remember, almost sacramentally, a lost relationship with their fathers, but they also hunt to discover their own emerging role as fathers themselves. These men, both real and fictional, find hunting essential because the experience brings them closer together in a variety of complex ways despite the fact (or because of the fact) that this bonding is an incomplete and fragile experience.

In one of Hemingway's most notable stories about the relationship between Nick Adams and his father, "Fathers and Sons," hunting is how the son best remembers his father. However, as Reynolds observes, Hemingway used the title ironically because the story reveals more emotional rifts than moments of bonding between these fathers and sons.7 Although Nick and his father do experience male bonding while hunting, it is not enough to transcend other aspects of their complex relationship. In this story, thirty-eight-year-old Nick is traveling cross-country with his son. The setting is pastoral:

> It was not his country but it was the middle of fall and all of this
> country was good to drive through and to see. . . . [He was] hunting
> the country in his mind as he went by; sizing up each clearing as to
> feed cover and figuring where you would find a covey and which way
> they would fly.8

It may not be Nick's country in a literal sense, but it is his in a psychological one; it is identified in Nick's memory as a special time of the year—fall and hunting season. Because of its similarities to his own childhood, the occasion of his return to this locality (which is a psychological homecoming and not an actual one) stirs Nick into a profound reverie, leading directly to his thoughts about hunting and finally to memories of his father:

> In shooting quail you must not get between them and their habitual
> cover, once the dogs have found them, or when they flush they will
> come pouring at you, some rising steep, some skimming by your
> ears, whirring into a size you have never seen them in the air as they

pass, the only way being to turn and take them over your shoulder as they go, before they set their wings and angle down into the thicket. Hunting this country for quail as his father had taught him, Nicholas Adams started thinking about his father. (152)

In an experience common with highly self-conscious, middle-aged men, Nick is not only thinking about his father; Nick is actually thinking like his own father, as the momentary shift from the third to second-person perspective in this passage suggests.

Conveying Nick's self-identification with his father is extremely diffi-cult in a third-person perspective because it distances the narrative from the story's primary agent, but the success of this narrative again demon-strates the brilliance of Hemingway's revisions and the valuable informa-tion that can be discovered in the manuscripts. In the final draft of this story, Hemingway decided to use Nick's full name to identify his protago-nist. This revision has an arresting effect on experienced readers of Hemingway's fiction who are all too familiar with the less formal, adoles-cent nickname. The formality of using Nick's full name does more than underscore a sense of his present-day maturity; it demonstrates the depths of Nick's self-identification with his father. Thus, caught off guard by his sudden, unexpected rush of memory, Nick, himself now a father, momentarily confuses himself with his own father. Such confusion in self-identity is a common experience when an adult man takes his child into the locality of his own childhood. Although the final version of this story ended up being told in the third person instead of in the original first-person, "Fathers and Sons" maintains the intimacy of a first-person story because the perspective is entirely limited to Nick's consciousness.

In addition to uncovering complex narrative techniques, this story's composition history indicates that, like Nick, Hemingway was also having problems with unpleasant memories of his own father. Robert E. Fleming, in *The Face in the Mirror: Hemingway's Writers*, provides the best biographical analysis to date on Hemingway's development of the story.[9] Fleming writes that in "Fathers and Sons," "Hemingway reacts to Clarence Hemingway's suicide, an event that troubled him deeply, with-out bringing the suicide of Dr. Henry Adams to the surface level of the story."[10] Fleming asserts that Hemingway's "difficulty in treating this sen-sitive subject is evident in the number and nature of the manuscripts that document the genesis and growth" of this story.[11]

As this analysis reveals, Nick and Hemingway had much to be con-fused about, and until this time, both had sublimated their feelings about their fathers into their art instead of talking about them. Fleming further notes that by "changing [the narrative] to the third-person point of view and attaching 'Fathers and Sons' to Nick Adams, Hemingway distanced the events of the story not only mechanically but psychologically."[12] However, despite the fact that the third-person perspective does distance the story somewhat from Nick and Hemingway, enough residue of these events remains to allow for Nick's intense self-identification with the father. Identifying Nick as a writer, Fleming writes that some "memories are better lost than retained, and writing about them can provide catharsis for the writer."[13] Commenting on Nick's emotional baggage, James Nagel observes that "even three decades later Nick still feels the emotions of these events keenly, particularly those involving his father."[14] Nagel also notes that the only way Nick is able to deal with these emotions is through his art.[15] Thus, art for both Nick and Hemingway serves as a place of refuge and release.

As "Fathers and Sons" also demonstrates, Nick has never been able to exorcise disturbing memories of his father: memories which ultimately prove very hard to contain. Flowing in a wide-ranging associative pattern, Nick's memories of hunting with his father eventually lead to recollections about an almost pathological desire to turn his shotgun against his father. Nick at one time felt such animosity for his father that he "had sat inside the woodshed with the door open, his shotgun loaded and cocked, looking across at his father sitting on the screen porch reading his paper, and thought, 'I can blow him to hell. I can kill him'" (159). These violence-laden memories eventually lead to thoughts about the father's own subsequent violence against himself. (These particular "unthinkable" thoughts were excised from the published version, an excision which underscores Nick's and Hemingway's desire to repress them.)

Writing about the implications of these memories, Fleming observes that a

> writer's capital is his experience, and Hemingway had already accepted the fact that unhappy love affairs, broken marriages, and psychological breakdowns must all be considered fair game for the writer. But it seems unlikely that any of these subjects had disturbed him [and Nick] as deeply as his father's death by suicide and his guilty feeling that he might have prevented his father's death if he had been more perceptive.[16]

As the complexity of these experiences would suggest, Nick has good reasons to keep his guilt about his father to himself; some things are truly best left unsaid. Richard B. Hovey, in *Hemingway: The Inward Terrain*, observes that the "ancient Oedipal urge to kill the father scarcely needs further comment. But when it goes so far that the son actually has a readied murder weapon in his hand, we gain a little more insight as to why the father's suicide, as a fulfillment of an obscure wish, might induce greater guilt than was normal."[17]

Because of the associative memory of fall and hunting, Nick and his son are now both at the right age for Nick to sense the psychological connection between himself and his father and between himself and his son. Nick's son, now stirred by thoughts of the grandfather, eventually asks: "Why do we never go to pray at the tomb of my grandfather?" (161). Obviously, Nick and his son have never had this conversation before, indicating, among other things, that Nick is still hurt by the fact that "[a]fter he was fifteen he had shared nothing" with his father (159). Thus, like Hemingway and his father, by the time Nick was fifteen, he and his father did not even share hunting experiences together. Still hurting from that fact, as well as from the other painful memories, Nick has not talked about his father in ordinary conversation until this partic-ular hunting season, even with (or especially with) his own son. The rea-son, therefore, they have never gone to the grandfather's tomb is that Nick does not want to commemorate the final resting place of a suicide victim: Nick prefers to remember his father shooting birds rather than shooting himself.

Interestingly, although Nick remembers aspects of his father's charac-ter apart from his ability to hunt, he does not share them with the son. The son asks, "What was my grandfather like?" (161). Nick responds by stating that he was a "great hunter" and that he had "great eyes":

> "Was he greater than you?"
> "He was a much better shot and his father was a great wing shot too."
> "I'll bet he wasn't better than you."
> "Oh, yes he was. He shot very quickly and beautifully. I'd rather see him shoot than any man I ever knew. He was always very disap-pointed in the way I shot." (161)

Hunting seems to be the way Nick prefers to talk to his son about the father (and probably about his grandfather as well). Having no other way to measure the man, Nick equates great shooting with greatness of char-acter. Thus, like his father before him, Nick teaches his son the sport of shooting as a way to become a good man.

Because of this emphasis on hunting and masculine identity, the shotgun becomes a phallic as well as a practical object of male bonding: Possession of a gun distinguishes the men from the women—you can-not be a man or a hunter without a "gun." For example, in the Nick Adams short stories which include both father and mother (such as "The Doctor and the Doctor's Wife" and "Now I Lay Me"), Nick's father is always carrying a shotgun.[18] In "Now I Lay Me," the narrator remembers one

> time when my father was away on a hunting trip she made a good thorough cleaning out in the basement and burned everything that should not have been there. When my father came home and got down from his buggy and hitched the horse, the fire was still burning in the road beside the house. I went out to meet him. He handed me his shotgun and looked at the fire.[19]

Seeing these prized possessions burning, the father gives the shotgun to the son, perhaps to protect the gun from the mother. The father says, "'Take the gun and the bags in the house, Nick, and bring me a paper.' . . . My mother had gone inside the house. I took the shotgun, which was heavy to carry and banged against my legs, and the two game-bags and started toward the house"(278). Carrying the heavy gun, young Nick can actually feel the differences between his father and his mother, and he can easily sense the similarities between his own phallus and the shotgun his father has just given him.

Another example of the importance of the shotgun to male identity is in "The Doctor and the Doctor's Wife." In this story, the father is cleaning his gun to get his mind off the argument he is having with his wife:

> The doctor wiped his gun carefully with a rag. He pushed the shells back in against the spring of the magazine. He sat with the gun on his knees. He was very fond of it. Then he heard his wife's voice in the other room.[20]

While he is being verbally emasculated by his wife, after being humiliated by Dick Boulton, the father seemingly has to clean his weapon to remind himself of his masculinity. One may wonder what else is going through Dr. Adams's mind in the short story besides an attempt to hold on to his masculinity. The narrator does emphasize that he is very fond of his gun.

The shotgun and male identity are important even in stories where the mother has been written out of the story, such as in "Fathers and Sons." Although the mother is absent in the published version of that story, in an earlier draft, Hemingway specifically mentions Nick's mother in describing the incompatible relationship between her and Nick's father.[21] This woman's residual presence is so strong that even though she is eventually erased from the story, the men still feel compelled to arm themselves.

In another short story, "A Day's Wait," which some critics regard as a Nick Adams story,[22] the father goes quail hunting to divert his attention from the sick son. As in "Fathers and Sons," Nick is a mature man.[23] In *Hemingway's Nick Adams*, Joseph Flora writes that the "hunting scene

serves to identify the story . . . as a Nick story—to remind us of the bond
that hunting was between Nick and his father, even as we sense it as a tie
between the narrator and Schatz."²⁴ While the father is away hunting, the
sick son is worried that his temperature is too high because he has con-
fused a Celsius reading for a Fahrenheit one. In "Up and Down: Making
Connections in 'A Day's Wait,'" Linda Gajdusek points out "that this is primarily a story about misunderstanding—*breakdown* in communication is
central."²⁵ Another important element coincidental to the boy's irrational
fear of death is Nick's taking his shotgun out to hunt. Gajdusek argues that
this "passage merits our special attention, for it is not only a splendid
example of Hemingway's taut, evocative, descriptive prose but the catalyst
that makes the story resonant."²⁶ Gajdusek also observes that in contrast to
the boy's sick bed,

> the father's world of the hunting scene is rich with the beauty of glis-
> tening landscape and the vitality of movement, even clumsiness,
> clatter, sliding, slithering. In fact, compared with the astonishing
> control demonstrated by his young son, this father, who slips and
> falls and drops his gun and misses half his shots, seems not all that
> much in control of things."²⁷

During this hunting adventure, Nick understates his own fearful
dilemma: "[I]t was difficult to stand or walk on the glassy surface and the
red dog slipped and slithered and I fell twice, hard, once dropping my
gun and having it slide away over the ice" (92).

   Because of Nick's understatement, we do not realize until the end of
the story that the father is in much more danger of dying than the son is.
(We know from statistics taught in gun safety courses that many hunters
kill themselves by slipping while carrying a loaded gun.) As it juxtaposes
the father's travails with the son's, this scene underscores the close psychological relationship between the two males: Each male seems helpless
without the other. When read as a companion piece to "Fathers and
Sons," this story clarifies the importance of hunting in the Adams family
by dramatizing the perils and circularity of fatherhood. This story also
illuminates the painful ramifications of miscommunication between
fathers and sons. Hovey writes that though the "twist is a child's tragi-
comic ignorance, we still feel that somehow Schatz could and should
have been spared, that somehow between him and his father the lines of
communication might have been clearer."²⁸ Nick learns that despite his
own sensitivity and desire to be better than his own father, he cannot be
the perfect, insightfully communicative father either.

   As "Fathers and Sons" reveals, the first thing Nick always remembered
about his father was his eyes. However, despite his father's ability to see as

a hunter, ironically, he has very little insight otherwise about life in general. In "Fathers and Sons," Nick states that the "quail country made him remember [his father] as he was when Nick was a boy and he was very grateful to him for two things: fishing and shooting. His father was sound on these two things as he was unsound on sex" (153). As this observation indicates, it is hard to know which topic was more important to Nick at the time: sex or hunting. However, both topics are forever linked in Nick's mind solely because his father had so much insight into one while having so little into the other. Dr. Adams was an awkward father, and as Nick now realizes, slipping and sliding on the icy ground with a loaded gun is figuratively what his own father would have done in a different time—abandoning Nick to suffer irrational fears alone, as he has just done with Schatz. Just as it had been for Dr. Adams, the pressures of fatherhood force Nick to the woods alone. The paradox of this situation is that while the grandfather, who was a medical doctor, could easily have diagnosed the grandson's physical malady, he also would have lacked the insight, as Nick himself does, to diagnose the boy's mental discomfort. Both men lacked the insight to see the cause of their respective son's troubles.

A father himself now, Nick can better understand how difficult a time his own father had had and how ill-equipped both men were at performing their fatherly roles. As he grows older, Nick is shocked to discover that in some ways he is becoming more like his own father. Flora writes that "Nick's relationship with his father had long haunted him. There was much that was good about his associations with his father [like hunting], but as he grew up he questioned Dr. Adams' ways increasingly."²⁹ By Dr. Adams's ways, Flora must mean that Nick especially questioned his father's Victorian notions of morality. However, despite his rejection of his father's sense of morality, Nick unquestionably recognizes that his own "ways" are becoming increasingly similar to his father's. Nick may not have a Victorian mindset, but as he grows older, Nick is now shocked to discover that he is becoming more and more like his own father.

Despite the fond memories of hunting and learning to shoot in these Hemingway stories, the importance of shooting instruction is negatively underscored in "I Guess Everything Reminds You of Something"—a revealing story that is thematically linked with the Nick Adams stories because of its emphasis on shooting and writing within the context of a father and son relationship.³⁰ In this story, the father is reminded of all the work he has done training his son to shoot:

> With all his unbelievable talent the boy had not become the shooter he was . . . by himself. . . . He had forgotten now all about the training. He had forgotten how when he started to miss live birds his

father would take his shirt off and show him the bruise on his arm
where he had placed the gun incorrectly.[31]

After discovering that his son has won a literary prize using a plagiarized
story, the father realizes that the son is more than just a cheat. Although
the awareness that his son is a plagiarist would be devastating enough,
even more devastating is the father's realization that the values he has
tried to pass on through shooting have not caught on. The story ends
with the father thinking that "he knew that the boy had never been any
good. He had thought so often looking back on things. And it was sad to
know that shooting did not mean a thing" (601). The father has not lost
faith in the value of shooting; rather he has lost complete faith in the son
instead. Just as the son has faked writing the award-winning story, he has
also faked learning the true lessons of hunting. However, what the father
does not realize here is that by abandoning the son because he does not
live up to his expectations, the father is reliving an experience similar to
that of Clarence and Ernest and Nick and his father: The son is left
alone.

As is the case with the Adams men, learning to shoot a shotgun also
seems to be the way the Hemingway men learned to relate to one
another. In *Papa: A Personal Memoir*, Gregory Hemingway wrote: "the
summer that really stands out was the summer of '42. That was the summer when papa taught me to shoot."[32] Ironically, Gregory, the best shotgun shooter of Hemingway's sons, was also the son that Ernest seemed to
have the most difficulty understanding. Yet, despite the difficulty of their
relationship, Gregory (like Nick) remembers receiving instructions about
how to shoot a shotgun as one of his fondest boyhood experiences.
Gregory recounts his father's instructions:

> If the gun isn't positioned correctly, a smaller percentage of your
> shoulder will receive its full recoil, and it will kick like hell. Then
> you'll start to flinch, jerking the trigger in anticipation of your pain of
> the recoil, and that will move your gun off target before the shot
> leaves the barrel.[33]

Hemingway's instructions here illustrate his deep understanding of
shooting; after all, he had been a lifelong follower of the sport. Moreover,
as Gregory's bitter memoirs indicate, these instructions seem to be the
clearest and best advice Papa would ever give this son.

As the importance of these instructions suggests, the roles of shooting
instructor and father were inextricably linked for Hemingway. Jackson L.
Benson observes that

the constant focusing and refocusing on the father in [some of Hemingway's short stories], as well as later emphasis on the father figure, the "tutor" or the professional, and assumption of the "Papa" figure role by Hemingway himself, would indicate that Hemingway's own father and the idea of "fatherhood" in general have far-reaching implications, serving as the foundation for an emotional structure that spreads out in many directions.[34]

Following this line of thinking, Fleming also notes that Hemingway first started using his Papa persona in *Green Hills of Africa*—his experimental hunting novel.[35] Probably without even realizing it, the simple title of Gregory's memoirs (*Papa*) forms a profound paradox underscoring the complexity of this father and son relationship. Hemingway's Papa persona as the quintessential sportsman (even non-readers recognized him as such) became such a public moniker that Gregory seems compelled to subtitle his book a "personal" memoir as if to clarify the nature of his relationship with his own papa, the man who was also his shooting mentor and hunting guide.

Thus, primarily through the sports of hunting and fishing, Papa Hemingway became not only father to his sons, but to the larger reading public as well. Throughout the generations, the love of shooting, and the values associated with this sport, may have been the most important skill the Hemingway (and the Adams) men handed down to each other. Jack Hemingway says that the love for fishing, hunting, and being outdoors is one of the most important aspects he inherited from his father.[36] Hunting in the Hemingway family would never be an exclusively male domain— women were often a part of the group—but for all practical purposes, hunting remained a very masculine (paternal) occasion.[37] Donaldson notes that in his adult life Ernest "took every opportunity to practice what he had learned as a boy, in the process moving from tyro to accomplished sportsman. Finally, he assumed the role of instructor himself, tutoring his family and his readers in the proper way to hunt."[38]

In a continual act of passing down a passion for hunting to the next generation, Ernest's relationship with his father and sons mirrors Nick's relationship with his father and son in that it was easier for them to talk about hunting than it was to talk about how to live their lives. Unlike his father, the adult Ernest had no interest in being a doctor or a conservative Christian. Moreover, except for Jack's and Gregory's memoirs,[39] none of Ernest's sons has had any interest in becoming a professional writer; in fact, Jack Hemingway notes that his father actually discouraged him from becoming one.[40] However, all three sons have remained keenly interested in hunting (and fishing) throughout their lives as their father had been himself.

As Gregory's memoirs demonstrate and a preponderance of the family photographs illustrate, shooting seems to have been one of the most pleasurable activities that the family experienced during the boys' adolescence. Maybe to assuage a sense of guilt about being absent from his own sons so much, Ernest could have been trying to compensate for the way his own father had initiated him into this sport only to desert him. Whatever the reason, Hemingway men spent an extraordinary amount of time hunting when they were together. Although the bonding experiences were very brief and would not be strong enough to keep the family emotionally intact indefinitely, taking a shotgun out to hunt birds was how the Hemingway and Adams men sought to bond; it was primarily how one generation of men learned to identify with the other. Although a shotgun is forever linked with Hemingway's suicide, an act that will always make a shotgun more than just a shotgun in Hemingway studies, his choice of an instrument of death may have had much to do with its familiar feel. Maybe because of the shotgun's associative power, linking him both with his father and his sons forever, it was the last object in life Hemingway chose to hold on to.

NOTES

1. Edward K. Roggenkamp, III, *American Roughshooting: The Practice and Pleasures of Sport Hunting* (New York: Howell Book House, 1996), 5.

2. Leicester Hemingway, *My Brother, Ernest Hemingway* (Sarasota: Pineapple Press, 1996), 22.

3. Scott Donaldson, *By Force of Will: The Life and Art of Ernest Hemingway* (New York: Viking Press, 1977), 83. For a fuller chronology of Hemingway's hunting development, see page 69.

4. Michael S. Reynolds, "Hemingway's Home: Depression and Suicide," *American Literature* 57.4 (December 1995): 600.

5. Jackson L. Benson, *Hemingway . . . The Writer's Art of Self-Defense* (Minneapolis: University of Minnesota Press, 1969), 9–10.

6. Ibid., 10.

7. Reynolds, "Hemingway's Home," 600.

8. Ernest Hemingway, "Fathers and Sons," *Winner Take Nothing* (New York: Scribner's, 1970), 151–52. Subsequent references will be given as page numbers in the text.

9. Robert E. Fleming, *The Face in the Mirror: Hemingway's Writers* (Tuscaloosa: University of Alabama Press, 1994), 62.

10. Ibid.

11. Ibid.

12. Ibid.

13. Ibid.

14. James Nagel, "The Hunting Story in *The Garden of Eden*" in *Hemingway's Neglected Short Fiction: New Perspectives* (Tuscaloosa: University of Alabama Press, 1992), 336.

15. Ibid., 337.

16. Fleming, *The Face in the Mirror*, 64.

17. Richard B. Hovey, *Hemingway: The Inward Terrain* (Seattle: University of Washington Press, 1968), 47.

18. In "Indian Camp," for example, the mother is not there, so neither is the shotgun.

19. Ernest Hemingway, "Now I Lay Me," in *Men Without Women* (New York: Scribner's, 1970), 218–32. Subsequent references will be given as page numbers in the text.

20. Ernest Hemingway, "The Doctor and the Doctor's Wife" in *In Our Time* (New York: Scribner's, 1970), 23–27.

21. Ernest Hemingway, "The Tomb of My Grandfather," ms. copy of "Fathers and Sons" in folder 383-84, John F. Kennedy Library.

22. See Paul Smith's commentary in *A Reader's Guide to the Short Stories of Ernest Hemingway* (Boston: G. K. Hall, 1989), 302–6.

23. Ernest Hemingway, "A Day's Wait" in *Winner Take Nothing* (New York: Scribner's, 1970), 91–94. Subsequent references will be given as page numbers in the text.

24. Joseph Flora, *Hemingway's Nick Adams* (Baton Rouge: Louisiana State University Press, 1982), 221.

25. Linda Gajdusek, "Making Connections in 'A Day's Wait'" in *Hemingway's Neglected Short Fiction: New Perspectives*, ed. Susan Beegel (Tuscaloosa: University of Alabama Press, 1992), 294.

26. Ibid., 297.

27. Ibid., 298.

28. Hovey, *The Inward Terrain*, 43–44.

29. Flora, *Hemingway's Nick Adams*, 218.

30. This story obviously hit too close to home as Hemingway never attempted to publish it during his lifetime, and even after his death, Mary Hemingway must have not wanted it published either. A manuscript copy of the story reveals that she wrote "NOT TO BE PUBLISHED" in 1-inch letters on the top of the first

page. Ernest Hemingway, "I Guess Everything Reminds you of Something" in folder 485a.5, John F. Kennedy Library.

31. Ernest Hemingway, "I Guess Everything Reminds You of Something" in *The Complete Short Stories of Ernest Hemingway* (New York: Scribner's, 1987), 597–601. Subsequent references will be given as page numbers in the text.

32. Gregory Hemingway, *Papa: A Personal Memoir* (Boston: Houghton Mifflin, 1976), 54.

33. Ibid., 55.

34. Benson, *The Writer's Art of Self-Defense*, 12–13.

35. Fleming, *The Face in the Mirror*, 3.

36. Jack Hemingway, "Memories of Papa" in *The Student* (Winter 1978): 31.

37. Rose Marie Burwell argues convincingly in *Hemingway: The Postwar Years and the Posthumous Novels* (Cambridge: Cambridge University Press, 1996), 17, that Ernest's early exposure to the outdoors was a relatively genderless experience. She notes that Grace could hunt and fish as easily as Clarence could cook and can food.

38. Donaldson, *By Force of Will*, 83.

39. Hopefully, Patrick will also publish a full-length memoir—besides his articles "My Papa, Papa," *Playboy* 15 (1968) and *"Islands in the Stream":* A Son Remembers" in *Ernest Hemingway: The Writer in Context*, edited by James Nagel (Madison: University of Wisconsin Press, 1984)—about his hunting experiences and life with Papa and his brothers, which will enrich our understanding of this topic.

40. Jack Hemingway, "Memories of Papa," 29.

Freedom and Motion, Place and Placelessness: On the Road in Hemingway's America

H. R. STONEBACK

I

"The center line of highways was the boundary line of home."
ERNEST HEMINGWAY, "THE STRANGE COUNTRY"

This essay is concerned with Hemingway's American landscape, actual and symbolic, natural landscape and *paysage moralise*, and with the roads that wind through it, the roads he figures in his fiction, the roads he follows in fact. One striking pattern in Hemingway's fiction, rarely if ever mentioned in critical commentary, is that so many of his stories begin on the road. For example, the first sentences of "Fathers and Sons" and "Wine of Wyoming" evoke roads and cars, and the first paragraphs foreground the road-and-car imagery. Other stories begin with roads and cars (e.g., "Che Ti Dice La Patria") and at least one story, "The Strange Country," is centrally concerned with the road, the act of driving, and the symbolic significance of roads and cars.

All too often, it seems, the Hemingway stories we remember best, those which are somehow sharpest in memory, are those which begin on the road—but on *carless roads*. We recall woods roads, logging traces, gravel roads, orchard lanes: young Nick Adams *walking* the logging road in "Indian Camp," the hemlock-woods path in "The Doctor and the Doctor's Wife," the orchard road in "The Three-Day Blow." We see Nick *riding* on the horse and wagon down the road in "Ten Indians," or *walking* "down the gravel road" and drinking from the roadside spring in "Summer People," or *skiing* down the mountain road in "Cross-Country Snow," or *walking* along the railroad tracks and the deserted road in "Big Two-Hearted River," or *bicycling* along the road in "A Way You'll Never Be." Or maybe we remember the American couple and Peduzzi *walking* down the road at the beginning of "Out of Season," or John and the narrator *walking* down the mountain road in the opening sentences of

"Alpine Idyll." If these roads opening into Hemingway's narratives are the ones we remember best, then we should recognize them for what they are: pastoral roads, roads free from cars and mechanization, roads with no machine-in-the-garden, roads that lead to and from real places with a living numinous *Deus Loci*, an authentic sense of place—not the car-ravished and ravaged roads of placelessness.

On the other hand, there are Hemingway stories—more of them than we might at first recall—in which roads and cars, road-and-car imagery, and the act of driving figure importantly. Consider the last five stories of the "first forty-nine" (i.e., those which conclude *The Short Stories of Ernest Hemingway*), all of which involve cars and roads either through rendered action or through metaphor and image: "Fathers and Sons," where the road and the car figure importantly to define place and place-lessness, freedom and motion, and the act of driving is a kind of medita-tive state; "The Gambler, the Nun, and the Radio," where Frazer, accident victim in his hospital bed, imagines himself riding every night in "the big white cabs (each cab equipped with radio. . .)" of Seattle; "Wine of Wyoming," where the car functions as implicit machine-in-the-garden, emblematic of the condition of displacement so central to the identity of the Fontans and the narrator, and to the curious placelessness or inau-thenticity of Hemingway's landscape: "It looked like Spain, but it was Wyoming"; "A Natural History of the Dead," where heavy trucks raise "great clouds of dust" on the disaster-strewn wartime roads; "A Day's Wait," where car imagery carries the burden of explanation of the differ-ence between Fahrenheit and Celsius to the fevered young Schatz: "It's like miles and kilometers. You know, like how many kilometers we make when we do seventy miles in the car."[1]

Since the *first* five stories of *In Our Time* have no references to cars and since they date from the early 1920s, and since the *last* five stories of the "first forty-nine" contain multiple references to cars and date from the 1930s, it is tempting to explain this pattern as a mere function of chronology, of historical "progress" or increasing mechanization. Indeed, since Hemingway's fiction written in the late 1930s, 1940s, and 1950s (e.g., "The Strange Country," *Across the River and into the Trees*, *The Garden of Eden*) is even more car-centered, the chronological explana-tion, the progressive mechanization argument seems obvious. All too obvious, however, if we consider carefully the early fiction, with its exquisitely crafted pastoral design and its primary concern with *authentic place* (e.g., northern Michigan). And if we recall that even in the earliest fiction cars occasionally figure significantly—for example, in "Soldier's Home" from 1924, where the car is associated with freedom (and motion away from home), where Krebs's mother tells him, "Your father does not want to hamper your freedom. He thinks you should be allowed to drive the car" (115). All of this taken together will lead to the recognition that the steadily increasing importance of road-and-car symbolism in Hemingway's fiction is not just a naturally occurring chrono-phenomenon fundamentally extrinsic to his fiction. It is also, far more importantly, deliberate aesthetic design and an index to his increasing concern with motifs of freedom and motion, identity through place, and placelessness. Jake Barnes, in *The Sun Also Rises*, knows that "You can't get away from yourself by moving from one place to another."[2] Many years later, in "The Strange Country," Roger, behind the wheel of his Buick, rolling west at seventy miles per hour, has forgotten—or not yet discovered—this knowledge.

In one sense, then, Hemingway's meditations on the road confirm the theories of place posited by practitioners of topistics and chorology, the conclusions of modern and postmodern geographers regarding the role of roads and cars in stripping America of a sense of place. Not the *old* roads, which connected authentic places, which were themselves imbued with place (as are the carless country roads of much Hemingway narrative), but, in E. Relph's words, "the New Road . . . an essentially twentieth century creation and an extension of man's vehicle; it does not connect places nor does it link with the surrounding landscape." This "New Road," one of the creators of and manifestations of "placelessness," "starts everywhere and leads nowhere."[3] This is the "New Road" of Hemingway's later fiction, the road of "The Strange Country," for example, where Roger thinks: "The center line of highways was the boundary line of home" (621). Displaced, disconnected from authentic place, Roger's driving and drivenness are a primary manifestation of the curse of American mobility which most writers of topistics view as the great destroyer of place.

Yet, in another sense, it could be argued that many of Hemingway's displaced characters are in motion in quest of authentic place. With the possible exception of Nick Adams in northern Michigan, there are no examples in Hemingway of the sense of place that informs, say, Faulkner's fiction. The deeply invested sense of "locality," fundamental to regionalism for two centuries, and essential to such a writer as Faulkner, has largely disappeared from the American landscape because, as J. Nicholas Entrikin puts it, "necessary connections between people and places have been replaced by contingent connections."[4] If Hemingway's fiction operates in this "betweenness" of "contingent place," if none of his characters are regionalist or Faulknerian autochthons, nevertheless many are—if I may coin a useful term—anachthons, seeking reconnection with authentic place.

In still another sense, the basic problems and paradoxes of freedom and motion, of place and placelessness, of the anachthon seeking to reconnect with place, are embodied in the American Romance of the Road. Hemingway's fictions (as well as his life) provide compelling evidence of his deep engagement with that irreducible and quintessential American mystery—the Romance of the Road, the Car, the Highway. Let us consider more closely some of that evidence.

II

". . . inside an automobile dealer's show window, lighted against the early dark, there was a racing motor car finished entirely in silver with Dans Argent lettered on the hood. This I believed to mean the silver dance or the silver dancer. . . ."
ERNEST HEMINGWAY, "GOD REST YOU MERRY, GENTLEMEN"

That Great American Dream of the Road, that love affair with the automobile, resonates in the opening paragraph of "God Rest You Merry, Gentlemen." After the story's first striking sentence—"In those days the distances were all different"—which I propose as a touchstone for our time-space/motion-place meditations on the road, the narrator looks in the window of an automobile showroom. A pilgrim at the shrine of the iconic car, he stares at "a racing motor car finished entirely in silver with Dans Argent lettered on the hood." He thinks this means "the silver dance or the silver dancer," a perfect metaphor for the romance of cars and roads. "Slightly puzzled which it meant but happy in the sight of the car and pleased by [his] knowledge of a foreign language," he walks on down the street (298). The reader, of course, recognizes that it means neither "silver dance" nor "silver dancer," sees that this mistranslation reflects the young man's romantic infatuation, his almost religious veneration and spiritual lust for this shining car and its road-promise. Perhaps, too, in the full context of the story, there is a suggestion of the dehumanizing, unmanning, castrating "eunuchhood" of the road and the machine, but this is not the place to consider in detail the many ironic variations on "rest" and "ride" which reverberate throughout the story. It must suffice to note this quintessential image of the car as romantic icon, and to observe that the text obliquely tells us that this distance-transforming "silver dancer," this fabulous car, really signifies money, that the driver of such a car must be "in the money"—*Dans Argent*. Of course, speaking grammatically, *dans argent* refers primarily to color—"in silver"—but the glamorous car in the showroom window also conveys this message: The very rich are different from you and me.[5] The car-rapt narrator does not know enough to respond that they are dull and play too much backgammon on the road, or to say: "Yes, they have shinier, faster cars."

This early instance in Hemingway's fiction of the familiar American obsession with the fabulous automobile provides a telling rubric for consideration of Hemingway's engagement with the road, the car: the "silver dance," the "silver dancer." And how can we, at 70 mph, know the dancer from the dance? In his life, Hemingway was particular about the cars he owned or rented—all shiny Buicks and Lincolns and Packards, all fast luxurious convertibles. (Perhaps I am not the only reader of biographies who is still waiting for some biographer to provide that crucial index of taste—a detailed list of all the cars Hemingway drove in his lifetime, and how many miles he put on them. You are what you drive, advertisements tell us. You are also where and how you drive, I would add.) Hemingway's fascination with cars, however, is rarely manifest in his fiction. One notable exception occurs in *Across the River and into the Trees*, where Colonel Cantwell is proud of his Buick, its speed and solidity. Cantwell has interesting things to say, too, about roads and motion, about the way speed blends and blurs things, and how—in a direct echo of the opening line of "God Rest You Merry, Gentlemen"—from the car, the country is different: "the distances are all changed." And he leaves us with these last words at the moment of his death in the Buick: "I'm now going to get into the large back seat of this god-damned over-sized luxurious automobile."[6]

It is also a Buick that provides the primary setting for Hemingway's most intensely car-and-road-centered fiction, "The Strange Country." This story, or posthumously published mutant manuscript, or discarded portion of early *Islands in the Stream* material, or intended but unfinished Great American Road Novel (whose manuscript, we note, bears the title "A Motor Trip" and indicates some intention of expansion, of extending the trip to the West), takes place, for the most part, on the road and in the car. It also provides Hemingway's most extensive and intensive meditation on roads and cars, their space and time and memory functions, their relation to place and placelessness, and to landscapes, actual and symbolic.

Almost every page of the story presents details regarding the road, the car, and the act of driving, with the exception of those passages dealing with the lost manuscript tale and intervals of eating and sex while the travelers pause on the road. The narrative begins with the act of acquiring the correct car. "Do you know anything about cars?" Roger asks Helena at the start. They each take one Miami newspaper and study the "classifieds on motorcars for sale." Roger tells her they're looking for a "convertible with good rubber. The best one we can get" (605). A few hours later they have purchased a Buick convertible, used, with six thousand miles on it.

Hemingway describes the car and its accessories precisely: "It had two good spares, set-in well fenders, a radio, a big spotlight, plenty of luggage space in the rear and it was sand colored" (606). They head west on the "straight and heat-welted" highway across the development of "what had once been the Everglades." Roger drives fast and the car's motion through the "heavy air made the air cool as it came in through the scoop in the dash and the slanted glass of the ventilators" (607). Feeling the car, already beginning to feel deeply centered in and at home in the car, Helena says: "She's a lovely car. . . . Weren't we lucky to get her?" "Very," Roger says (607).

In the first few pages the car is established as a major presence in the story, as is the road. Roger looks down the road he has so often driven before, "seeing it stretch ahead, knowing it was the same road . . . knowing that only the car was different, that only who was with him was different" (607–8). Three pages of details about the road follow, demonstrating Roger's precise knowledge of this particular road and relating exact details of the road to specific events in his past. These passages, and others in "The Strange Country," define the act of driving as a meditative state, a kind of Composition of Place and Memory, much in the manner of "Fathers and Sons."

One feature of Hemingway's car-road Composition of Place is the observation of wildlife, of the natural landscape that the comminatory road slashes through. For example, Roger remembers a rattlesnake, a wild turkey, and a buck deer seen on this road. And he knows the exact place in the road where they will see a "big osprey's nest in the dead cypress tree" (608). (As an interesting aside, I note that when I retraced the route of "The Strange Country" a few years ago I saw the osprey's nest in the dead cypress, still there in the precise spot indicated by Hemingway.) More crucial to the Composition of Place are the spiritual components. Helena asks Roger, for example, if "it's possible to be happy" and urges him to "say it is anyway." Roger *says* he thinks it is and then *thinks*: "He'd always said it was. Not in this car though. In other cars in other countries. . . . Everything was possible once. It was possible on this road" (609–10). And the reader thinks: Ah but that was in another car, and besides . . . the battery's dead.

As they ride down the road, Roger thinks and Helena talks about the past. The past leans in on them, gnaws at the present, and Roger declares: "Look . . . We'll throw it all away. All of it. We'll throw it all away now right here beside the road . . . we've thrown it all away now and we've really thrown it away" (611). The "it" that is emphatically discarded is the past. Thus the memory-laden road functions here in its familiar mythic character as a place of disburdenment, flight, and freedom from the past. With the past discarded, they concentrate on another kind of flight, the flight of birds. They watch "the way they brake with their wings and the long legs slant forward to land"; then they watch "the wood ibis crossing the sky with their pulsing flight to wheel and light" in an island of trees (612). In the past, Roger notes, they roosted much closer to the road. Thus Hemingway's road-rhythms and car-counterpoint play variations on past and future, on natural landscape and the inner spiritual landscape, on the road as flight and freedom and the road as depredation.

Timing their driving by the number of drinks, they drive on into the night "with the swamp dark and high on both sides of the road and the good headlights lighting far ahead. The drinks drove the past away the way the headlights cut through the dark" (613). The forward motion of the car and the straight-ahead focus of the "good headlights" provide the tunnel-visioned illusion of tomorrow, of the future, and freedom from the dark threatening swamp of memory. They check into a roadside cabin and immediately take their dose of another sovereign road-anodyne against the past—sex: "In the dark he went into the strange country . . . taking away all things before . . . bringing the beginning of bright happiness in darkness . . . to drive toward happiness suddenly, scaldingly achieved" (615). Even the notation of sex is grounded in car-road imagery, in road-past-driving resonances, with sex rendered here as another kind of bright "headlight," a "drive" through pastless darkness toward "happiness."

After sex they drive to a restaurant, aptly named the Green Lantern (green light for "go"). After dinner, accompanied with barefoot foreplay under the table, they drive back to the tourist cabins; the car enters its place between cabins, and as they go inside for more sex, Helena says:

> "The car knows about us already. . . . I was sort of shy with him at
> the start but now I feel like he's our partner."
> "He's a good car. . . ."
> "The car will protect us. He's our good friend already. Did you
> see how friendly he was coming back. . . ."
> "I saw the difference." (617)

Surely this is one of the most extraordinary descriptions of a car in American literature. The car has been elevated from a major narrative presence to major character, protagonist, exemplar—"partner," "friend," protector. Also we note that the Buick has undergone a gender-change; even cars, it appears, may be androgynous in Hemingway's fiction.

With the car firmly established as a friendly character, an enabling conspirator and accomplice in all the actions of the road, the motif expands to include the car as a *place*, the car as *home*. "Home," Roger thinks. "That's a laugh. There isn't any home. Sure there is. This is home. All this. This cabin. This car. . . . The center line of the highways was the boundary line of home" (621). Roger checks himself in this meditation, wary of beginning to think "like one of those Vast-Spaces-of-America writers" (621). Roger, the displaced *man*, feels his placelessness, and, as displaced *writer*, renders the car and the highway as place, as home. At the same time, he cautions himself against any simplistic mythicizing about the American Road, and Whitmanesque-Kerouacesque-Steinbeckian-Wolfean "Vast-Spaces-of-America" Romance of the Open Road.

On the road again, they continue on their ultimately westerly route, through the Peace River Valley and Arcadia. Hemingway continues to render the natural landscape with precision even as symbolic landscape—*paysage moralise*—shapes and informs the narrative more and more. The route they follow—through the Valley of the Peace to Arcadia, through springs country where numerous springs are claimed to be the Fountain of Youth, through a "wicked stretch of country" to the symbolic Suwanee-crossing and Cross City—is profoundly charged with symbolic landscape reverberations.[7] For example, the crossing of the Suwanee—"like a river in a dream" (631)—underlines the motif of displacement, of roaming "all up and down the whole creation," yearning for home. Or, as they drive at a "steady seventy," "making their own breeze . . . and feeling the country being put behind them," as they approach the country of springs, Helena declares that it's fun to drive fast because it's "like making your own youth . . . sort of foreshortening and telescoping the world the way youth does" (629). Although there is no direct allusion to the various Fountains of Youth, they do discuss spring water, and the Fountain of Youth metaphor does resonate as the deepest layer of the textual iceberg, as geomoral landscape. This youth passage further develops the motifs of freedom and motion, of putting country "behind" and speeding forward toward the illusion of renewal, toward a remade pastless "youth."

Increasingly, narrative emphasis falls on the act of driving, of "making time," speeding west. Even the instrumentation of the car figures in image-patterns that serve the themes of time and space, past and future, the cycle—or wheel—of youth and age, experience and memory. After Roger and Helena discuss the age difference between them, Roger looks "through the wheel at the clock on the dashboard" (630). The car radio brings the news of the world—and the Spanish Civil War—into the car-home between installments of soap operas. Roger becomes somewhat obsessed with the speedometer, with "making fast time," with holding it at seventy, with clocking as much over sixty miles in each hour as he possibly can. The road becomes "monotonous"; Roger doesn't like to "waste country but on a long trip you had to" and he drives now "only to put it behind him" (633). In this final passage concerning the act of driving, Hemingway plays new variations on the freedom-motion and place-placelessness motifs. Roger is bored now with the no-longer-new strange country, feels guilty about wasting country yet concentrates on speed as he labors to put country behind him. Put another way, he is trapped in the riddle of the road, caught in the anxiety, the tension between the speedometer and the odometer.

In his long interior monologue following this final driving reference, Roger tries to convince himself that he "really can start it all over now," that this journey west is a new beginning (635). After the gap in the story, the non-rendered driving omitting all the country between Tallahassee and New Orleans, there are no more driving or road allusions. But in the New Orleans sequence, as Roger gets "scared" about his new relationship, his future with Helena, as things begin to go wrong, the final car image occurs: "What woman in the world did you think could be as sound as a good secondhand Buick car? You've only known two sound women in your life and you lost them both" (643). So the road West through the "strange country" ends in New Orleans, in the actual and symbolic French Quarter, not in some visionary liberating "Vast-Spaces-of-America" West, not in renewal and freedom from the past, but in the strangest country of all—darkest memory—as Roger closes the narrative with his anguished memories of his first wife and the lost manuscripts.

One conclusion a reader may draw might go something like this: Roger has gone across the road and into the Buick one too many times. Another conclusion might be that Roger's burden, his fundamental dilemma, is rather like Jack Burden's in Robert Penn Warren's *All the King's Men*. Jack Burden's story is, for me, the richest tale of the road and flight, of the confusion of motion with freedom, of place and displacement in American literature. We read Jack and we hear Roger: "That was why I had got into my car and headed west, because when you don't like it where you are you always go west. We have always gone west. That was why I drowned in West and relived my life like a home movie."[8] We flee West, like Roger, trying to believe we "really can start it all over." And Jack Burden's words reverberate: "So there is innocence and a new start in the West, after all. If you believe the dream you dream when you go there" (311). Jack Burden comes to understand this at last, in Burden's Landing, Louisiana, and his final vision is crystalline, redemptive. It is doubtful that Roger, whose story also ends in Louisiana, understands much of it, and his final vision is murky, absinthe-cloudy.

That may, in part, be a function of this so-called short story's identity as manuscript fragment, unfinished tale, or discarded material from a novel which, in the view of many, should never have been published.

Manuscript evidence does clearly indicate that Hemingway intended to expand this road narrative, to put in, for example, all the country between Tallahassee and New Orleans that the published version lacks. Hemingway made specific notes to himself to add Wakulla, Carrabelle, Apalachicola, Panama City, Fort Walton, Pensacola, and Mobile. In the same manuscript note he reminds himself to get exactly the way the country feels, to make it as compelling as the road trip from France into Spain in *The Sun Also Rises*. His intention is to write it with such precision and design that the rendered country will produce the desired emotion in the reader. He must be mindful, his notes continue, that he has driven through that country many times and that he has always been profoundly moved by it, without observing exactly the details that created the emotion. This entire remarkable passage throws another light on Roger's regrets over his "waste" of country, in his westward haste. Hemingway admonishes himself to get precisely all the details of the landscape he passes through, the natural world, as well as the details of the act of driving, all the sensory qualities that make the intense physicality, the good feeling of driving. He is well aware that he usually drives this stretch in an almost anesthetized condition because of the need to cover long distances, that he absorbs his delight in the landscape unconsciously, without registering the details that produce the feeling, which moves him deeply.[9]

These revealing and illuminating manuscript notes serve to reinforce several of my conclusions about "The Strange Country." First, Hemingway's actual title, "A Motor Trip," is a better and more precisely descriptive title than the editorially-created title which has the unfortunate effect of centering attention on the obvious sexual metaphor. Second, Hemingway's central concern was the delight and good emotion of the road, of the act of driving, of the car, of the connection with the passing country, and all the symbolic undertones and mythic overtones that accompany that catalogue of delight. Third, he did indeed intend this narrative to be a kind of Romance of the Road, regardless of whatever other themes figured in his physical and spiritual Composition of Place. And he *does* use the country to produce the emotion. But then he had always done that, from the very beginning.

I nominate "The Strange Country," then, as Hemingway's *On the Road*, his contribution to a great American genre. He writes from deeply within the knowledge that every American is, at least in part, as Wallace Stegner puts it, "the displaced person . . . always in motion." Hemingway writes from the center-line of the American "tradition of restlessness," as Stegner has it, that distinctly American vision that urges "motion . . . as a form of virtue."[10] That the American Road promises renewal, that motion promises freedom, that car and road together simultaneously figure place and placelessness—all this constitutes the triumph and the tragedy of what we might still be permitted to call The American Dream. The problems and paradoxes of the Song of the American Road may not be resolved, may be immune to resolution, closure. Yet still Merle Haggard sings it, calls it "White Line Fever"; Hemingway sings it, calls it "the boundary line of home." Hank and Merle and Willie and all the others sing it, with Hemingway, the delight and feeling of being "on the road again."

III

"[Ernest] bought a beautiful Buick Roadmaster convertible, royal blue with bright red leather lining and seats . . . he flew to Miami to join Toby and the car for a leisurely detoured voyage to Sun Valley via his childhood haunts in northern Michigan."

MARY HEMINGWAY, *How It Was*[11]

"Papa loved being on the road. He liked to see every detail, every bird and animal . . . it was amazing the things he saw and pointed out to me. Sometimes he took notes. And he knew the history of places we drove through, too, and he'd make weird connections. . . . He liked convertibles because you could see more, you were closer to the country you went through, "more inside" it, Papa said. . . . He loved to drive, too, even if maybe he wasn't a very good driver—he liked looking too much. . . . No, he wasn't a very good driver but he was one hellacious looker and seer. And we'd take our own sweet time. If he wanted to see something close up or more exactly, we'd stop, or we'd make a detour to see something he wanted to see. Or somebody. There was this one cross-country trip that was mostly detours. We went to Oxford to see Faulkner. . . ."

TOBY BRUCE, INTERVIEWS WITH H. R. STONEBACK[12]

Before we conclude we might note, as a small service to biographers and students of Hemingway's life, to biographically-oriented readers and critics, a few hitherto unpromulgated facts and an engaging anecdote or two regarding Hemingway on the American Road. For example, it seems to be widely (and incorrectly) assumed that "The Strange Country" is a thinly veiled account of a road trip Hemingway made with Martha Gellhorn, and Helena is assumed to be modeled on Martha. Clearly, as much internal and external evidence argues, this is not the case. Helena is, in fact, much more closely a portrait of Jane Mason. There is far too much evidence to go into here, and, to be sure, it is of little *critical* interest. Yet we might note that since many details in the story are straight from life, are directly based on Hemingway's relationship with Jane Mason, and since the omitted part of the drive, the road west through Apalachicola which Hemingway intended to add, is probably based on a trip to Apalachicola he made with Jane, perhaps that is one reason he discarded this manuscript, left it unfinished. Because he knew that he was not *making* it true and "made up," not creating character, not inventing story, not transmuting fact into fiction.[13]

What was it like to drive down the road and cross-country with Ernest Hemingway? In *How It Was*, Mary Hemingway describes Ernest's "beautiful Buick Roadmaster convertible, royal blue with bright red-leather" seats and upholstery in which he made a "leisurely detoured" maiden voyage in 1947 with Toby Bruce (208). In conversation, Mary told me that Ernest "especially loved Buicks, all the details about them," and that he loved "convertibles above all." Mary allowed that she did not share his passion for cars, nor his "passion for driving": "he loved to drive, to ride, to be in a car and look at passing country and talk about it," while observing precisely all the "natural and historical facts" of the landscape.[14]

My conversations with Toby Bruce, who was often with Hemingway on long road trips, marked the turning point in my view of Hemingway as a train and ship person, a man who did not care much for cars and roads. Toby told me that "Papa loved being on the road," and added that "he was a lot of fun to ride with, always cheerful, always looking, and he saw everything." He said the best trips were the ones when they were not in a hurry, and could make unscheduled stops and detours. And then he told what is, for me, by far the most remarkable and revealing Hemingway on-the-road anecdote, which has escaped the notice of all biographers and commentators and is here revealed for the first time. Driving cross-country in that shiny new Buick convertible, on one of his "leisurely detoured" pilgrimages on the American Road, en route to Sun Valley with a planned detour to northern Michigan, Hemingway directed a sudden and substantial and profoundly symbolic detour: "We went to Oxford," Toby said, "to see Faulkner."

When they got to Oxford they drove by Faulkner's place, but nobody was home. There was "a lot of commotion in town that day," Toby said: "There was some kind of celebration honoring Faulkner. . . . I think we saw a sign or banner or something saying it was 'William Faulkner Day' in Oxford. So we left, and didn't get to see Faulkner." I asked Toby when this trip occurred: "Let's see, it was after the war. We were in that new blue Buick Roadmaster so it must have been '47 or '48. And it was after

Papa had that blowup with Faulkner—you know about that?" Yes, I said.
"Actually," Toby continued, "there were two or three different trips when
he talked about making a detour to see Faulkner; one other time we got
pretty close to Oxford but Papa changed his mind. As far as I know, this is
the only time Papa actually went to Oxford looking for Faulkner."[15]
Clearly, from Toby's description, the Oxford pilgrimage must have
occurred in September 1947, when Bruce and Hemingway drove from
Miami to Sun Valley via Walloon Lake.

Since it sheds significant light on Hemingway's Oxford trip, let us
rehearse briefly the well-documented facts referred to by Toby Bruce
as "that blowup with Faulkner." On 14 April 1947, Faulkner suggested
to a class of students at the University of Mississippi, among other
things, that Hemingway didn't take enough risks in his writing. On May
11 the New York *Herald Tribune* printed an account of Faulkner's
remarks, Hemingway read them, thought Faulkner had called him a
coward, and feverish letters ensued: Hemingway to his World War II
comrade-in-arms "Buck" Lanham, Lanham to Faulkner, Faulkner to
Lanham and Hemingway.[16] On June 28 Faulkner wrote briefly to
Hemingway, saying he was "sorry" about this "damn stupid thing," it
was just a misconstrual of informal remarks not made for publication
and he hoped it would not "matter a damn" to Hemingway.[17] On July 23
Hemingway wrote a long and revealing letter to Faulkner which is a
crucial document, indispensable for any consideration of Hemingway's
personal sense of place and placelessness. Hemingway tells Faulkner:
the "difference with us guys is I always lived out of country . . . since
kid. My own country gone. Trees cut down. Nothing left but gas stations, sub-divisions. . . . Found good country outside [i. e., abroad] . . .
and lost it the same way." And here is the phrase that reverberates:
"Been chickenshit dis-placed person since can remember." Sharply to
the point, then, Hemingway acknowledges Faulkner as a man and
writer with place, who is deeply *placed*; and he laments his own lack of
place, his displacedness. After some praise of Faulkner's writing,
Hemingway ends this July 23 letter by telling Faulkner that he would
like to keep up the correspondence: "I am your Bro. if you want one
that writes and I'd like us to keep in touch."[18] There is no record of
Faulkner's response. But we now know that a few weeks later
Hemingway, self-styled "chickenshit dis-placed person," made his pilgrimage to the Capitol of Place in American literature to see Faulkner.
But Faulkner was not at home, because he was being honored by his
place. Then Hemingway leaves Oxford, goes on up the long road to the
only location where he ever felt truly *placed*, to northern Michigan.
There is no more poignant moment in American literary history.

This sequence of events, to be sure, serves as profound commentary on the haunting paradigm of place and placelessness in Hemingway's life and work. Was he really a "chickenshit dis-placed person," always in motion on a road that started every place, led to no place, started everywhere, ended nowhere? What *do* all those miles, burning up the road in Buick Roadmasters and all the other cars, add up to? Was Hemingway Master of the Road? Perhaps we can agree with Michael Reynolds: "What we see is a man more comfortable on the road than at any place called home."[19] Or perhaps we can write much of it off to Tax Strategy. Or perhaps we had better rethink the paradigm, recognize that Hemingway, after his fashion, had many places—Paris, Roncevaux and the country around, the pilgrimage of St.-Jacques/Santiago (the ultimate example of a road that is *placed*), or corrida-country, or Key West in the old days, or Wyoming, Idaho, the Finca, the Pilar, the Sea, the Gulf Stream and all the Big Two-Hearted Rivers where he could feel authentically "there," in the "good place." Hemingway was *never* a mere "tourist" in place (as he said in his letter to Faulkner that Dos Passos "always" was). If Hemingway was never a rooted autochthon like Faulkner, he was—and so were many of his created characters—an anachthonous pilgrim.

The design of Hemingway's life and work, then, reveals a pattern of freedom and motion, place and placelessness, or deracination and the lost authentic place, of the constant quest for and pilgrimage to the hoped-for numinous place. The quest is always in the optative mood, often goes through strange country and Arcadian landscapes, is frequently conducted in the shadow of a Poussinesque landscape, under the rubric: "Et in Arcadia Ego." Sometimes this famous motif in literary and art history is understood as a configuration of melancholy place and displacement. Sometimes it is read as romantic yearning, sometimes as death-haunted brooding. Yet the common romantic mistranslation—"I too have been in Arcadia"—does not preclude or contradict the actual signification: "Even in Arcadia, there am I" (i.e., death). Hemingway has it both ways, all ways; his complex vision of place simultaneously evokes all of these readings, as he and his created characters go down the road in their Roadmasters, chanting: Et in America Ego.

NOTES

1. Ernest Hemingway, *The Complete Short Stories of Ernest Hemingway* (New York: Scribner's, 1987), 363, 353, 336, 334. Subsequent references will be given as page numbers in the text.

2. Ernest Hemingway, *The Sun Also Rises* (New York: Scribner's, 1926), 11.

3. E. Relph, *Place and Placelessness* (London: Pion Limited, 1976), 90.

4. J. Nicholas Entrikin, *The Betweenness of Place: Towards a Geography of Modernity* (Baltimore: The Johns Hopkins University Press, 1991), 11.

5. *"Dans argent"* is not a familiar idiom or equivalent of "in the money," which should take the form *"dans l'argent."* Yet it is possible that a car manufacturer or customizer would omit the "l" and apostrophe through ignorance, as wordplay, or to avoid clutter in a logo or emblem. I should also note here that my efforts to locate references to an actual car of the period which had "Dans Argent lettered on the hood" have thus far yielded no result. My first hunch was that this might have been a Rolls Royce model name, given the Rolls proclivity toward names "in silver." But a Rolls enthusiast and amateur of automotive history could not confirm the existence of a "Dans Argent" Rolls model. Perhaps, since Hemingway's car is a "racing motor car," it is customized, one-of-a-kind.

6. Ernest Hemingway, *Across the River and into the Trees* (New York: Scribner's, 1950), 12–14, 307.

7. I have treated this matter in more detail in a forthcoming essay, "'Et in Arcadia Ego': Deep Structure, *Paysage Moralise*, Geomoral and Symbolic Landscape in Hemingway," a version of which was presented at the Conference on American Literature of the American Literature Association, Baltimore, Md., May 1995.

8. Robert Penn Warren, *All the King's Men* (New York: Harcourt Brace Jovanovich, 1982), 309. Subsequent references will be given as page numbers in the text.

9. Ernest Hemingway, "The Strange Country"/"A Motor Trip" manuscript. Hemingway Collection: John F. Kennedy Library, Item 102B.

10. Wallace Stegner, "A Sense of Place" *The Hudson Valley Regional Review* 11.2 (September 1994): 47–48, 52.

11. Mary Hemingway, *How It Was* (New York: Alfred A. Knopf, 1976), 208.

12. Otto (Toby) Bruce, interview by author, Key West, Fla., 9–13 January 1978. When I recently relocated my original notes from my earliest conversations with Toby Bruce, I was struck all over again by the amount of time we spent talking about those cross-country drives Hemingway and Bruce made together. These road anecdotes seemed to be Toby's most vivid and compelling memories of Hemingway; or perhaps they seemed so to me because he was telling me things I had not heard or read elsewhere. In later conversations Toby also talked a good deal about being on the road with Papa, cars, trips made together. When I wrote the original draft of this essay, I had not consulted my notes on these conversations for over a decade; thus they played no conscious role in the formation of my critical views regarding roads and cars in Hemingway's fiction. Yet I have from time to time referred in class to a few of Toby's road remarks that I

had partially transcribed on the flyleaf of a Hemingway volume that I have taught from hundreds of times since 1978; so perhaps a touch of what some may be pleased to regard as the biographical fallacy may have crept in at the edges of my explication de texte.

13. The assumptions regarding Martha as Helena which I cite here are both conversational and from conference panel discussions; I have not seen any published material dealing with this matter. The mass of details regarding Helena-Jane, internal narrative evidence and external biographical evidence, will appear in a forthcoming essay primarily concerned with the Hemingway-Mason relationship. It must suffice here to note that Jane Mason had relatives in Apalachicola and that Hemingway seems to have made just such a road trip with her as "The Strange Country" describes. Eyewitnesses and Mason family connections place Hemingway in Apalachicola a number of times, at least once with Jane.

14. Mary Hemingway, conversations with author, New York, N.Y., 1977–85. I cite Mary's mention of Ernest's "passion for driving" because until this and other conversational references from Mary and those who knew best changed my view I had a picture—gathered from multifarious biographical sources—of Hemingway as someone who did not like to drive, who liked to be driven. The first time Mary told me of Ernest's "passion for driving" I was driving her from New York City to my home in the country; she said she had not been in a car (except for cabs) for some time and she didn't like to drive, but it was pleasant riding. I asked if it wasn't that way with Ernest, too, but she insisted that no, he loved to drive. The driving details of "The Strange Country" (and, of course, *The Garden of Eden*), both of which appeared years after these conversations regarding cars, confirmed Hemingway's passion for the act of driving.

15. Bruce, interview. Toby repeated the story of this Oxford trip to see Faulkner several times in later conversations with me, with no substantial variation, after our original 1978 interviews. I told him it was an extraordinary story and tried to get him to write it all down—with no result. For decades, in every possible source, published and unpublished, and with every possible resource (e.g., persons who knew Hemingway well in this period), I have sought secondary confirmation of Toby's story of the Oxford visit. I asked Mary Hemingway repeatedly if she knew anything about this trip—had Ernest called her from Oxford, maybe, or had he made some remark about it? She said she thought Ernest had gone through Oxford hoping to see Faulkner once, but she was not with him, and she had no idea he had done it on the 1947 Miami-Sun Valley drive. She thought "quite possible." Bill Walton said he had some vague notion Hemingway might have gone to Oxford to see Faulkner—"didn't they know each other?" (he also said)—but he had "no earthly idea when." (He and Ernest had, "of course," talked about Faulkner, his art, his writing, and about Faulkner as the "prime example of a writer who had place": Conversations 1988–94). As far as the

precise dates of the trip, it is difficult to pinpoint. Toby Bruce did not remember the dates, or the routes they followed. The most reliable biographers do not agree on the general dates of the Miami-Sun Valley excursion during which the Oxford detour (of which they are not aware) occurred. Carlos Baker has Hemingway setting off "in September in a new Buick Roadmaster with Otto Bruce as driver. They varied the usual itinerary in order to pay a call at Windemere on Walloon Lake. . . . Late in the evening of the 29th they reached Sun Valley" (*Ernest Hemingway: A Life Story* [New York: Scribner's, 1969], 462). Michael Reynolds has them leaving in late August "for Idaho via Walloon Lake," arriving at Sun Valley on September 29 (*Hemingway: An Annotated Chronology* [Detroit: Omnigraphics, 1991], 111). Mary Hemingway has Ernest and Toby leaving Miami in "mid-September" (*How It Was*, 208). My efforts to fix a precise date for the event from the Faulkner-Oxford perspective have thus far yielded no firm result. Faulkner's biographers provide no information pertinent to the matter. In the late 1970s and early 1980s my conversations with Faulkner family members (e.g. Jimmy Faulkner) and friends (e.g. Mac Reed) produced anecdotal evidence of several events that might fit Toby Bruce's description of a celebration of "Faulkner Day" in Oxford, but no hard data. In my perusal of the files of the *Oxford Eagle* I was only able to find the account of the Faulkner celebration in Oxford in December, 1950, when Faulkner returned from the Nobel Prize ceremonies in Stockholm: the high school band, cheerleaders, and majorettes gave Faulkner a rousing homecoming. But in December 1950 Hemingway was in Cuba. In September 1947, then, Hemingway was in Oxford, Mississippi; so was Faulkner, but they did not meet. This seems the appropriate place to record my view, after decades of interviews and conversations with scores of persons who knew Hemingway, that Toby Bruce was the most reliable, most consistent witness in matters of fact. Others may tell better stories, but they don't always check out. Toby's always did, especially stories of this kind, where he was a central actor, where he was behind the wheel.

16. For biographical overviews of this situation, see Joseph Blotner, *Faulkner, A Biography* (New York: Random House, 1974), 1230–35; and Baker, *Life*, 461.

17. Joseph Blotner, ed., *Selected Letters of William Faulkner* (London: The Scholar Press, 1977), 251–52.

18. Carlos Baker, ed., *Ernest Hemingway: Selected Letters 1917–1961* (New York: Scribner's, 1981), 623–25.

19. Michael Reynolds, *Hemingway: An Annotated Chronology* (Detroit: Omnigraphics, 1991), 8.

Vardis Fisher: Ernest Hemingway's Stern Idaho Critic

JOSEPH M. FLORA

Ernest Hemingway is a writer we associate intimately not just with place, but with places: northern Michigan, Paris, Spain, Italy, Key West, Cuba. Idaho had never driven his imagination as these places had, but following his suicide on 2 July 1961, in Ketchum, his association with Idaho took on a meaning it had not had before.[1] In a sense, Idaho also changed. Hemingway became an Idaho writer.

When Hemingway first visited Sun Valley, he was not entering a state void of a literary tradition. In fact, 1939 had brought Vardis Fisher, Idaho's most famous writer, the greatest public acclaim and highest monetary reward he had ever known. Attention to Fisher for his Harper Prize-winning novel *Children of God* was at its peak when Martha Gellhorn and Hemingway arrived at Sun Valley Lodge that September. So the odds are good that Hemingway had heard of Idaho's chief novelist that fall if he had not before. But he might have known of him earlier. In the 1930s, Fisher had made his biggest literary stir, bringing considerable attention to Idaho, first with novels set there, including an autobiographical tetralogy, and especially with *Idaho: A Guide in Word and Picture* (1937)—the first state guide completed under Roosevelt's Federal Writers' Project. Fisher directed Idaho's effort and wrote most of the text. But I know of no hard evidence that Hemingway ever read a book by Fisher. It's doubtful that he would have liked many of them, though *Dark Bridwell* (1931) and *In Tragic Life* (1932) might have won him over. It is clear, however, that by 1939 Fisher had an abiding antagonism toward Hemingway; it would become an obsession.

In the only published biography of Fisher, Tim Woodward affirms that Hemingway knew about Fisher and that the two authors came close to meeting. According to his story, Hemingway had hired a guide for pheasant hunting along the Snake River. Near Hagerman, he told the guide he would like to see Fisher's ranch. The guide obliged. From a rimrock, Hemingway stared at the Fisher home for some time, finally breaking silence with the observation that "all the time he'd been in Idaho, Fisher had never bothered to look him up."² The story sounds apocryphal. Its source is Fisher's widow, who got it from the guide. She would be inclined to believe the story, to see it as a demonstration of an arrogant Hemingway, a man she did not admire. Had Hemingway ever knocked at the Fisher house, he might have been invited in, but his entrance might well have produced a companion story to the famous fight between Hemingway and Wallace Stevens.

Whether or not Hemingway knew about Fisher, Fisher had been a long-time observer of Hemingway and had read several of his books, though increasingly he came to read *about* Hemingway, the Hemingway of the popular press, rather than to read him. Once Hemingway moved to Ketchum (little more than an hour's drive from Hagerman), Fisher would certainly have been aware of his new neighbor and likely would have heard accounts about him.

Certainly Fisher took keen interest in Hemingway's last Idaho sojourn, as I can testify. For if Hemingway never called on Fisher, I was fortunate enough to have been able to do that. The time was summer 1963. A recent Ph.D., I was working on a book on Fisher. We had had some correspondence, and I wrote to ask about the possibility of a visit. He replied that I would be welcome. And so in late summer I made my first trip to Idaho. Vardis and Opal Fisher met my flight in Boise, then drove me to their Hagerman home.

The last event of the day was "night caps"—a lengthy process. One of the things that Fisher and Hemingway shared was a large capacity for alcohol. Fisher believed that alcohol facilitated conversation—and honesty.

Hemingway was among the topics of conversation that night, especially his death. Like Hemingway, Fisher had given a great deal of thought in his lifetime to the concept of suicide. As a young man, he had threatened it, though he may never have seriously pondered it until after his first wife committed suicide, an event for which Fisher, then twenty-nine, bore much blame and for which he never forgave himself. Unquestionably, Fisher took special interest in Hemingway's ending at Ketchum. Fisher believed that suicide could be a rational and honorable choice. What bothered him was not that Hemingway committed suicide, but that he had managed it so poorly—in the house, a terrible mess for Mary, a characteristic mistreatment of a woman. Eyes a-twinkle, Fisher joked about better ways to achieve the deed. He envisioned rigging himself up with hand grenades all over his body and then pulling a master pin, thus blowing himself into a million pieces—leaving no mess, no body for cremation or burial.³

Fisher died five years later, at age 73. As I learned the details of his death, I thought back to my Hagerman visit. Apparently, Fisher and his wife had argued. Fisher had gone to the guest cottage to spend the night. He had been drinking heavily and then took a large number of sleeping pills. He was rushed to the hospital in Jerome; two hours later he was pronounced dead. The cause was overdose of alcohol and sleeping pills. Some who knew Fisher well (many had heard him discourse on suicide) had no doubt that his death was by choice. Others were free to consider it an accident.[4] The widow could console herself with this view—even as Mary Hemingway had at first claimed Hemingway's death an accident.

Opal Fisher was a gracious hostess for my brief stay in Hagerman. But she held some harsh views about Hemingway—views that Fisher seemed to share. She was not so much distressed by Hemingway's mistreatment of women as by his mistreatment of the natural world. She prized all living forms. She was loathe to disturb a spider, as I who stayed in her guest cottage can attest. The Hemingway who hunted for sport and trophies had only her scorn; she put bullfighting in the realm of the pathological.

Evidence that Hemingway was important to Fisher's life and thought is not dependent, however, on conversations that he had with me or others, nor on statements in letters. Hemingway had proven immensely useful to Fisher in a literary sense. In 1953 Caxton Printers of Idaho published Fisher's *God or Caesar?*. Subtitled *The Writing of Fiction for Beginners*, the book is a good deal more than that. With twenty-five years of writing books behind him, Fisher wanted to share his views on writing and publishing in America. He shares as well his philosophy of life—what he wishes he had known when he had started writing. His book is strongly polemical, vigorously iconoclastic—full of warning and admonition.

Fisher divides writers into two groups, God's writers and Caesar's. For those who write for God, by which he means true artists, those intent on fully realizing their talent, acclaim may come after death—as with Melville and Stendhal. God's writers probe deeply and seek important truth; often their contemporaries misunderstand and ignore them. Caesar's writers have their eye on money and acclaim here and now. They specialize in what is marketable.

It's clear that Fisher (an energetic atheist) counts himself among those writing for God in this metaphorical sense; he himself is the hero of his book. *God or Caesar?* is partly autobiography—though Fisher's examples are by no means all personal. The contemporary writer he praises most often is James Branch Cabell. Neglect of Cabell, Fisher claims, is not a result of Cabell's mannered style, but consequence of the truths he continuously reveals: Cabell is unrelenting in his unflattering presentation of human vanity and in his depiction of a humanity intent on masking realities with comforting myths.

Fisher had little patience for those writing for Caesar, but he provides examples of writers rendering much too much to Caesar. Chief among these is Ernest Hemingway, the counterpoint in *God or Caesar?* to Cabell. A very inadequate index demonstrates that Hemingway was much on Fisher's mind, but not how much. It lists thirteen references, not even half of the listings an accurate index would have cited. Hemingway is a constant motif in *God or Caesar?*. References to him thread the book.

Although the references are often condemning, Fisher at least pays Hemingway the tribute of imitation, twice. In a chapter on dialogue, he imitates three writers (Hemingway, Wolfe, Robert Nathan), beginning, he says mockingly, with Hemingway as "the easiest of all writers to imitate."[5] In the following chapter Fisher moves to scene, again offering a trio of imitations of a love scene. He begins "inevitably" with Hemingway; *A Farewell to Arms* lurks behind his effort. Fisher follows his imitation with a brief analysis of the "hardboiled" style, then quotes Charles Angoff:

> Hemingway is probably the only respectable author in all world literature who does not think that civilized people need poetry for authentic love-making. He fails to distinguish between the means and the end. He considers the means as the end. No wonder so many women readers find him revolting, and no wonder so many men readers look upon him as the perennial adolescent. (116)[6]

Fisher then follows by putting the poetry in the scene, using Cabell as model.[7]

Still, Fisher found Hemingway worthy of inclusion in a novel course he taught at New York University. *A Farewell to Arms* was on the syllabus, doubtless as exemplar of the popular novel.[8] Fisher's students, he says, grasped the novel "without any trouble at all, and liked it" (53)—though only a few were able to grasp the truths in the two Cabell novels also in the course. With the Angoff quotation in mind, we might imagine the slant the teacher put on Hemingway's novel. In spring 1968, because I had included Fisher's *Mountain Man* in a course, I sent him my syllabus. The same syllabus listed two works by Hemingway, *In Our Time* and *The Old Man and the Sea*. Fisher let the first title stand unchallenged; by *Old Man* he wrote: "Do you really think this has any literary worth?"

The praise that Hemingway gets in Fisher's book is decidedly faint, though Fisher does acknowledge that study of Hemingway can be useful to the beginning writer of fiction. He recommends that the beginner who wishes to study "almost wholly impressionistic delineation of (for the most part) relatively simple extroverted people" read Hemingway (98).

He suggests further that a writer with a tendency toward the ornate and flamboyant would do well to read the early Hemingway (103). In his discussion of title selections, Fisher credits Hemingway with selecting good ones. *The Sun Also Rises* is on his list of novels with excellent titles. Still, Fisher finds it necessary to undercut even the Hemingway he most admires. Having stood with Hemingway in choosing the commonplace word for the unusual or pretentious, preferring *said* as the verb for tags identifying dialogue, he reports that his students found the continuous use of *said* in Hemingway dull. For some, Fisher says, the repetition is "an offensive mannerism, for others it is 'lean athletic prose'" (103). Having written a Ph.D. dissertation on George Meredith, Fisher had great affinity for the Victorian writers. At the end of his chapter on dialogue, he says it may be that "we have gone too far in brisk, brittle, staccato repartee. Dialog in the older books had more depth and richness but much less sincerity." He ends the chapter by suggesting that the reader put "side by side . . . any good novel of the last century and any book by Hemingway" (110). We sense the conclusion he would have us reach.

Mainly, however, Hemingway appears in *God or Caesar?* as a warning. In a single reference to Fitzgerald, Fisher admonishes the aspiring young writer to be familiar with a good Fitzgerald biography (218).[9] Had Fisher lived to see the proliferation of Hemingway biographies, he would have taken sardonic note of them—and not been surprised at any revelations, though he would have found the number of biographies excessive and indicative of cultural neuroses. Still, he might be advising the young reader to be familiar with one of them as a cautionary tale. As it is, he takes special note of Lillian Ross's profile of Hemingway. For Fisher, it is a revealing text:

> There you will find egoism and doubt in the most naked conflict. There you see his fear that he may not be a great writer after all, even while he places himself . . . above all novelists but Tolstoy. Even while he cries out that he was 'champion' in his twenties, again in his thirties, again in his forties, and then recently in his fifties, doubts rise to challenge him. There is revealed, almost too painfully, his morbid fear of age and death; his scorn of formal education and of erudition even while he shows pride in the fact that he had a son at Harvard; and his obsession with the jargon of fighting and killing, in which alone he seemed able to express himself. It may indeed be a horrendous caricature but it is also a pitiless revelation of an artist's soul. (19)[10]

In Fisher's view, Hemingway had not arrived at this sorry state entirely through his own doing. Fisher, who deplored myth making of all kinds, views Hemingway as a victim of mythologists, a victim of his "votaries" who had marked him for apotheosis. Fisher excoriates Malcolm Cowley and John O'Hara as chief culprits. He sees Cowley's essay in *Life* ("A Portrait of Mister Papa," 25 [10 January 1949]) as rampant myth making, and he is especially appalled at Cowley's revelation that each morning Hemingway reads, at least until he is halfway finished, what he has already written on his novel, when two or three chapters may suffice.[11] Fisher points out that for a novel of a hundred thousand words, the writer who composes an average of five hundred words a day will have read the first half a hundred times. If what Cowley reports is true, Fisher says that "we can only stand aghast at the indulgence" Hemingway feels for his "stuff" (46).[12] Fisher points scornfully to a 1950 *Collier's* editorial ("and New Champion," *Collier's* 126 [18 November 1950], 86) that was accompanied by Al Hirschfeld's drawing showing Hemingway "as a hairy and triumphant colossus [standing] with his left foot on a prostrate Shakespeare, his left hand grasping his dripping spear, while around him in postures of grotesque defeat are a score of the greatest writers of the past three hundred years." The editorial quotes approvingly the first paragraph of O'Hara's New York *Times* review of *Across the River and Into the Trees*. In it O'Hara calls Hemingway "the most important, the outstanding author since the death of Shakespeare" (45–47).

Many reviewers and readers of *Across the River* had doubted that the 1950 novel enhanced Hemingway's literary reputation. Fisher seems to have taken special note of the controversy—particularly responses from other authors who came to Hemingway's defense. Evelyn Waugh faulted those who attacked the novel: "I believe the truth is that they have detected in [Hemingway] something they find quite unforgivable— Decent Feeling. Behind all the bluster and cursing and fisticuffs he has an elementary sense of chivalry—respect for women, pity for the weak, love of honor" (47). William Faulkner praised Waugh's response; deriding those who threw "spitballs," Faulkner said that the author of *Men Without Women* and *The Sun Also Rises* and the African pieces needed no defense. Responding, Fisher wrote:

> Camaraderie in authors is a fine thing; but why, one wonders, if Hemingway needed no defense did Faulkner with such pretentious derision come to his aid? If some reviewers were smug and conde-scending, they have been so in other times and with other authors, when Waugh and Faulkner were silent. The plain truth is that a god was under attack and his votaries sprang to the temple. (47)

Thus, when Fisher ends his chapter on "Myths and Legends"—one of the most important in the book—Hemingway is the paramount bad example:

Unless you are sure that your mind can perceive the motives and your vanity resist the blandishments[,] flee from your idolaters as you would from bedlam. Unless you wish to exploit the credulity, superstitions, ignorance and hero-worshipping tendencies in people, and at last get hung up in a web, abjure the mythmakers. Abjure the efforts of the god-abandoned or god-seeking to bring you to the apotheosis, for they have no interest in the gods they create but only in the reflection of their image in their creations. The life of an artist has enough hazards without being put in the way of a god-creating and god-eating mankind. For in ancient times—let me repeat it— people ate their gods, and in ways subtly and wondrously refined they still destroy them. (49)

Nevertheless, Fisher could find evidence that Hemingway aided and abetted this process. He condemns him for endorsing ale and fountain pens in magazine advertisements (209–10). He notes, "That sort of thing is done by people swimming with the current and seems to have become, generally, an acceptable aspect of American life. We are startled only when we find one endorsing a product of whom we had thought he was on the side of God" (211). More vociferously, he mocks the Hemingway who aspired to a fourth and even a fifth dimension in prose—and the critics who argued he had achieved those dimensions. For Fisher, such theorizing was another form of mystification, mythmaking, and would certainly not be helpful to the young writer.[13] Though we may find Fisher's treatment strident (as in so much else), he identifies a legitimate theme, one that John Raeburn later gave extended and more balanced treatment in *Fame Became of Him: Hemingway as Public Writer* (1984).

Fisher's stridency can be distressing, as when he faults Hemingway for his "prodigious scorn for learning" (31), a charge Fisher makes more than once. The charge stemmed, doubtless, from Hemingway's imprudent statements about "intellectuals" and professors. Fisher thought that Hemingway's great mistake was in having read mainly fiction. Although throughout the pages of *God or Caesar?* Fisher recommends various fiction (including Hemingway) to the aspiring writer, he expects the serious writer to read a good deal besides fiction. Fisher's last appendix recommends to the aspiring writer a list of books—none novels. Their subjects are history, anthropology, religion, psychology. Had Hemingway known more, Fisher implies, he would have been less taken in by his cultists.

Fisher had not, of course, the advantage of reading Michael Reynolds's *Hemingway's Reading, 1910–1940* (1981), or he might have broached this topic more temperately. Hemingway's reading more than made up for the background that he would have gotten at an American college or university. As Reynolds notes, in Anderson, Stein, Pound, and Ford, Hemingway had had excellent mentors to guide him in his "crash course." Reynolds also makes clear that Hemingway did not restrict his reading to fiction and poetry.

Recognizing that some of his choices in his list of one hundred books for the aspiring writer may reflect his own prejudices, Fisher claims that many of them would appear "in any well-chosen list calculated to give a young person a broad knowledge of the past" (264). Reynolds shows three of those books in his inventory of Hemingway's reading: Coulton's *Life in the Middle Ages* (Hemingway borrowed volumes II & III from Sylvia Beach's bookstore), Havelock Ellis's *Erotic Symbolism* (Hemingway's reading of Ellis was extensive), W. E. Lecky's *History of European Morals*. Fisher lists Edvard Westermarck's *Origin and Development of Moral Ideas*; Reynolds shows Hemingway owning Westermarck's *The History of Human Marriage* (three volumes). Though Reynolds does not inventory Freud's *Totem and Taboo*, it is likely that Hemingway had read it; similarly he knew about and likely read some of the work of James Frazer. "Books [Hemingway] once told a friend, were his ammunition."[14]

In attacking Hemingway's reading, Fisher, of course, leaves himself open to the charge that he did not spend enough time reading contemporary novels. In his review of *Mountain Man*, Larry McMurtry, himself a Fisher collector, suggests that Fisher's scholarly training may not have served him as novelist. "Fisher has a strong desire to be a scholar-artist, but his gift for narrative has not always been compatible with his yen for scholarship. His talent and his subjects are sometimes not congruent."[15]

Clearly, books were Fisher's ammunition for his historical novels and especially for his autobiographical novel *Orphans in Gethsemane*. No novelist ever barraged readers with so many quotations as Fisher did there. But more than Fisher knew, and as Reynolds asserts, Hemingway was correct in identifying books as his ammunition. The difference in how the two writers used their ammunition is crucial to the difference between them.

As Hemingway was useful to him for issuing a strong caution about myth makers, Fisher also found Hemingway extremely useful in his opening chapter as he defines the artist's nature. In this attempt Fisher was in advance of his time. Although Fisher had been dead several years before "androgyny" became current in the vocabulary of literary criticism, he had come to recognize the concept as central to his notion of the artist. He explains:

> The artist is a kind of hybrid, half-man and half-woman, half-woman
> and half-man. You have only to look at the photographs of most of

them to perceive that. I do *not* have homosexuality in mind. Real
homosexuals are rare, even if homosexual practices may be commonplace. I have in mind what psychologists call cross-identifications—
that is, identifications in childhood with the opposite sex. (20–21)

Admonishing his readers to be mindful of "the psychological truths in the
bi-sexual gods of ancient times," he grants that some artists look very feminine or masculine in appearance, citing Millay and Hemingway. And then
he makes a statement that anticipates some of the most current
Hemingway biography and criticism: "But those who try to understand
Hemingway will fail until they realize that his nature is essentially feminine. It is not for nothing that he has devoted so much of his life to guns,
war, and killing" (21). In the next chapter, Fisher reaffirms that
Hemingway's nature is "largely feminine," explaining Hemingway's
"obsession" with guns, killing, and war as "a simply symbolic and childlike
effort to believe in his maleness" (48). Such studies as Kenneth Lynn's
Hemingway (1987), Mark Spilka's *Hemingway's Quarrel with Androgyny*
(1990), James Mellow's *Hemingway: A Life Without Consequences*
(1992), J. Gerald Kennedy's *Imagining Paris: Exile, Writing and American
Identity* (1993), and Nancy Comley and Robert Scholes's *Hemingway's
Genders: Rereading the Hemingway Text* (1994) would have confirmed
Fisher in his view and perhaps made him more compassionate to the man.
Likely he would have wondered why it took the academy so long to catch
up with him!

Affirming Hemingway's androgynous nature, Fisher finds Waugh's
assertion that Hemingway had a chivalric attitude toward women exceed-
ingly superficial. At the same time he finds too simplistic the view that
Hemingway hated women, a view that Gershon Legman vigorously
asserts in his 1949 *Love & Death: A Study in Censorship*. There, in a
chapter called "Open Season on Women," Legman declares, "No modern
writer has taken the hatred of women farther than has Ernest
Hemingway" (47). Legman, Fisher states, has failed to recognize the
feminine in Hemingway.[16]

Fisher returns to Legman in a chapter concerned with writing the
bestseller. Legman had noted the triumph of the bitch-heroine in contemporary fiction, which he sees as foreshadowing a rebellion of women
against the controlling patriarchy. Legman claims that women, as they
anticipate a new social order, "fiercely delight in tales of triumphant
bitchery" (190). Margaret Mitchell made her fame creating a bitch heroine; in Legman's reading, Scarlett O'Hara ruins the life of every man she
touches. Other examples Legman provides come from W. Somerset
Maugham, James Hilton, and—of course—Hemingway. Legman credits

the popularity of these writers to "their bitch-heroines, killings, death motifs" (191). Fisher acknowledges that "Hemingway, [Philip] Wylie, and their school" deserve rebuke for their portrayal of love and their portrayal of women, but he again faults Legman for not looking deeply into the causes of their negative portraits of women. Fisher's chapter on the best-seller instructs less on the writing of such books than on understanding gender in the Western world. Noting that "the struggle between the sexes, which Edmund Wilson thinks Hemingway dragged out into the open, has been going on for some thousands of years" (188), he refers his readers back to Ovid and the myth of Hermaphrodite. Fisher's research into myth and history for his Testament of Man novels had led him to conclude: "The way men degraded women in ancient times and later under the Christians constitutes the most revolting chapter in human history" (198).

While Fisher was writing *God or Caesar?*, he was already planning to rewrite and expand his autobiographical tetralogy to make it the last volume of his Testament of Man series, a series of twelve novels that traced human development from pre-speech life to the present day. Looking at the modern world as a "darkness at noon," Fisher had ample opportunity in that revision to remind his readers of Ernest Hemingway. In *Orphans in Gethsemane* he makes virtually all of the criticisms of Hemingway that he makes in *God or Caesar?*, though Hemingway is not as important to the totality of the long novel (almost a thousand pages) as he is to Fisher's treatise on writing. In the novel, Hemingway represents the child artist of the lost generation. Whereas Hemingway is important throughout *God or Caesar?*, he plays across only the final third of the novel. References to him are brief and not always (though usually) by name. We learn that Vridar, like Fisher, had taught Hemingway's work at New York University. Amusingly, Fisher reverses what he had reported as his experience in the earlier book. In the novel, students liked Cabell's novels (after Vridar had told them what they mean), but almost none of them liked Hemingway.[17] Hemingway is more of a motif than a theme in the complex ménage of quotation and allusion that make Vridar's story a novel of ideas as well as an autobiography.

The first references to Hemingway in *Orphans* are casual, even glib. But they become more insistent when the protagonist, Vridar Hunter, determines to embark on a series of novels that will depend on research into anthropology and human evolution. He asks Athene, his second wife: "Is the greater writer the one who stands on his generation, like Hemingway, or beyond it, like Hunter?"—close to a paraphrase of the God or Caesar dichotomy (690). Vridar's life is pointedly contrasted to Hemingway's as he undertakes the enormous reading program that will underlie his intellectual series. We are told: "From libraries all over the nation books would be sent to his mailbox, and he would find joy in reading them that some men found in killing defenseless things in Africa" (791). Later, the narrative mocks "the modern bullfighters, and the lovers of bullfighting, and all the lovers of the lovers of bullfighting" (804). Vridar and his third wife, Angele, are united in their feelings about bullfighting. Hemingway may well have made his move to Ketchum when Fisher wrote these lines: "[Angele] would not have invited to her home, nor would Vridar, any person who went to bull fights for the pleasure of it. When in Spain, as she was to be again and again, she always sent to her friends postcards of bull-fights in which the bull had the man down and was goring him" (821).[18]

Not all the dialogue having to do with Hemingway originates with the protagonist. The first reference comes from a student of Vridar's who asks if his teacher has read Hemingway's "a farewell to screwing" (851). Some years later, a friend tells Vridar that he should take a lesson from Hemingway, who knew that including lots of sex helps sell books (851). The comment allows Fisher, with some humor, to state the major thesis of *God or Caesar?*. But there is no humor implied later when Vridar thinks of Hemingway, but doesn't name him:

> He would observe that a popular novelist, with an income in six figures, would say pompously for a news magazine, 'Whores find their own level,' and a few weeks later sell his name to an ale or a fountain pen. He wondered at the inner nature of the uncommon people who, to keep their purses filled and their faces before the public, endorsed almost any product that was aimed at the common people. He thought all this a shameless form of exploitation of ignorance and credulity. (886)

A few pages later, by name, he mocks Hemingway for saying that he had read *Across the River and Into the Trees* 206 times.

Never one to make a point only once, Fisher returns to the notion of awed reading of one's own work in a cluster of Hemingway references as the novel nears its close. He connects Hemingway with Waugh (as in *God or Caesar?*) as children rereading their books in acts of great self love (950) and then reminds us of O'Hara's ranking of Hemingway with Shakespeare (955). These references are focused by Vridar's reading of Van Wyck Brooks's *The Writer in America* (Brooks's topic is major to Fisher's novel as it was to *God or Caesar?*). Vridar notes, humorously, that in his lamentation for a neglected artist, Brooks makes no mention of Hunter. Without humor he states, "Mr. Brooks seems not to know that the neglect, even the torture and killing, of its greatest minds and hearts has always been one of mankind's sports. And what do you suppose he's asking now?—if Fitzgerald and Hemingway ever grew up!" Angele is surprised that Brooks, beyond three score and ten, hasn't learned that Hemingway and Fitzgerald "are only boys" (957). Vridar grants her point, citing novelist Edward Dahlberg's view: "Hemingway has no intellectual virility and is a slack gawk in amorous scenes." But Vridar challenges Dahlberg's contention that "it's hatred of women that dominates such writers." He says that Dahlberg "smells the right odor but comes up with the wrong corpse" (957). (The reader familiar with *God or Caesar?* will recall Fisher's consideration of Legman on Hemingway.)

This conversation with Angele comes when Vridar is deep in despair, uncertain that he will ever complete his Testament, or if he does, that the novels will be published. As Vridar recovers from pain and despair and ultimately completes his vast project, the novel's tone lightens considerably; we hear more joy, more hope. And in these more buoyant pages there are no direct references to Hemingway, though Fisher refers as always to numerous writers, artists, intellectuals, and historical persons. But the reader is not meant to forget Hemingway. Criticism of him lurks behind the several references to Ellen Glasgow's biography, especially in the final chapter. Both Vridar and Athene have read with approval Glasgow's biography *The Woman Within*, admiring her courage, her intelligence, her compassion for animals and the oppressed. She—like Vridar and Fisher, the reader is meant to conclude—belongs in God's camp.

Although Hemingway's place in *God or Caesar?* was doubtless heightened by the following publication of *Across the River and Into the Trees* and the ensuing debate about it, that publicity does not account for Fisher's sustained attention to Hemingway. Fisher's Hemingway-watching had been going on for a long time. Eventually, of course, Hemingway's residency in Idaho put a sharp focus on Fisher's long-time preoccupation. Conditioned by Fisher to suspect such links, we may well ask if on some deep level Fisher identified with Hemingway. I think it likely, especially as Fisher might have pondered Hemingway's portrayal of love and women. As we have seen, Fisher rejected Legman's portrayal of Hemingway simply as "woman hater." When he was writing *God or Caesar?*, Fisher knew that Hemingway had seen three marriages end in divorce and now had wife number four. Fault Hemingway as he might on other counts, Fisher was reluctant to batter him on this one. And much as he seemed to despise Hemingway, Fisher was aware that they shared some decisive psychological traits. We have seen his strong affirmation of the feminine side of Hemingway, and his acknowledgment of a strong identification with the female in himself. He placed Hemingway and himself in the androgynous camp.

[232]

In *Orphans*, the strongest overt connection between Hemingway and Fisher comes in a late scene when Vridar visits his brother Marion, a psychologist now teetering on insanity but capable of profound insight. Marion, always eager to goad his brother, is amused at Hemingway's statement about *The Old Man and the Sea*: "Don't you think it is a strange damn story that it should affect all of us (me especially) the way it does. I have had to read it now over two hundred times and every time it does something to me." Anticipating Gerry Brenner's 1983 reading, Marion says that the story reveals that Hemingway had a castration complex.[19] Marion asks, "Does the guy know what he was doing?—when he goes out into the ancient symbol of the womb and the mother, and fishes something out of it? His father. He really worked him over, didn't he?" According to Marion, "Hemingway has a castration complex"—and then he taunts Vridar "and you never got over yours" (930). As Fisher had made clear in *God or Caesar?*, he knew that he indeed had such a complex, and he made it an important aspect of the revised portrait of his autobiographical hero. Vridar does not comment on Marion's statement, but both Vridar and the author of *Orphans* seem to accept the validity of Marion's reading. Whether or not Hemingway had a "castration complex," Fisher thought that Hemingway did and considered it a link between them.[20]

Fisher does not advance other connections, but his readers might. Although Fisher distances himself emphatically from Hemingway's devotion to blood sports, he was certainly aware of Hemingway's so-called fascination with death; Hemingway had been charged with it often enough. Some readers have found Fisher too focused on blood and violence, even perversely so, all the way to his last novel, *Mountain Man* (1965), whose protagonist Sam Minard (Jeremiah Johnson in the movie version) ate the livers (raw) of the Indians he killed. Readers of *Orphans in Gethsemane* can chart Vridar's obsession with death, particularly violent death. Late in the novel, Vridar acknowledges "his fantastically morbid consciousness of death"—did it come, he wonders, "from having seen so many creatures die brutally" (810). Could not this same Vridar read, say, Hemingway's "Indian Camp" or "The Killers" with keen identification? Fisher's short stories were collected in 1959 under the title *Love and Death*. That title could serve for any of Hemingway's story gatherings. Responding to Lillian Ross's portrait, Fisher had pointed to Hemingway's "morbid fear of age and death." Fisher's own fascination with suicide and his revulsion at what aging had done to his parents, especially his mother, and his increasing sense of what aging was doing to him, might permit a similar judgment on himself.

During my 1963 visit with him, Fisher expressed disgust that Grace Hemingway had sent her son the gun with which his father had committed suicide. He thought that incident went far in explaining Ernest

Hemingway. He could not know that Ernest had asked her to send the gun. He was prepared, as so many have been, to come down hard on Mrs. Hemingway. He had some sense of Hemingway's view of her from the fiction. Could he have read her letters to her son (not available in his time), he might have made her another target in *Orphans*. Instead, Franklin Roosevelt's mother gets labeled archetypal mother tyrant.

More tellingly, his own mother, as the fictional Prudence Hunter, comes in for increasingly harsh analysis as the source of many of his own problems. Near the novel's end, Vridar says: "What woman was ever good enough for her manly little Vridar. God bless his mewling and pewling soul. What a dean of women she would have made! What a Mother Superior in a nunnery!" (953). Ernest Hemingway might have liked those exclamations! In any case, Fisher's readers will find many striking parallels in the lives of the two authors. In responding to Hemingway, Fisher was often close to key conflicts in his own psyche.

In this connection, no conflict was more telling than that of his own sense of his worth as a writer. As we have seen, Fisher sensed the insecurity behind Hemingway's bravado in the interview with Lillian Ross. In his painful decline, Hemingway was keenly troubled by the specter that he could no longer produce. What point was there in living if he could not write? Fisher knew about such agony. In *Orphans*, Vridar Hunter goes into profound despair over his inability to produce; he experiences severe writer's block. The novel's dedication makes clear how close the fictional presentation is to life. Fisher dedicated *Orphans* to his wife and to Alan Swallow, who had approached him about publishing the Testament after Fisher had despaired of finding a publisher willing to continue with the series. The dedication reads: "For Opal Laurel Holmes and to Alan Swallow—who was a candle when the night was deepest / who was a haven when the home was lost." It is a telling moment in *Orphans* when Vridar receives Angele's wrath for saying, "I may be only a damned mediocre writer—" (789). That is the great fear of Vridar's life, the notion that he dare not contemplate.[21] The fault must be, as in the case of Stendhal, with the public, with the critics. (In *God or Caesar?* the analogies to Stendhal are between Fisher and the French writer; the critics also get their due for obtuseness and worse.)

However numerous the parallels between the lives of Ernest Hemingway and Vardis Fisher, finally it is as writers that they must be compared. In fact, Fisher insists on that comparison. Both *God or Caesar?* and *Orphans in Gethsemane* invite it, anticipating especially the evaluation that would come after the deaths of the two writers. In *God or Caesar?*, Fisher mocks and challenges Hemingway's position in modern literature; he declares that Hemingway's place would eventually find the

JOSEPH M. FLORA

level where it belongs—or descend below that level "as artists too commonly do who are betrayed by those who glorify them" (48–49). One of Fisher's aims in *God or Caesar?* was to speed the reassessment. In *Orphans* he continually plays his autobiographical protagonist against Hemingway, the writer of his time as opposed to the writer in advance of his time.

It is now over forty years since Fisher called for the reassessment of Hemingway, and both writers have been dead for at least thirty years. Fisher was certainly right that reassessment of Hemingway's literary reputation would come. Hemingway has not lacked for detractors (he never did—as many of Fisher's examples illustrate), but his importance in the literary world is abundantly clear. His life and works have been continuously studied and reappraised; the person who can read everything published on Hemingway in a year is indeed kept busy. Although some have complained about the vastness of the Hemingway "industry," Michael Reynolds, a chief Hemingway biographer, reports that there is still much work to be done.[22] Meanwhile, Hemingway's works have remained in print; virtually every title is available in either hardback or paper, usually in both. If not an inevitable inclusion on course syllabi to the extent he once was, he is still regularly taught in America and throughout the world. Every anthology of twentieth-century American literature recognizes his importance. Writers continue to pay tribute to him for his artistry, acknowledging his influence on them. To be sure, he remains a popular cult figure as well.

A look at 1995 *Books in Print* reveals how different the case has been with Fisher, though there is an encouraging sign or two. The last book Fisher published, *Gold Rushes and Mining Camps of the Early American West* (1968) is still available from Caxton. Opal Fisher reprinted several titles under the name Opal Laurel Holmes; the process was photocopy of the original publication. Marketing of these books was a problem Opal Fisher was not equipped to deal with. A few Fisher titles are available from Gordon Press, but at prices only a wealthy or very serious collector would pay. Two novels are available in paperback: *The Mothers* (Holmes) and *Mountain Man* (Pocket Books) are the best possibilities for inclusion in college courses. *Mountain Man*, Fisher's last novel, has not only remained in print since its 1965 publication, but has sold well. Doubtless, the success of the film *Jeremiah Johnson* has been a factor in that success. Were Fisher reviewing the listings in *Books in Print*, he would be most disappointed that none of the Testament of Man novels, the work he saw as the culmination of his career, is in print. (By 1962 Pyramid Books had put the entire Testament series in paper.) The *Books in Print* list, nevertheless, gives encouragement that Fisher will not be forgotten. The

University of Idaho Press had taken over distribution of Fisher titles, and lists four in its 1995 catalog. (With settlement of Opal Fisher's estate, Boise State now lists those titles.)

A review of the annual bibliographies of *Western American Literature* shows only a trickle of activity on Fisher. Most revealing is the perspective of Tim Woodward's biography. *Tiger on the Road* (1989) was written to check neglect of Fisher. Woodward wrote with the hope that Fisher "will take his place among the nation's distinguished regional writers" (266). Fisher aimed higher than that. Although western and proud to be so, he did not wish to be relegated to "regional writer." Nevertheless, he is now viewed primarily as a Western writer, and not usually in the first tier. The reason for the ranking is not his unpopular views, but his artistry. Perhaps his former student Wallace Stegner puts that into focus as well as anyone. Stegner, while aiming to give Fisher credit where it was due, said that Bernard DeVoto overpraised *Children of God*. As he was finishing *The Big Rock Candy Mountain*, Stegner tried reading Fisher's prize-winning novel aloud to his wife Mary. "It didn't read aloud. It wasn't good prose. It hurt my ears, it seemed so blunt. It was made with an axe."[23] Fisher's manner more than his matter has worked against him. In *Orphans in Gethsemane* Vridar feared the charge of mediocrity; Stegner, a skilled Western writer, makes that very charge against Fisher.

Fisher faulted Hemingway for an inadequate sense of irony (*God or Caesar?*, 48), an accusation that would baffle most Hemingway scholars. At a minimum, it indicates how deficient was Fisher's memory of *The Sun Also Rises*. When Hemingway took up residence in Ketchum, Fisher likely saw the irony that a long-time antagonist had become his neighbor. Were he alive now, his own sense of irony would be sorely tested by the position granted Hemingway as an Idaho icon. It would be tested by the choice of Sun Valley for the 1996 International Meeting of the Hemingway Society. Busy idolaters, he would charge! The Sun Valley meeting came one year after the centennial of Fisher's birth, an event not marked in Idaho by conference or festival.[24] His sense of irony would be tested, too, by my notice of his deep identification with Hemingway.

NOTES

1. The poet Radcliffe Squires portrays the moment of this transformation in Idaho in "In Memoriam: Ernest Hemingway." The poem is collected in Radcliffe Squires, *Fingers of Hermes* (Ann Arbor: University of Michigan Press, 1965), 31.

2. Tim Woodward, *Tiger on the Road: The Life of Vardis Fisher* (Caldwell, Idaho: Caxton Printers, 1989), 203.

3. Hemingway had also envisioned an ideal scenario for completing the deed. See Carlos Baker, *Ernest Hemingway: A Life Story* (New York: Charles Scribner's Sons, 1969), 167 and 485–86.

4. For details about Fisher's death, see Woodward, *Tiger on the Road*, 245–55.

5. Vardis Fisher, *God or Caesar?: The Writing of Fiction for Beginners* (Caldwell, Idaho: Caxton Printers, 1953), 163. Subsequent references will be given as page numbers in the text.

6. Following his imitation of Nathan, Fisher returns for commentary on the three imitations. He again uses Angoff to suggest limitation in Hemingway's ability to create character. Angoff says about Hemingway's characters: "they love, they lie, they swindle, they talk and talk and talk, but they never come to life. One knows as much about them after reading ten pages as after reading two hundred pages. . . . The men can be interchanged as can the women. Catherine is an English Maria, and Maria is a Spanish Catherine. Similarly with Jordan and Henry" (120).

7. The Hemingway manner, according to Fisher, "sometimes makes it appear that men and women are nothing but genitals" (193).

8. Fisher taught at Washington Square College, New York University, from 1928–31. *A Farewell to Arms* was a national bestseller at the time Fisher included it in his course, something of an avant-garde selection for the period. Fisher pronounced the students at NYU above the national average as he had experienced it. (He had taught at the University of Utah from 1925–28 and at the University of Montana during the summers of 1932 and 1933.)

9. Not one of the expatriates, Fisher considered the "lost generation" writers "pathetically adolescent" (38), including, of course, Hemingway, as this essay will make abundantly clear. We sense Fisher's notion of the artist's responsibility when he faults these writers for "making the world vulnerable to a second great war."

10. Fisher errs in reporting Hemingway's account of his "championship." Ross reports Hemingway as saying of the "title," "I won it in the twenties and defended it in the thirties and the forties, and I don't mind at all defending it in the fifties," (Lillian Ross, "How Do You Like It Now, Gentlemen?" *New Yorker* 26 [13 May 1959]: 49). This is a significant difference from Fisher's saying Hemingway claimed he was champion "in his twenties" and defended his title in his thirties, forties, and fifties.

11. Other instances of Cowley's aiding myth: Hemingway's sons "worship" their father; Hemingway doesn't smoke in order to preserve "his keen sense of smell"; "he has scars from his crown to his feet" and is "always getting hurt"; he is "romantic by nature and falls in love like a big hemlock crashing down through the underbrush" (46).

12. Fisher mocks Hemingway for having read one of his novels 206 times (165), an extreme of self-devotion. Fisher also faults Hemingway for counting his words, a practice he finds a waste of time and the essence of self-absorption (225).

13. Lambasting a critic (Fisher does not name the critic) who claims that the sixteen principal characters in *For Whom the Bell Tolls* have "three solid dimensions" and are "more absolutely memorable than the characters of any contemporary American novel, with the possible exception of *The Grapes of Wrath*," Fisher says the characters in both novels are "fairly simple extroverts, which is to say, persons whose depth of consciousness is shallow." He mocks the same critic for declaring that in one story, Hemingway achieved "the 'fourth and fifth dimension' of prose, which speaks simultaneously on several levels and whose effect is to leave us aware of an experience at once more real than reality, and with overtones that can only be called extra-natural, of this world and beyond it" (90). For Fisher, such criticism is "rhapsodizing over the intimation of a shadow on an invisible leaf in the dark" (90). He continues to mock the notion of "fourth and fifth dimensions" (92 and 120).

14. Michael Reynolds, *Hemingway's Reading, 1919–40* (Princeton: Princeton University Press, 1981), 33.

15. Larry McMurtry, "Icy Grief and a Fire of Vengeance," *Saturday Review*, 48 (6 November 1935): 33.

16. Anyone who thought that feminist criticism was the first to excoriate Hemingway for his portrayal of women would do well to read Legman. Legman's work first appeared in pamphlet form, privately printed. (It was republished in 1963 by Hacker Art Books.) So it may have escaped Hemingway's notice. One hopes so. Reynolds reports that Hemingway was a "compulsive" reader of literary criticism: "His clipping service sent him reviews for each new publication. He subscribed to most of the literary journals. His letters to Perkins show him acutely aware of published criticism" (Reynolds, *Hemingway's Reading*, 25). Probably Hemingway had not discovered *God or Caesar?*. It would not have pleased him. Should Opal Fisher's story to Woodward about Hemingway's awareness of Fisher be true, we would be certain that he had not.

17. Vardis Fisher, *Orphans in Gethsemane* (Denver: Alan Swallow, 1960), 781. Subsequent references will be given as page numbers in the text.

18. Near the end of his life, Fisher journeyed to the University of South Dakota, where he was interviewed by John R. Milton in the studio of KUSD. In the interview, Fisher again contrasted himself and Hemingway as polar opposites. He saw himself more as teacher in his novels and Hemingway as reflector of his age. Hemingway "certainly was a man of his times, which I don't think I have been. . . . I don't know what writer better expressed his age, the aspect of his age [violence, guns, wars, killings], than Hemingway." John R. Milton, ed., *Three West: Conversations with Vardis Fisher, Max Evans, Michael Straight* (Vermillion: University of South Dakota Press, 1970), 26.

19. See Gerry Brenner, *Concealments in Hemingway's Works* (1983) or Gerry Brenner, *"The Old Man and the Sea": Story of a Common Man* (1991). Brenner

finds Hemingway's novel teeming with personal anxieties, the deepest of these a result of Hemingway's complex relationship with his father. Brenner discovers "unconscious homosexual feelings toward Manolin that [Santiago] cannot accept in himself" (*Story of a Common Man*, 94).

20. As early as 1934, Dr. Lawrence Kubie, a psychiatrist, wrote a psychoanalytical analysis of Hemingway based on Hemingway's writing; he identified "male erotic aggression" and "fear of genital injury" as important Hemingway themes. Hemingway was outraged by the article and blocked its publication, though it was eventually published in 1984. Psychological studies of Hemingway, many of which identify latent homosexuality and castration anxieties, have proliferated since Kubie. For a review of such analytical studies, see R. J. Craig, "Contributions to Psychohistory: XXIII. Hemingway 'Analyzed,'" *Psychological Reports* (1995): 1059–79.

21. The importance of this line in the chapter and this section of the novel (it ends Part II of Book II) is emphasized in the short paragraphing when it occurs and in the ending of the chapter, when the fear resurfaces. Angele says, "I wonder if you want to be a successful writer. If so, why did you weep when you got the prize?" (Vridar's prize is based on Fisher's 1939 Harper Prize.) Vridar recalls the time: "Yes, it was the shameful truth! He had gone absolutely hell-roaring mad. He had poured bitter grief out of him like a stupid blubbering lubber, moaning out of anguish that he would never be worth a hill of terds [*sic*]" (794). Angele's words, we discover, "had stirred something hiding deep within him, some evil furtive thing down there in the dark of his nature" (795). As the chapter ends, Vridar is weeping profusely, replaying the emotional response to the prize.

In this section of the novel Vridar often fears for his sanity. Such fears are by no means unique to Vridar at the time of angst over his career, but they are intensely insistent in this period. As Fisher struggled over problems similar to Vridar's, he could not have known the extent of Hemingway's mental turmoil in the same years, but he lived long enough to learn something of their severity and could have found ample grounds to see some parallels.

22. See Michael Reynolds, "Prospects for the Study of Ernest Hemingway," *Resources for American Literary Study*, 21 (1995): 1–15. Reynolds's essay builds on a presentation he made for the meeting of the Hemingway Society held in Boston, Massachusetts, in July 1992. In itself, the existence of an active Hemingway society underscores the huge gulf in the attention the two writers receive. Efforts to create a society dedicated to Fisher scholarship have not been successful.

23. See Wallace Stegner and Richard W. Etulain, *Conversations with Wallace Stegner on Western History and Literature*, (Salt Lake City: University of Utah Press, 1983), 39–40. Acknowledging that Fisher might have had an influence upon him that he didn't understand, Stegner nevertheless has definite views about Fisher the artist: "I never had the highest respect for Vardis's novelistic

skill"—though he grants that Fisher had told some good stories (29). (Stegner had been a student in Fisher's freshman English course at the University of Utah. Stegner gives his account of that experience on pages 24–25.) But check the index of *Conversations* for Hemingway. It is clear that Stegner found Hemingway a major writer and used him, not Fisher, to articulate his views on modern writing.

24. Boise State University dedicated its renovated and expanded Albertsons Library on 6 September 1995. Dr. Dorys Grover, professor emeritus of literature and languages at East Texas State University, gave a lecture "Reminiscences of Vardis Fisher" as part of the day's activities. Among exhibits in the library was one marking the one hundredth anniversary of Fisher's birth. "Vardis Fisher: A Centennial View—1895–1995" circulated in libraries throughout Idaho during the centennial year. Sponsored by the Pocatello Public Library, the exhibit was funded by the Idaho Humanities Council, the Community Hospital Corporation of Idaho Falls, and the Idaho Commission on the Arts. It should be noted, however, that on the occasion of the twenty-fifth anniversary of Hemingway's death, Boise State launched a year-long celebration of his life and works, and the Hemingway Center for Western Studies was established on that campus. A further irony, in 1993 the University of Idaho Press became publisher of the *Hemingway Review*.

Dateline Sun Valley: The Press Coverage of the Death of Ernest Hemingway

JOHN R. BITTNER

*You can go. But I've been to all those places and I've left them
all behind. And where I go now I go alone. . . .*
ERNEST HEMINGWAY, *The Fifth Column*

On a bright summer morning in Idaho, not unlike the morning in 1939
when he first arrived in Sun Valley, Ernest Hemingway met death in his
Ketchum home.[1] Blaine County authorities listed the cause of death as a
"self-inflicted gunshot wound to the head." Speculation led to talk of suicide.
Regardless of how he died, that split second on a summer Sunday morning
in 1961 riveted the attention of the press on Ketchum and Sun Valley. For
the hundreds of millions of people worldwide who knew of Hemingway and
the millions who had read his works, it was not the biographers or academicians who formed the general public's perception of the man. It was the
press: A press that in 1961 had an average United States daily newspaper
circulation of 60 million copies per day. Although he had a love-hate relationship with the press, sometimes guarding his privacy while simultaneously demanding of his publisher promotion of his books, Ernest
Hemingway understood early in his career the relationship between journalism, press coverage, and his literary reputation.[2] As he became famous, the
press found him all the more interesting. At the time of his death, Ernest
Hemingway had become an author whose personal life—well publicized
and often misrepresented—was inextricably linked to his literary works.

He was also well known to the local residents of Sun Valley, but more
as one of them than most celebrities. He hunted with them, drank with
them, and helped bury their dead. The week after his death, some people
in Sun Valley and Ketchum resented the attention outsiders gave to his
death, even to the point that the resentment became the topic of newspaper reports.[3] Few Ketchum and Sun Valley residents wanted to talk about
him to the press, and if they did, they didn't want to be quoted.

On July 2, in Idaho, reporters called early. Small towns keep few
secrets, and before Sun Valley publicity director Dorice Taylor was out of

bed, the Associated Press was on the phone from Boise. Taylor, not knowing that Hemingway had just returned from the Mayo Clinic, told AP,
"He's not even in Sun Valley."[4] Sun Valley publicity assistant Jerry Noling
called next, asking, "Have you heard anything about Ernest Hemingway?"
Taylor told him Hemingway was at the Mayo Clinic. "But he isn't," Noling
answered. "He was having dinner in the Christiania with Mary and some
man last evening." Taylor next called local resident and Hemingway family
friend Chuck Atkinson, who confirmed that Hemingway was dead but
hedged when Taylor asked whether it was suicide.

As the press contact person for events in Sun Valley, Taylor then asked
Atkinson whether he could get Mary Hemingway to make a statement.
Taylor asked Atkinson to instruct Mary to turn all calls over to the Sun
Valley Publicity Office, from which Taylor would give out Mary's state-
ment and nothing else. Atkinson complied.[5] Mary's statement read,
"Ernest Hemingway has been accidentally killed by a blast from a shot-
gun he was handling."[6]

At the Publicity Office the phones were already ringing. From New
York, London, Italy, the calls came into the night, and Mary Hemingway's
accidental-death statement was repeated over and over. Later that day,
Blaine County Sheriff Frank Hewitt and Coroner Ray McGoldrick, who
also doubled as funeral director, issued their own statement, saying,
"Ernest Hemingway died this morning at about 7:30 at his home near
Ketchum from gunshot wounds. His wife thinks it was accidental while
he was cleaning his gun."[7] Over the next twenty-four hours the two statements would be combined by the press in various ways, but national
newspapers on July 3, with a few speculative exceptions, reported the
death as an accident, not a suicide.

Hemingway's death would have made news regardless of how, when,
or where he died. However, in addition to his stature as a writer, multiple
factors converged in Idaho in July 1961, factors that had a profound
effect on the amount and type of press coverage his death received.
These factors included his adventurous personal life; his work as a journalist; the time, day of the week, and month of his death; the violent
nature of his death; and the location of his death near Sun Valley.

First, Hemingway's personal life—his world travels, African safaris,
four marriages, correspondent reports during the Spanish Civil War and
World War II, two plane crashes, and public appearances at bullfights in
Spain—over many years stocked newspaper and wire service photo files
and contributed to Hemingway's status as a newsmaker.

Second, he was a journalist before becoming a novelist, and he continued to write nonfiction well into his career. As the new medium of television was changing the face of the fourth estate, Hemingway stressed what

editors told reporters, that one true sentence was important, and the printed word could still eclipse the cosmetics of a soundbite. This literary icon was one of their own, and like police officers who attend *en masse* a fallen comrade's funeral, newspapers paid him their respect.

Third, the time of the suicide, early Sunday morning, is significant because it provided editors with enough time to lay out the next day's edition and collect additional information to background a story. In 1961, lead time was even more important than it is today because newspaper type was set on Linotype machines, a much slower process than today's computerized layout and printing processes. Even the day of the week on which Hemingway died played a part, especially during the initial phase of coverage. Sunday is considered the slowest news day of the week, and the news hole is large because traditional news sources—the courts, government meetings, etc.—do not function on the weekend. Hemingway's death was an international news event of high news value, and the news hole was waiting for it. The month of July is a slow news month, and one of the slowest times of the month is the July 4th holiday, especially when it falls near mid-week. In 1961, July 4th fell on Tuesday and that meant the news hole extended all week, providing opportunities for additional coverage.

Moreover, Hemingway died violently. A celebrity shooting himself in the head with a double-barreled shotgun, whether in private or public, whether accidentally or deliberately, makes news. High-intensity words like "gun," "shotgun," "blast," and "shot" make headlines.

In addition to the factors noted above, the place of his death, a mile from Sun Valley, brought to bear on the event an area that for more than twenty years had tied its fortunes to the press publicity generated by celebrities. A promotion campaign based on "mountain sunshine" had one of its first celebrities when Ernest Hemingway arrived in 1939. By 1961, in or near Sun Valley, President Harry Truman fished; Groucho Marx married; Lowell Thomas broadcast; Clark Gable skied; Gary Cooper hunted; and Marilyn Monroe made a movie. Union Pacific Chairman Averell Harriman's image of a world-class ski resort growing out of sheep and cattle pasture at the end of a railroad spur was calculated by design, embellished by a willing press, and driven by public relations professionals. Sun Valley became the dateline of choice for many celebrity reporters, a dateline as familiar to the world press as Hemingway himself. During the Hemingway era, Sun Valley was a well-oiled, celebrity-fueled, publicity machine.

Directing on-location publicity at Sun Valley were Gene Van Guilder—Van Guilder was later killed in a duck hunting accident—and Van Guilder's photographer, Lloyd R. "Pappy" Arnold.[8] Admitting later he was "publicity property," but credited by Arnold with coming to Idaho for the hunting and fishing, Hemingway immediately became the subject of Arnold's camera. Along with Sun Valley guide Taylor "Bear Tracks" Williams, Hemingway, Van Guilder, and Arnold hunted and fished together. For more than twenty years, whenever Ernest Hemingway visited Sun Valley, Pappy Arnold's and other staffers' cameras were snapping pictures. For an author who liked hunting, fishing, and the outdoors, finding Sun Valley and pals who liked the outdoors as much as he did was an ideal match. When Hemingway went hunting and fishing with Pappy Arnold, it was like having his own personal press photographer along. When Ernest Hemingway died in 1961, there was no shortage of press photos of this Idaho hunter, fisherman, and sportsman.

A review of fifteen major daily metropolitan newspapers found every paper gave the story of Hemingway's death extensive front-page coverage.[9] The *Atlanta Constitution*'s July 3 front-page headline was subdued, reading, "Hemingway Found Dead, Gun at Feet." But the lead sentence read, "Ernest Hemingway, a 20th-century literary giant who wrote of wartime violence and death in the afternoon in blood-soaked bullrings, shot himself fatally in the head Sunday with a double-barreled, 12-gauge shotgun." The *New York Times* headlined the death across three columns, "Hemingway Dead of Shotgun Wound; Wife Says He Was Cleaning Weapon." The *Boston Globe, San Francisco Chronicle, Des Moines Register, Chicago Daily Tribune*, and the *Washington Post* all ran headlines across the entire front page, with the *Chronicle*'s, the *Register*'s, and the *Tribune*'s in large, boldfaced, capital letters. The *Register* headline read, "Gun Blast Kills Hemingway." The *Chronicle*'s headline read, "Accident in Idaho: Hemingway Dead—Shotgun Blast."[10] Expanded coverage of his death in the *Chronicle* was significant. Counting the front page and book review columns, the *San Francisco Chronicle*'s July 3rd edition carried twenty-six columns and twenty photographs about Hemingway, including photographs of his four wives, with Fidel Castro in Cuba, with a leopard in Africa, with the Royal Air Force in England, and two photographs with Gary Cooper in Sun Valley.

From Hemingway the spectator at bullfights, to Hemingway the hunter in Idaho, America read about Hemingway the writer and Hemingway the man. In addition to the *San Francisco Chronicle*, all of the other papers studied ran additional stories on inside pages. Readers read epitaphs from around the world, of shock in France, of reaction in Cuba, of dedicated programs on Moscow television, and of comments in the Vatican Paper which stated, "he was a great writer but not illuminated by Christian grace."[11]

Many newspapers ran front-page companion features. In Kansas City readers were told the *Star* was where Hemingway learned to write.[12] The

Accident in Idaho

HEMINGWAY DEAD
---SHOTGUN BLAST

WEATHER FORECAST
Bay Area: Variable cloudiness with little change in temperature. Low temperatures Monday 52 to 57; highs 62 to 74. Westerly winds.
Full Report, Page 17

San Francisco Chronicle
THE VOICE OF THE WEST

FINAL

97th YEAR No. 184   CCCCAAA   MONDAY, JULY 3, 1961   10 CENTS   GArfield 1-1111

Arson Probe

Fires Sweep
S. F. Buildings

Firemen battled two raging blazes in San Francisco's warehouse district yesterday—a half hour and three blocks apart.

Almost immediately, investigators were probing the smoldering ruins on the theory the two fires might be the work of an arsonist.

The first, a three-alarmer with the first alarm sounding at 4:28 p. m., sent flames roaring through a two-story frame warehouse at 55 Morris street.

Size Isn't Everything

Last week, one of our giant competitors asked Jack Davis about the size of his staff.

"There are usually five salesmen," said Jack, "and Lorraine, and Ernie, and the 3 people in the tailor's shop."

"Why, counting you, that's a dozen people! Surely there isn't enough work in this small store to keep twelve of you going?" the competitor asked.

"Well," said Jack, "there isn't, but if we weren't here, there would be."

Where else in town would you find such a selection of superb Louis Roth suits? Who else offers so many expensive and original sportcoats? Then, too, wouldn't this space in the Chronicle look funny with nothing printed in it?

Anyway, we're open today, then it. Have a hang-up in!

jack davis
LOUIS ROTH CLOTHES
116 KEARNY STREET

Owned and occupied by the Austin Drayage Company.

What appeared to be the first indication that the two trucks parked inside were destroyed.

INFERNO

The inferno sent billowing clouds of black smoke into a clear blue sky. Flames seared the rear of an adjoining two-story frame building owned by the Gonzales Draying Company, causing slight damage.

The fire also leaped to a billboard in full view of the

See Page 2, Col. 1

Oust British,

Iraq Asks
U. N. Council

New York Times Service
UNITED NATIONS, N.Y., July 2—Iraq asked the Security Council today to order the withdrawal of British forces from the Sheikdom of Kuwait.

The Iraqi delegate, speaking in an unusual Sunday session of the Council, did not, however, ask for immediate action. He said he would prefer discussion of the British action in Kuwait to a later meeting.

He said Iraq would support Iraq's claim to the former British protectorate, recently given its independence, came during a procedural wrangle at the start of the meeting.

Such support would align the Russians and only against Great Britain, but also against a number of Arab States led by the United Arab Republic, that back Kuwaiti independence.

This morning's holiday

See Page 4, Col. 2

Cold Horror

After Car
Leaps Cliff

A young San Francisco commercial artist survived a 600-foot plunge in a car down a mountainside near Stinson Beach, then huddled through the chill night waiting for rescue.

The artist—John Wanek, 25, of 1004 Tennessee street—told Highway Patrolman Joseph Kennedy he apparently dozed and went off the walkout to a halt. Shoreline Highway at a point about two miles south of Stinson Beach.

His car went crashing end over end down the steep (45 degrees) canyon side, banging to a halt in a clump of decae brush about 190 feet from the ocean.

BROKEN LEG

Wanek, critically hurt, crawled out of the wreckage, but found he was unable to climb the slope. His right leg was fractured.

He lay on the edge of a

See Page 2, Col. 1

Injunction in

Ship Strike
Likely Today

The Kennedy Administration may resort in its first Taft-Hartley injunction today to halt the 17-day national maritime strike.

New York negotiations yesterday produced another spate of union-ship-owner agreements, but it was a patchwork pattern—there were too many pieces missing to bring full agreement to a halt.

Most ship operators had reached agreement with one or more of the five major unions involved. But most also were still at least one agreement short of an over-all settlement.

Labor Secretary Arthur J. Goldberg, en route to Hyannis Port, Mass., to confer with President Kennedy this morning, was reported as most convinced that only a Federal injunction could end the dispute.

And David L. Cole, head of the fact-finding panel set

See Page 2, Col. 1

ERNEST HEMINGWAY
"The manner of his life, and death, was hard, violent, sincere"

Epitaph for a Friend

By Donne Pretitcher

Ernest Hemingway is dead.

And I've been asked in vain something, because he was my teacher, my friend. I loved him, and I owed him money.

These are all reasons involving debt, and you do not like to write much about the people you are indebted to so

deeply and from so many different directions.

High Blood Pressure

But the manner of his death, like the manner of his life, was hard and violent -and sincere, and there will be critics who will tell that what he wrote was phony because he himself was phony, his death tends to prove it.

It is not my intent to deprive anybody...

See Page 10, Col. 1

Marina Green Festival

Fireworks Fun Tomorrow

Thousands of eager youngsters, followed by as thousands more eager adults, will converge on the Marina Green tomorrow to take part in The Chronicle's annual Fourth of July Fireworks Festival.

Entertainment, contests and competitive racing will continue throughout the day until the traditional fireworks display, sponsored by The Chronicle, begins about 9:15 p.m.

The display will be high-

lighted by the detonation of an "atomic bomb" created by way at 2 p.m. the Golden State Fireworks Co.

Activity at the Marina Green will begin at 10 a.m. when hundreds of youngsters will compete for prizes in a series of field events.

At noon there will be a pet contest open to animals of varying shapes, sizes and zoological classifications.

A variety show, featuring singers, dancers, musicians

and acrobats, will get under way at 2 p.m.

The San Francisco Municipal Band will give a two-hour concert beginning at 7 p.m.

The Chronicle's Folkbout Invitational yacht race will be run in the waters off the Marina at 7:15 p.m. About 40 25-foot sloops are entered in the competition.

For a complete schedule of events, see page 2.

At Idaho Home

Novelist Killed
In Gun Accident

New York Times Service
KETCHUM, Idaho, July 2—Ernest Hemingway, the Nobel-prize-winning author whose writings revealed a fascination with danger and violent death, was found dead of a gunshot wound in the head at his home here today.

His wife, Mary, said he had killed himself accidentally with his shotgun.

He would have been 62 years old July 21.

Blaine county Sheriff Frank L. Hewitt announced after a preliminary investigation that "it looks like an accident" and "there is no evidence of foul play."

Later, Coroner Ray McGoldrick said that, upon the advice of County Prosecutor V. K. Bergquist, it had been decided no inquest would be necessary for the time being.

"His wife thought it was accidental and there was no one with Mr. Hemingway at the time," the coroner added.

The body of the bearded, barrel-chested writer, clad in robe and pajamas, was found by his wife, Mary, in the foyer of their modern house. She told friends she could find no note.

A double-barreled, 12-gauge shotgun lay beside him with one barrel fired. The blast had entered his head.

For a literary analysis of Hemingway by The Chronicle's Book Editor, William Hogan, see Page 26.

Mrs. Hemingway, the author's fourth wife, whom he married in 1946, issued this statement: "Mr. Hemingway accidentally killed himself while cleaning a gun this morning at 7:30 a.m. No time has been set for the funeral services, which will be private."

The widow, the former Mary Welsh, was then placed under sedation for shock.

High Blood Pressure

The world-famous writer was discharged from the Mayo clinic in Rochester, Minn., last Monday after two months of treatment for hypertension (high blood pressure) and what a Mayo spokesman called a "very old" case of hepatitis.

Hemingway had been hospitalized at Mayo last year for the same conditions and was released after 50...

About a month ago, Hemingway's physician at the clinic described his health as "excellent." The author had been worried about his weight—200 pounds distributed over a six-foot frame.

A friend, Les Jankow, said residents had told him...

See Page 8, Col. 1

THE INDEX

Another report on Skyline San Francisco by Allan Temko on Page 30

S. F. Stores Open Until 9 o'Clock Tonight

Where to Find It:

Comics	6	Weather	12
Editorials	4	Wilson	6
TV, Radio	12	Women	7

*****

THE WEATHER — Sunny, a little warmer today. High in 80s. Fair to partly cloudy tonight and Tuesday. High Tuesday 93. Sunrise 4:45; sunset 7:52.

The Des Moines Register

The Newspaper Iowa Depends Upon

Des Moines, Iowa, Monday Morning, July 3, 1961—16 Pages—Two Sections

Price 10 Cents

GUN BLAST KILLS HEMINGWAY

Find Famed Novelist With Shotgun Beside Him

HOFFA SEEKS 'WAR CHEST,' MORE POWER

For All-Out Fight On Justice Dept.

By Clark Mollenhoff

Of The Register's Washington Bureau

MIAMI BEACH, FLA. — Teamster President James R. Hoffa has drawn plans to revamp the Teamsters Union constitution to extract more money from union members for an all-out war against the justice department.

Top officials of the Teamsters Union and union lawyers have been drawing up the constitutional revisions in the last few days, and are ready to spring them on convention delegates later in the week.

Headquarters Move

One of the most important moves that the Hoffa forces are making is the proposal to move the International Teamsters headquarters to Detroit, Mich., an area in which the courts have always dealt most kindly with Hoffa and his henchmen.

The International Teamsters headquarters is in Washington, D. C., in a palatial building across the Capitol plaza from the U. S. Capitol.

Headquarters in Washington are under the nose of congressional investigating committees, and the investigations of Teamsters financing can be conducted in grand juries and in a federal court system that is observed closely by the FBI and Attorney General Robert F. Kennedy.

It is reported that the major reason for moving the headquarters to Detroit is to get Teamster records out from under the direct jurisdiction of the federal courts in the District of Columbia.

Other high Teamster sources report that Hoffa is planning a series of personnel changes to solidify his personal control of Teamsters finances and activity.

Convicted Twice

It is reported that Hoffa will boost William Presser, twice-convicted Ohio Teamsters boss, to a position as one of the three trustees of the International Teamsters Union funds.

Other trustees will be Frank Matula, Los Angeles, Cal., Teamsters boss who has been convicted of perjury in connection with a garbage collection racket, and Roy Cohen, Philadelphia, Penn., Teamsters leader who is currently under indictment on charges of misappropriating large sums from the local union treasury.

All three — Presser, Matula and Cohen — are

HOFFA—
Continued on Page Eight

British Troops Arrive in Kuwait

Lieut.-Col. E. R. Bridges (left), commander of British Royal Marine commandos, and Marine Maj. John Taplin watch landing operations as British forces arrive in Kuwait Saturday. Radio control post is in right background.

Iraq to U. N.: Make Britain Quit Kuwait

By New York Times News Service

NEW YORK, N. Y. — Iraq Sunday asked the United Nations security council to order the withdrawal of British forces from the sheikdom of Kuwait.

The Iraqi delegate did not, however, ask the council to act immediately.

He said he would defer detailed discussion of the British action to a later meeting.

Soviet Support

What appeared to be the first definite indication that the Soviet Union will support Iraq's claim to the former British protectorate, recently given its independence, came during a procedural wrangle at the start of the meeting.

Such support would align the Russians not only against Great Britain, but also against a number of Arab states led by the United Arab Republic, that support Kuwaiti independence.

The Russians supported the Iraqi contention Sunday that the complaint of Kuwait itself could not be considered directly, but only those of Britain and Iraq. Iraq took the position Kuwait is not a nation, but a part of Iraq.

Meanwhile:

1 **In Kuwait, British tanks, commandos and paratroops dug into a solid defensive ring in the Kuwait desert, their guns poised to meet any threat from Iraq. By nightfall the landing of reinforcements for 750 men sent in Saturday had been completed.**

A British spokesmen declined to say how many men were in the "brigade level" force, but it was believed to be well under 3,000.

In position at the border also are units of Kuwait's 2,400 man army and thousands of armed desert tribesmen.

2 **In London, Prime Minister Harold Macmillan conferred with senior cabinet ministers and defense chiefs including the ...**

TRAFFIC TOLL REACHES 283

CHICAGO, ILL. (AP)—The toll of traffic deaths pushed upward rapidly in the midst of the long Independence Day weekend.

At 1 a. m. today the toll had reached 283.

Seven persons had died in Iowa accidents (Story: Page 3).

Driver Arrests In Iowa at 502

Improper passing continued to be the largest single offense by drivers in Iowa Sunday during the Fourth of July weekend.

Highway patrolmen reported a total of 502 summonses issued between 6 p. m. Friday and 8 p. m. Sunday. Eighty-three were for improper passing, nine for speeding.

The others were for a variety of offenses.

The summonses are being issued in an all-out highway safety drive by the highway patrol through the Fourth of July weekend.'

Governmental Offices Open

In case you're confused about whom you will or will not be able to see today because of the long Fourth of July weekend:

Federal offices in Iowa will be open for business.

State offices will be closed.

The Des Moines city hall and the Polk county courthouse will be open.

There will be no Des Moines city council meeting tonight; the next meeting will be Monday, July 10.

All of the federal, state, county and city offices will be closed Tuesday, July 4.

The Des Moines post office and substations will be closed Tuesday. Only special delivery mail will be delivered. Regular holiday collection schedules will be followed and all mail will be dispatched as usual.

INDIAN QUADS

BOMBAY, INDIA (AP) — **Girl quadruplets, each weighing 3 pounds, have been born ...**

Killed When Home-Made Plane Falls

McGREGOR, IA. (AP) — Lloyd Eddings, 58, of Marquette died Sunday when his homemade plane crashed into a wooded area six miles south of here.

H. C. Hartley, Federal Aviation examiner from Cedar Rapids, said the one-seat plane was built by Eddings from plans issued by a national firm.

Had Parachute

Hartley said Roy Thomas, a farmer near McGregor, saw the plane go down and a search party found wreckage of the craft scattered over a wide area on the Carol Olson farm.

Authorities said Eddings was test-flying the plane prior to applying for a permit for its regular use. He was wearing a parachute.

One witness said a wing appeared to fail before the plane crashed.

Hartley said he would investigate the crash today to determine the cause.

Made Bows

A former carpenter and cabinet maker, Eddings began manufacturing bows for target archers and hunters at Marquette and about 12 years ago moved his factory to McGregor. Many of the bows were used by big game hunters in Africa.

Eddings learned to fly about the same time he started his bow plant in McGregor and used an airplane to call on dealers. He continued to live in Marquette.

Surviving are his wife and a daughter and several grandchildren.

Clear, Warm For the Fourth

Snakes and sparklers will burn under clear skies and in warm air July 4.

The weather bureau said that the next two days will be slightly warmer than Sunday's balmy low 80s ...

TIE, ASSAULT 2 WOMEN AT 3919 GRAND

Landlady, Tenant; 2 Men Held

By William Holden

Two women were bound and raped early Sunday morning when two men broke into a rooming house at 3919 Grand ave., police were told Sunday.

The two men, wearing white cloth masks, assaulted Mrs. Madge Howard, 55, the landlady, then went upstairs to the third floor where three young women were sleeping and assaulted one of them, Mary Glider, 20.

Two Arrested

Both women were taken to Broadlawns Polk County Hospital for treatment.

From a description and other facts furnished by the women, police Sunday morning arrested two men.

They were identified as Dale Milton Buteaux, 29, of 1515½ Harding road, and George Henry Trust, 36, of 627 Des Moines st. They were being held for investigation by detectives Sunday night.

Mrs. Howard described the two-hour ordeal as "a night of terror."

She said it was about 3:30 a. m. Sunday when she heard someone walking around in a second-floor apartment. She had been asleep in her bedroom on the first floor. She said she thought possibly it was some of her working-girl roomers returning home.

"A Holdup"

Shortly thereafter she heard a noise and saw a man standing near the bedroom door. He said, "This is a holdup," Mrs. Howard said.

She said she tried to run out the door but fell over a chair. The two men carried her back into the bedroom where she was tied hand and foot with scarves and assaulted by one of the men.

The two then carried her television set out of the living room and put it on the porch. Another television set which was in the hallway also was taken to the porch.

Then one of the men blindfolded her and made her walk down Grand avenue to what Mrs. Howard thinks was Fortieth street, where she was told to get into a car.

The man then drove the car back to the house, presumably into the driveway, and the two men loaded one of the television sets into the car. They also took $10 in bills from Mrs. Howard's purse and about $6 in change from a drawer.

3 Girls In

Still blindfolded and with her hands tied, Mrs. Howard

ATTACK—
Continued on Page Five

INSIDE THE REGISTER

See Kennedy Strike Step

KENNEDY is expected to invoke the Taft-Hartley law today to compel striking seamen to return to their ships .... Page 16

REPORT links between 170 and 260 deaths in New York City 7 years ago to ...

Ernest Hemingway

Death In The Morning

Hemingway: One of 3 Most Influential Writers of Era

By Charles Poore

New York Times News Service

NEW YORK, N. Y.—"Writing is architecture, not interior decoration," Ernest Hemingway once said, "and the Baroque is over."

In a way lucky for him, the Baroque was not over. Against its weary, ornamented excesses the spareness of his style stood out. With that style he did something to change the course of storytelling in our century.

Simple—As A Fugue

If it was a simple style it had the simplicity of a Bach fugue or a landscape by Cezanne. The thousand and one writers who—consciously or unconsciously — imitated its elementals found that out.

None could quite catch his harmonies and cadences. Others wrote pages spattered with three-word sentence dialogues. Their pages fell apart.

He stands now, with William Butler Yeats and James Joyce, as one of the three most influential writers of an era.

He appeared in the sky of our literature like a meteor —and then stayed there. A strange way for a meteor to act. Yet as each book appeared, savants dutifully issued final announcements that he was burned out. The Nobel prize judges apparently believed those announcements until they read "The Old Man and the Sea."

He was sustained as effectively by his enemies as by his friends. The millions who enjoyed his stories were not particularly troubled by his skill in writing about violence. They had probably noticed that the world around them was generally in a state of considerable turmoil and that he found patterns of significance in its embroilments. Also, he created some heroines who brought about vicarious fatalities of the heart.

They Read Him

Those who candidly deplored Hemingway and all his works sacrificed awesome amounts of time to the documentation of their disapproval. They seemed to have read every single word he wrote. Since no statute required them to do so, one wondered where they found marginal leisure to enjoy authors they wholeheartedly admired.

There is an unassailable mythology about any writer's themes and characters. In Hemingway's case the salient idea is that he wrote about big-gamesters, pugs, thugs, girls with long legs and tawny hair, soldiers of fortune and misfortune.

villan life the hero of "A Farewell to Arms" was an architecture student, or that the hero of "For Whom the Bell Tolls" was a schoolteacher, or that the hero of "The Sun Also Rises" was a working newspaper man with an editor barking at him through the other end of a cable, must be guilty of some sort of weakness for obnoxious irrelevance.

Hemingway was no dove for the lit'ry coteries, but he was a gregarious man. He had more friends than any other writer of his stature, in more astonishingly varied circles, from Africa to Montana, from Key West to New York to Madrid, Paris and the Venetian plain.

He was aware that many wanted him to settle down and cultivate the surburbanalities. Once he wrote a parody of the clucking intellectual herdsmen of literary nationalism. It was spoken by a fishing-trip companion to Jake Barnes, the hero of "The Sun Also Rises":

"You're an expatriate," the man tells Jake. "You've lost touch with the soil. You get precious. Fake European standards have ruined you. You drink yourself to death. You become obsessed by sex. You spend all your time talking, not working. You're an expatriate, see? You hang around cafes."

An Idyll

One of Hemingway's friends was Bernard Berenson, connoisseur of life in art, art in life, who called "The Old Man and the Sea": "An idyll of the sea as sea, as un-Byronic and un-Melvillian as Homer himself, and communicated in a prose as calm and compelling as Homer's verse. No real artist symbolizes or allegorizes — and Hemingway is a true artist—but every real work of art exhales symbols and allegories."

Arrest 5 More Freedom Riders

JACKSON, MISS. (AP)—Five "Freedom Riders" arrived by bus from Montgomery, Ala., Sunday and police arrested them shortly after they entered the terminal's white waiting room here.

The riders—three white and ...

WIFE CALLS THE SHOOTING ACCIDENTAL

Death Comes in Idaho Home

SUN VALLEY, IDAHO (AP) —Ernest Hemingway, the Nobel prize-winning author who became a legend in his own time, was killed by a shotgun blast Sunday while his wife was asleep upstairs.

Mrs. Hemingway, the "Miss Mary" who accompanied him on his world travels, was awakened by the shot, found the body and summoned a doctor.

A double - barreled, 12-gauge shotgun, one barrel fired, lay beside Hemingway. The blast had entered his head.

Calls Friend

Mrs. Hemingway called a local motel man, Chuck Atkinson, a family friend, and asked him to put out a statement that the creator of ment that the creator of "A Farewell to Arms," "The Old Man and the Sea" and "For Whom the Bell Tolls" was dead.

"Mr. Hemingway," the statement said, "accidentally killed himself while cleaning a gun this morning at 7:30 a. m."

No Note

Atkinson said it was the statement Mrs. Hemingway wanted, that she feels the death was accidental. He said no note was found.

The county coroner, the sheriff and the prosecuting attorney talked for more than an hour and then decided not to call an inquest.

Wound in Head

"I can only say at this stage that the wound was self-inflicted," said Coroner Ray McGoldrick. "The wound was in the head. It could have been accidental or otherwise. There is no evidence of foul play, and no witnesses. Nothing could be gained by an inquest. But one could be called at any time if there was some reason to justify it."

Hemingway, 61, was released only last week from the Mayo Clinic in Minnesota where he underwent treatment for high blood pressure.

Some of the people here who knew Hemingway as their most celebrated citizen, talked openly of rumors that it was more serious than that.

They said he had appeared most depressed at the death of actor Gary Cooper, who played some of Hemingway's heroes in films. Cooper died of cancer in May.

Sun Valley and the little neighboring community of Ketchum where Hemingway

HEMINGWAY—
Continued on Page Five

Page One, *The Des Moines Register*, 3 July 1961

CHARLOTTESVILLE, VA.,
July 3 (UPI)—Nobel Prize-winning novelist William Faulkner wrote this brief statement in tribute to his close friend and contemporary Ernest Hemingway who died Sunday:
"One of the bravest and best, the strictest in principles, the severest of craftsmen, undeviating in his dedication to his craft; which is to arrest for a believable moment the antics of human beings involved in the comedy and tragedy of being alive. To the few who knew him well he was almost as good a man as the book he wrote. He is not dead. Generations not yet born of young men and women who want to write will refute that word as applied to him."

Story, *San Francisco Chronicle*, 3 July 1961

Star's editor C. G. Wellington was quoted as saying that he did not teach Hemingway how to write. "Hemingway taught himself."

Readers were introduced to matador Antonio Ordoñez tossing his cap to Hemingway at a bullfight where Ordoñez dedicated a bull to the author as a measure of his friendship and admiration.[13] Writing about bullfights in Madrid and Pamplona had brought Hemingway some of his earliest visibility as a newspaper correspondent for the *Toronto Star Weekly* in 1923. On 4 July 1961, a UPI dispatch told of Ordoñez killing two bulls in honor of Hemingway.[14] The matador won both ears and the tail of one bull and one ear of the other, but not before standing with other matadors in the middle of the bullring before the event and joining a standing crowd in a minute of silent tribute to Hemingway. UPI reported Ordoñez "wept openly," saying, "I am sure that Papa Hemingway would have liked this form of praying for the repose of his soul."

Another feature story from Spain began with a lead sentence that read, "Men spoke in whispers today in Calle Victoria, which runs straight as a matador's sword past 15 bars and eight bullfight ticket offices." The dateline from Madrid offered a poignant perspective of Hemingway from the "aficionados who can afford only inexpensive seats on the sunny side of the arena."

> "I shake the hand . . .," said one man, shriveled by age and seared by sun. "I drink with him," another said proudly. He lifted his glass of raw red wine the way a Hemingway hero would have liked it and smiled a tobacco-stained salute. . . . Across the city in the restaurant Botin, which is more than 200 years old, a table stood vacant . . . set for one. . . .[15]

PAMPLONA, Spain,

July 7 (UPI)—The late Ernest Hemingway's favorite Spanish fiesta got underway today when a rocket was fired into the sky and six brave bulls spurted through Pamplona's narrow streets.

The bulls were bred by Hemingway's closest friend in the bullfight world, matador Antonio Ordoñez.

Hemingway had hoped to be back here for this year's "San Fermin" fiesta, and had promised Ordoñez he would be on hand to see his bulls in action.

Only a few days before his death, the famed American author canceled his reservations here.

The San Fermin ceremonies officially opened yesterday, and the first of ten bullfights went off this afternoon.

But early this morning shortly after dawn, the wild dash of the bulls through the streets began.

Pamplona youths, along with a few foreigners, raced in front of the bulls, jumping to safety when the beasts came too close.

The town was packed with visitors for the festival. Many sat up all night waiting for the rush of the bulls.

Story, *San Francisco Chronicle*, 7 July 1961

The Boise *Statesman*, more than most other papers, carried the reaction from Cuba. In a story headlined, "Cuba Village Mourns Loss of Hemingway," the *Statesman* reported

> Old men by the sea at the fishing village of Cojimar wept . . . in learning Ernest Hemingway was dead. At the late writer's villa . . . servants and neighbors sat in stunned silence among his many hunting trophies from African safaris.[16]

Hemingway the hunter appeared often during the week. His expert knowledge of firearms caused early speculation about his possible suicide. Readers in San Francisco opened their papers to find a photograph of Hemingway and Sun Valley guide Taylor Williams. Between them lay a pronghorned antelope. The photo, taken 26 September 1940, was set against the sprawling Idaho mountains and topped with a headline reading, "A Reunion in Death."[17]

Two other Sun Valley area photos appeared frequently that week, both with Hemingway and Gary Cooper, showing the two men as sportsmen with guns. One showed Cooper and Hemingway standing next to each other shortly after the first Sun Valley meeting of the two men in 1940.[18] Cooper, looking like a Hollywood dandy, is wearing what appeared to be a tailor-made new shirt and new jeans with the cuffs rolled up. Ernest is wearing a leather vest and rough, wool-looking pants, belt outside the loops, often his customary dress for hanging around Idaho. The *San Francisco Chronicle* ran the photo with a caption reading, "Gary Cooper, Hemingway in 1940: Friends were on a hunting trip near Sun Valley."[19] The *Seattle Post-Intelligencer* carried the photo with a headline reading, "Hunter and Writer," and a caption reading, "In 1940, Hemingway and late actor Gary Cooper, carried shotguns on an Idaho hunting trip."[20]

In addition to his hunting in Idaho and the West, his adventures on safari in Africa received wide coverage, partly because of the news items generated by his two plane crashes there in 1954, and partly by the availability of African safari photos shot by *Look* magazine photographer Earl Theisen. In the *Chicago Daily Tribune* Hemingway is pictured on safari with two African natives looking at hunting arrows.[21] Hemingway, wearing a safari hat and looking authoritative as the great white hunter, is holding the arrows upright, as the natives look on. Another safari photo has him bare-chested, holding his stomach and stretching outside his tent. Under a *Boston Globe* headline reading, "Fist Fights or Bull Fights, Hemingway Lived as He Wrote," the photo is displayed with the caption reading, "In His Element—Ernest Hemingway stretches as hot day begins in East Africa, scene of his famous 'Snows of Kilimanjaro.'"[22]

One photo, which looks posed because of the arrangement of the accessories, shows the studious-looking author seated at his makeshift table-desk in the bush. Another posed supreme-hunter photo, which appeared in color in *Look* magazine in January 1954, shows a dead leopard in the foreground with Hemingway sitting directly behind the animal's head—the leopard's eyes submissively closed—with his right hand holding his gun, pointed diagonally upwards across the photo.[23]

By coincidence, at the time of his death, two books with Hemingway as their subject were already in the hands of newspaper editors for possible book review. One was Carlos Baker's *Hemingway and His Critics*, the other was Leo Lania's *Hemingway: A Pictorial Biography*, part of the Viking Press series on famous people. The Lania book contained a full-page photograph of Hemingway with a hunting rifle slung over his left shoulder, with pine trees and mountains in the background. The same photograph appeared in the *Washington Post* book review column on July 9, with the caption, "Hemingway, the young hunter, in a pose that foreshadows his death by shotgun last Sunday,"[24] but Lania's book was not reviewed. A bandaged Hemingway sitting up in bed after a London auto accident appeared in the *San Francisco Chronicle* and was credited to the Lania book.[25] Other photos in the Lania book are identical to those published by newspapers in the coverage of Hemingway's death.[26]

Although not as dominant a theme as hunting, Hemingway the fisherman also appeared in the posthumous coverage. In one photograph he stands with his cap on, pot-bellied, bare-chested and barefoot, on the stern of a craft—not identified—with the wake trailing behind him and the caption reading, "Hemingway bared his chest to the sea air after a little fishing in the Caribbean."[27] In another photo we see a tiny Hemingway standing dwarfed alongside a hanging giant marlin caught during the filming of *The Old Man and the Sea*. Although that's the way a docked marlin hangs, the nose-down fish and the upright Hemingway offer David-and-Goliath symbolism.[28] Also on the fishing theme was a reprinted 1937 dispatch Hemingway authored for the North American Newspaper Alliance from Spain.[29] The *Kansas City Times* reprinted the dispatch and brought Hemingway's description of a trout stream to a new generation of readers:

> We shot no more snakes that day, but I saw three trout in the stream which would weigh over four pounds apiece; heavy, solid, deep-sided ones that rolled up to take the grasshoppers I threw them, making swirls in the water as deep as though you had dropped a paving stone into the stream. All along the stream, where no road ever led until the war, you could see trout; small ones in the shallows and the biggest kind in the pools and in the shadow of the bank. It's a river worth fighting for, but just a little cold for swimming.

The fragments of speculation that Hemingway's death was not accidental grew into full-blown stories as the first-day's coverage moved into the large July 4 news hole.[30] While the words "cover-up" did not appear, the front page July 4 *San Francisco Chronicle* carried a story with an underlying tone of tension between reporters and Blaine County officials, especially Blaine County Coroner and Hailey Funeral Director Ray McGoldrick, who said, "People can make up their own minds," whether Hemingway committed suicide. The *Atlanta Constitution*'s front page asked readers to decide, "Was Hemingway Suicide? You Judge."

Hemingway's family found the news hole when the press learned about his sister Ursula's flight from Honolulu and met her at the Los Angeles airport. Ursula was photographed wincing, with her hand against her face, and in a checked suit coat, ideal for black-and-white newspaper reproduction.[31] Distributed as an AP Wirephoto, Ursula's photograph became the single most prominent visual symbol of Hemingway family grief.

Madelaine and her son, Ernest Hemingway Mainland, flew to Idaho from Michigan and met Ursula at the Salt Lake City airport. There, the Hemingway sisters hid in the ladies' room while Ernest Mainland kept the press at bay.[32] When the three got off the plane at Hailey, Idaho, a press photographer captured them walking through the Hailey airport. The *San Francisco Chronicle* reported: "They refused to tell newspapers their names. But it was learned later they were."[33] The Hailey airport photo appeared as an AP Wirephoto in the *Chicago Daily Tribune*, with the caption, "Sisters of Author Ernest Hemingway at airport in Hailey, Ida., as they arrive to attend the funeral."[34]

More than a dozen columnists, many who knew Hemingway personally, or said they did, wrote about Hemingway during the week. One who did know him personally was Charles McCabe of the *San Francisco Chronicle*, who in his younger days had been an assistant for the Sun Valley Publicity Office. McCabe wrote, "I recall him best as a burly fellow who liked to fish for rainbow trout at 4 A.M. in the Idaho lakes with four bottles of aquavit cooling off in the trail of his canoe. . . . He thought Flaubert and Tolstoy were the greatest things since sin."[35] The slice of humor in the week came from columnist Bill Vaughan, who wrote in a column published on the front page of the *Kansas City Star* that it was the loneliest week of his long years of writing columns. He was the one person, he mourned, who had never met Ernest Hemingway—had never even laid eyes on him, had never received a letter from him, had never even been in Ketchum, Idaho.[36]

By mid-week, just how big the news hole had become could be seen in the *Idaho Statesman* and the *Minneapolis Morning Tribune*, where each paper carried an AP Wirephoto of the tractor digging the grave in the Ketchum cemetery.[37]

Hemingway's possible suicide and his three divorces—two as a Catholic—caused reporters to inquire about the appropriateness of a Catholic funeral ceremony. On that subject the Rev. Robert J. Waldmann, the Roman Catholic pastor of St. Charles Church in Hailey and Our Lady of the Snows in Ketchum, became the quoted source on Catholicism. On the subject of accident versus suicide, Waldmann said, "We pass no judgment on that and ask no questions."[38]

Had it not been for a reporter in Sun Valley, the issue of whether the death was an accident or a suicide might still be hotly debated. Enter Emmett Watson, reporter-columnist for the *Seattle Post-Intelligencer*. Sun Valley was Watson's beat. In 1959, he met Hemingway at the bar in the Duchin room at the Lodge. Hemingway liked him and gave him an interview, later published in the *Seattle Post-Intelligencer*. Friday, July 7, the day after the funeral, Watson decided to put in print what others were thinking, that the death was definitely a suicide. A front-page *Post-Intelligencer* headline read, "Emmett Watson Learns: Real Story of Death Of Hemingway. Speculation Clarified On Fatal Shotgun Blast." Watson increased the impact of his story by copyrighting his story to help assure attribution elsewhere, and by providing detailed information about the gun and the scene of the incident.

> The *Post-Intelligencer* learned that the death weapon was a silver-inlaid double-barreled shotgun with a hammerless tandem trigger mechanism. Both barrels had been fired. The 12-gauge hunting gun was an Angelini & Benardon, made by W. C. Scott and Sons, of London. The make of the gun was described on the right barrel. On the left barrel was inscribed "55 Victoria Street, London, Scott's Improved Bolt, Monte Carlo B."

He reported the details of a "rough sketch of where the body was found," that Sheriff Hewitt drew "following the funeral." Emmett Watson then penned his personal paragraph of closure.

> However, inquiry by the *Post-Intelligencer* along other channels disclosed that the author's death definitely was a suicide. Thus ends speculation which may well have plagued Hemingway scholars for years to come.[39]

Under normal circumstances the news value of the Hemingway death story would have ended with the funeral Thursday morning, July 6. Mary Hemingway had sent word to reporters that she didn't wish to talk to anyone for at least ten days. But in a letter to Mary sent through Sun Valley publicity director Dorice Taylor, reporters Emmett Watson, and Barry Farrell of *Time* magazine, asked Mary for an interview.[40] Mary agreed, and that agreement in itself made the national press.[41] The interview, with Watson, Farrell, and two other reporters, took place Saturday, July 8, and was the first confirmed news that Hemingway had stored in safes and vaults other written works not yet published.

The weekend news hole was waiting again. Extensive Sunday coverage of Mary's interview occurred, with some newspapers carrying the story on the front page. Watson, in more detail than most reporters, described the setting. "Wall length magazine racks held virtually every publication and many book shelves were filled. . . . On one wall is a working map of Idaho's saw-tooth mountain range and on another, next to the foyer, is a photographic reproduction of an early Picasso."[42]

Mary's interview was another catalyst for the Hemingway news agenda, and more background stories appeared. UPI found sixty-nine-year-old economist Harold Loeb still smarting over Hemingway's unflattering portrayal of him as Robert Cohn in *The Sun Also Rises*. UPI reported, "Loeb is no longer as angry as he was in 1926."[43]

Hemingway once complained to Maxwell Perkins, his editor at Charles Scribner's Sons, about the amount of promotion and advertising dollars

Scribner's was spending on Hemingway's works. In reporting his death, newspapers ran stories on multiple pages with illustrations. The press coverage was remarkable for its breadth and depth, spanning hard news, book reviews, columns, features, photographs, quotes, letters, and editorials. If a publisher or press agent had deliberately tried to obtain that much exposure for an author, not only would the cost of newspaper advertising alone have been prohibitive, but most newspapers do not sell display advertising on the front page. Also, news coverage has more credibility than advertising.

Recapping the way the week's press coverage developed, only a television script writer could have created a plot with as much news value. Near daybreak on Sunday, July 2, an internationally famous literary figure dies violently on the slowest news day of the week, in one of the slowest news weeks of the year. Reporters and editors have both a big news hole to fill and the time to fill it. The incident takes place in a world-renowned resort that has developed its reputation through celebrity press relations. For an entire week, a publicity office staffed by a working professional handles major communication matters for both the family and the press. When privacy and bereavement should exist, they're replaced by press coverage of controversy over how the victim died. Tension erupts between reporters and local officials. The story should end early in the week, but one son's delayed arrival from Africa and the July 4 holiday extend the news hole. When the funeral should bring closure, the widow, who has been in seclusion, decides to emerge and hold a press conference. Suspense creates more publicity over what she'll say about her husband's death. The press conference takes place on Saturday morning, almost as slow a news day as Sunday. Again, reporters and editors have a news hole and the time to fill it. The week ends waiting for a sequel about the victim's unfinished novels. In July 1961, the life and the literature of Ernest Hemingway created more press coverage than any other literary event in history.

NOTES

1. The Sun Valley resort and Ketchum are about one mile apart. Hemingway and his wife Mary bought their Ketchum home from Henry J. (Bob) Topping for $50,000 in 1959.

2. See for example, Michael Reynolds, *The Young Hemingway* (New York: Basil Blackwell Inc., 1986), 18. James D. Brasch, "Invention from Knowledge," in *Ernest Hemingway: The Writer in Context*, ed. James Nagel (Madison: University of Wisconsin Press, 1984), 203–4. Robert E. Fleming, *The Face in the Mirror: Hemingway's Writers* (Tuscaloosa: University of Alabama Press, 1994), 6.

3. "Townspeople Resentful," *New York Times*, 7 July 1961, p. L68.

4. Accounts of the role of the Sun Valley Publicity Office the week following Hemingway's death are from Dorice Taylor, *Sun Valley* (Sun Valley: Ex Libris, 1980), 145–47. Hemingway suffered from various ailments during his lifetime. See for example "Hypertension For 15 Years: Author's Physician Reports," *Seattle Post-Intelligencer*, 9 July 1961, Sec. 1, p. 15; Susan Beegel, "Hemingway and Hemochromatosis," *The Hemingway Review* 10 (Fall 1990): 57–66; Peter L. Hays, "Hemingway's Clinical Depression: A Speculation," *The Hemingway Review* 14 (Spring 1995): 50–61.

5. Taylor, *Sun Valley*, 145–46. This is Taylor's recollection twenty years later. The *Oregonian* and some other papers reported it was Mary who called local resident Chuck Atkinson and asked him to put out a statement.

6. Taylor, *Sun Valley*, 145. Variations of the statement appeared. The *Kansas City Times* reported on the front page a statement from Mary saying that Hemingway "accidentally killed himself while cleaning a gun this morning at 7:30 A.M." See "Hemingway is Killed in Shotgun Blast," *Kansas City Times* 3 July 1961, p. 1+.

7. "Hemingway Killed Cleaning Gun," *Washington Post* 3 July 1961, p. 1+. It is not uncommon for funeral directors to serve as coroners, although the issue of a conflict of interest can arise.

8. The account of the friendship of Van Guilder, Arnold, Williams, and Hemingway is from Lloyd R. Arnold, *High on the Wild with Hemingway*. (Caldwell, Idaho: Caxton Printers, 1969). Still married to Pauline, Hemingway, with Martha Gellhorn, drove to Sun Valley from Montana via Galena Summit in a black Buick convertible. When Pappy Arnold first saw Hemingway and Gellhorn headed for breakfast, he described Hemingway as "dressed like a ranch hand slicked up for a night in town" (3). Arnold, along with Don Anderson, Forrest H. Mac Mullen, Chuck Atkinson, George Brown, Leonard "Bud" Purdy, and Dr. George Saviers, served as active pallbearers.

9. The fifteen metropolitan daily newspapers studied were published during the week of July 2 through July 9, 1961. The papers were the *Boston Globe*, *New York Times*, *Washington Post*, *Atlanta Constitution*, *Chicago Daily Tribune*, *Minneapolis Morning Tribune*, *Kansas City Times* and *Star*, *St. Louis Post Dispatch*, *Des Moines Register*, *Houston Post*, *Seattle Post-Intelligencer*, *Idaho* (Boise) *Daily Statesman*, *Portland Oregonian*, *Denver Post*, and *San Francisco Chronicle*. To make the project manageable, other media, such as magazines, books, radio, television, and weekly newspapers were not examined.

This research was supported in part by a grant from the University Research Council of the University of North Carolina at Chapel Hill. The author wishes to thank professors Linda Wagner-Martin and Joseph Flora, and Kay Phillips, for their suggestions on an earlier draft of the paper.

10. "Accident in Idaho: Hemingway Dead—Shotgun Blast," *San Francisco Chronicle*, 3 July 1963, p. 1. Among other *Chronicle* stories were "Hemingway

Tribute From Faulkner," *San Francisco Chronicle*, 4 July 1961, p. 8; and "A Festival Hemingway Will Miss," *San Francisco Chronicle*, 8 July 1961, p. 12. The sub-headline in the *Register* stated, "Find Famed Novelist With Shotgun Beside Him." See "Gun Blast Kills Hemingway," *Des Moines Register*, 3 July 1961, p. 1.

11. For reactions see, for example, "France Shocked Over Hemingway," *New York Times*, 4 July 1961, p. L9. "Vatican Critical of 'Nihilistic Image of Life,'" *San Francisco Chronicle*, 4 July 1961, p. 8. "Moscow Dedicates TV Program to Ernest Hemingway," *Boston Globe*, 5 July 1961, p. 19. "Death in the Afternoon . . . and a Matador Weeps," *Boston Globe*, 3 July 1961, p. 7. For the UPI lead see "A Farewell Toast to Don Ernesto," *San Francisco Chronicle*, 4 July 1961, p. 8.

12. Robert K. Sanford (untitled story under headline "Hemingway is Killed"), *Kansas City Times*, 3 July 1961, p. 1.

13. The AP Wirephoto appeared on July 3 front pages of the *Oregonian*, *Kansas City Times*, *Denver Post*, *Atlanta Constitution*, *Boston Globe*, and *San Francisco Chronicle*.

14. "Ordóñez Kills Two Bulls in Honor of Hemingway," *New York Times*, 4 July 1961, p. L9.

15. "A Farewell Toast to Don Ernesto." *San Francisco Chronicle*, 4 July 1961, p. 8.

16. "Cuba Village Mourns Loss of Hemingway," *Idaho* (Boise) *Statesman*, 5 July 1961, p. 12.

17. The photo is dated in the Caxton Printers edition of Arnold's *High on the Wild*, 60–62.

18. See for example the *Boston Globe*, 3 July 1961, p. 7.

19. "Hemingway's Life Read Like a Book," *San Francisco Chronicle*, 3 July 1961, p. 9.

20. "Hunter and Writer," (photograph), *Seattle Post-Intelligencer*, 3 July 1961, Sec. 1, p. 1.

21. "Scenes from the Robust Life of Ernest Hemingway, Killed by a Gunshot Wound," (photographs), *Chicago Daily Tribune*, 3 July 1961, p. F8.

22. "Fist Fights or Bull Fights, Hemingway Lived as He Wrote," *Boston Globe*, 3 July 1961, p. 4.

23. See for example the *Washington Post*, 3 July 1961, p. B2.

24. David Sanders, "Hemingway Influence Lives On," review of *Hemingway: A Pictorial Biography*, by Leo Lania, *Washington Post*, 9 July 1961, p. E7. It's the only mention of the Lania book in four columns of reviews that include a discussion of the Baker book and two about writer William Faulkner. See also Robert S. Fogarty, "Critic's Corner: Hemingway's Story Real," review of *Hemingway: A Pictorial Biography*, by Leo Lania, *Denver Post*, 5 July 1961, p. 21.

25. Photograph captioned, "Was Accident Prone," *San Francisco Chronicle*, 3 July 1961, p. 9. The photo appears on page 104 of Lania.

26. See for example the *San Francisco Chronicle*, July 3, 1961, p. 8. The *Chronicle's* cropped photo of Pauline appears in Lania, page 86. The *Chronicle's* cropped photo of Hemingway the correspondent appears in Lania, 12. See also the *Kansas City Times*, 6 July 1961, p. 32; the photo of Hemingway standing at his typewriter also appears in Lania, 103.

27. *Washington Post*, 3 July 1961, p. B2.

28. See for example "Hemingway's Prize-Winning Works Reflected Preoccupation with Life and Death," *New York Times*, 3 July 1961, p. 6.

29. "Daring Young Man in the Spanish War," *Kansas City Times*, 6 July 1961, p. 40.

30. For Ray McGoldrick's statement on the cause of death see for example "Hemingway Shooting: No Official Decision on Novelist's Death," *San Francisco Chronicle*, 4 July 1961, p. 1+. Also, "Was Hemingway Suicide?" *Atlanta Constitution*, 4 July 1961, p. 1.

31. See for example "Hemingway Shooting," p. 8.

32. Madelaine Hemingway Miller, *Ernie* (New York: Crown Publishers), 139.

33. See for example, "Hemingway Shooting," p. 8.

34. *Chicago Daily Tribune*, 4 July 1961, back page.

35. Charles McCabe, "The Fearless Spectator—How Hemingway Taught Writing," *San Francisco Chronicle*, 4 July 1961, p. 24.

36. Bill Vaughan, "Alone in Crowd of 'Papa' Columnists," *Kansas City Star*, 8 July 1961, p. 1.

37. The photograph appeared in the *Idaho Statesman*, 5 July 1961, p. 10; and the *Minneapolis Star Tribune*, 5 July 1961, p. 10.

38. "Services Slated for Hemingway," *New York Times*, 5 July 1961, p. 68.

39. Seattle Post-Intelligencer, 7 July 1961, p. 1.

40. Letter from Barry Farrell to Mary Hemingway, undated, Ketchum Public Library Historical Collection, document RM-04 #74. See also Taylor, *Sun Valley*, p. 146.

41. See for example "By Wife: Hemingway Press Meet Called," *Seattle Post-Intelligencer*, 8 July 1961, Sec. 1, p. 6.

42. See for example, Emmett Watson, "'We Sang Together:' Mary Hemingway Describes Famous Writer's Last Hours," *Seattle Post-Intelligencer*, 9 July, 1961, p. 1+.

43. Bruce Agnew, "How Hemingway Book Infuriated His Friend," *Boston Globe*, 9 July 1961, p. 18.

Contributors

John R. Bittner is a Professor in the School of Journalism and Mass Communication at the University of North Carolina at Chapel Hill. Professor Bittner is the author of numerous scholarly articles, professional papers, and sixteen communication texts under the Simon & Schuster imprint.

Fredrik Chr. Brøgger is Professor of American Literature and Civilization at the University of Tromso, Norway. He has published essays on American Studies theory, American literature, and American popular culture and two books: *Culture, Language, Text* (1992) and *American Culture: An Anthology of Civilization Texts* (1996).

Suzanne Clark is Associate Professor of English at the University of Oregon. She has published essays on Julia Kristeva, Edna St. Vincent Millay, Annie Dillard, and Bernard Malamud. She also published *Sentimental Modernism: Women Writers and the Revolution of the Word* (1991) and has a book in progress, *Cold Warriors*, that will deal with Hemingway among others.

David N. Cremean is currently ABD at Bowling Green State University and is a Lecturer in English at the University of Wisconsin—Whitewater. His dissertation, in progress, is "With God Obsessed: The Writings of Cormac McCarthy." He has published in *Western American Literature*.

Cecilia Konchar Farr is Assistant Professor of English at the College of St. Catherine, St. Paul, Minnesota. She has published articles on ecology and literature, and on Willa Cather, Herman Melville, and Henry Roth. She is currently working on a book on autobiographical fiction and women modernist writers.

Robert E. Fleming is Professor of English at the University of New Mexico. He has published articles on Hemingway in *American Literature*, *Arizona Quarterly*, *Hemingway Review*, *Journal of Modern Literature*, *Midwest Quarterly*, and *North Dakota Quarterly* and a book, *The Face in the Mirror: Hemingway's Writers* (1994).

Joseph M. Flora is Professor of English at the University of North Carolina at Chapel Hill. He is author of *Vardis Fisher* (1965), *William Ernest Henley* (1970), *Frederick Manfred* (1974), *Hemingway's Nick Adams* (1982), and *Ernest Hemingway: The Art of the Short Fiction* (1989). He is co-editor of *Southern Writers: A Biographical Dictionary* and *Fifty Southern Writers Before 1900*.

Robin Gajdusek is Professor Emeritus at San Francisco State University. He has given a paper at every international conference of the Society and has published widely. Among his books are *Hemingway's Paris* (1978) and *Hemingway and Joyce: A Study in Debt and Repayment* (1984). A memoir of his war experiences will be published by Notre Dame University Press.

Peter L. Hays is Professor of English at the University of California, Davis, where he has been chair of the department. He is the author of some two dozen articles and notes on Hemingway as well as *The Limping Hero* (1971), *Ernest Hemingway* (1990), and *A Concordance to Hemingway's "In Our Time"* (1990).

Robert W. Lewis is Professor of English and chair at the University of North Dakota, where he also edits the *North Dakota Quarterly*. Past two-term President of the Hemingway Society, Professor Lewis has published extensively on Hemingway, including his books, *Hemingway on Love* (1965) and *A Farewell to Arms: The War of the Words* (1992).

Lawrence H. Martin is Elliot Professor of English at Hampden-Sydney College, Virginia. He has treated nature and sporting themes in Hemingway's short stories, novels, and journalism in conference papers and in articles in *Hemingway Notes*, *Hemingway Review*, and *New Critical Approaches to the Short Stories of Ernest Hemingway*.

James H. Meredith, a Lieutenant Colonel, is Assistant Professor at the U. S. Air Force Academy. He has published articles on Hemingway in the *Hemingway Review* and *War, Literature, and the Arts*. Presently he is working on a book about the literature of World War II for Greenwood Press.

Charlene M. Murphy is Professor of English at Massachusetts Bay Community College, where she teaches composition, American literature, and a special course on Hemingway. She presented a paper at the 1995 Hemingway colloquium in Havana, Cuba, and has published in the *Hemingway Review*.

James Plath is Associate Professor of English at Illinois Wesleyen University and Director of the Hemingway Days Conference in Key

West, Florida. His essays on Hemingway have appeared in the *Hemingway Review*, *North Dakota Quarterly*, *Studies in Short Fiction*, and *Hemingway Repossessed*. He was featured on a recent WPBT public TV special on "Hemingway in Key West."

Ann Putnam teaches creative writing and American literature at the University of Puget Sound in Tacoma, Washington. She has published fiction, personal essays, and scholarly articles in a number of journals and collections and has presented papers at Hemingway conferences in Pamplona, Havana, and Sun Valley.

Rod Romesburg is a doctoral candidate at the University of California, Davis. He has presented scholarly papers at several meetings of the Western American Literature Association and at a conference of the North American Interdisciplinary Wilderness Association.

H. R. Stoneback is Professor of English and Director of Graduate Studies at the State University of New York—New Paltz. He has edited and written several books and scores of articles, including many essays on Hemingway and Faulkner. He has been a Senior Fulbright Scholar at Peking University. He is presently at work on two critical volumes on Hemingway.

Lisa Tyler is an Assistant Professor of English at Sinclair Community College in Dayton, Ohio. Her essays have appeared in a number of scholarly journals, including the *Hemingway Review*, *Doris Lessing Newsletter*, *Studies in Short Fiction*, and *Woolf Studies Annual*.

Terry Tempest Williams is currently Naturalist-in-Residence at the Museum of Natural History in Salt Lake City, Utah. A winner of the Southwest Book Award, she is the author of *Pieces of White Shell* (1984), *The Secret Language of Snow* (1984), *Refuge: An Unnatural History of Family and Place* (1991), and *An Unspoken Hunger* (1994).

Index

Untitled